ONE HUNDRED YEARS
OF
SCOTTISH FOOTBALL

From Charles to Tom

Christmas 1974

Scotland *v*. England at Hampden Park, 1972. Bobby Clark punches ball away from Rodney Marsh and Martin Chivers, England's strikers. Asa Hartford watches.

ONE HUNDRED YEARS of SCOTTISH FOOTBALL

by

JOHN RAFFERTY

PAN BOOKS LTD · LONDON

First published 1973 by
Pan Books Ltd, 33 Tothill Street, London, SW1

ISBN 0 330 23654 7 (paperback edition)
ISBN 0 330 23687 3 (case-bound edition)

Printed in Great Britain by
Fletcher & Son Ltd, Norwich

Contents

Presidents of the Scottish Football Association

1873–75	A. Campbell (Clydesdale)
1875–76	A. S. McBride (Vale of Leven)
1876–77	W. C. Mitchell (Queen's Park)
1877–78	R. Gardner (Clydesdale)
1878–79	R. B. Colquhoun (Lennox)
1879–81	Don Hamilton (Ayr)
1881–82	J. Wallace (Beith)
1882–84	T. Lawrie (Queen's Park)
1884–86	J. E. McKillop (Cartvale)
1886–87	R. Browne (Queen's Park)
1887–88	A. McA. Kennedy (Dumbarton)
1888–89	J. A. Crerar (Third Lanark)
1889–90	C. Campbell (Queen's Park)
1890–91	T. R. Park (Cambuslang)
1891–92	G. Sneddon (Edinburgh)
1892–95	A. Sliman (Battlefield)
1895–96	R. F. Harrison (Ayr)
1896–97	W. Crighton (Arbroath)
1897–98	D. Mackenzie (Rangers)
1898–99	J. A. D. McLean (Ayr Parkhouse)
1899–1900	J. H. McLaughlin (Celtic)
1900–03	A. R. Kirkwood (Airdrieonians)
1903–04	R. M. Christie (Dunblane)
1904–06	A. Stevenson (Falkirk)
1906–07	W. T. McCulloch (Arbroath)
1907–09	J. Liddell (Queen's Park)
1909–10	W. Lorimer (Heart of Midlothian)
1910–14	A. M. Robertson (Stenhousemuir)
1914–19	D. Campbell (Morton)
1919–27	T. White (Celtic)
1927–33	R. Campbell (St Johnstone)
1933–37	J. Fleming (St Mirren–Moorepark)
1937–45	D. Bowie (Ayr United)
1945–49	D. Gray (Airdrie)
1949–52	J. Lamb (Arbroath)
1952–56	H. S. Swan (Hibernian)
1956–60	J. W. Park (Queen's Park)
1960–64	R. Kelly (Celtic)
1964–68	T. Reid (Partick Thistle)
1968–70	P. Scott (Morton)
1970–	H. S. Nelson (Arbroath)

Secretaries of the Scottish Football Association

1873–74	A. Rae
1874–75	J. C. Mackay
1875–80	W. Dick
1880–81	J. S. Fleming
1881–82	J. S. Fleming R. Livingston
1882–1928	J. K. McDowall
1928–57	G. G. Graham
1957–	W. P. Allan

1

In the Beginning there were Eight

On the morning of Monday, March 3, 1873 a notice appeared in Scottish newspapers under the heading, 'Scotch Challenge Cup'. It read: 'It has been proposed by the committee of the Queen's Park club that Scotch clubs playing Association rules should subscribe for a cup to be played for annually, and retained for the year by the winning team, the competition to begin next season. Scotch clubs who may wish to join this movement are invited to send two representatives to a meeting to be held to consider the matter in Dewar's Hotel, 11 Bridge Street, Glasgow, on the evening of Thursday the 13th inst. at eight o'clock'.

It was strange that in the *North British Daily Mail* the next paragraph should be headed, 'Scotch Football Union', and read: 'Those interested in Rugby football are reminded of the meeting to be held in the Elmbank Academy at half past four today for the purpose of inaugurating a Rugby Football Union'. The handlers and the dribblers, as they were called then, were taking sides.

The meeting was duly held in Dewar's Hotel and seven clubs were represented. They were Queen's Park, Clydesdale, Vale of Leven, Dumbreck, Third Lanark Volunteer Reserves, Eastern, and Granville. Kilmarnock sent a letter stating their willingness to join. These eight clubs that night formed the Scottish Football Association.

They unanimously resolved, 'That the clubs here represented form themselves into an association for the promotion of football according to the rules of the Football Association and that the clubs connected with this association subscribe for a challenge cup to be played for annually, the committee to propose the laws of the competition'. Mr Archibald Campbell of the Clydesdale club was elected the first president, and appropriately, Mr Archibald Law, who issued the notice calling the meeting, was appointed first secretary.

And so, in that little hotel to the south of Jamaica Bridge and just around the corner from Carlton Place, where later the Scottish Football Association were to have their offices, order was brought to a game which had been played for centuries in Scotland but in a crude form which was at best a rowdy kickabout.

The Scots at that time did need some new form of recreation. Their main pastime till then was under some pressure. On the day that the S.F.A. was formed, a group of ratepayers in the South Side of Glasgow met to demand that pubs should close at nine o'clock. They were alarmed and disgusted that, in 1872 in Glasgow, 54,446 persons had been apprehended for being drunk, incapable, and disorderly.

There was need, too, for an extension of sport and more liberal thinking about it for, even ten years later, Sir James Paget, speaking on recreation, defined true amusement as consisting largely in variation of employment.

The Scots, and, indeed, the English, had for many years been partial to kicking anything which would roll. The best ball of the period was an inflated pig's bladder but a craftily rolled school bonnet would do. In prose and in poetry football was mentioned but the game played had little relation to the orderly game which the Scottish Football Association established in Scotland.

Until the S.F.A. brought rules to the play the game was a mob exercise dangerous to life and property and frowned upon by every Scottish king of the 15th century. They had seen the game as a threat to the practice of archery and had not recognised its own warlike potential. By repressive measures they sought to turn the Scots from football.

In the first parliament of James the First 'Halden at Perth the XXI day of Maii, the year of God, ane thousand foure hundreth tuentie foure ziere, it was ordained – That na man play at the fute-ball, under the paine of fiftie schillings, to be raised to the Lord of the land, als often as he be tainted or to the Schireffe of the land of his ministers, gif the Lordes will not punish sic trespassoures'.

The parliament of James II held in Edinburgh in 1457 decreed that 'the fute-ball and the golfe be utterly cried down'. In 1491 the Parliament of James IV decreed, 'that in na place of the Realme there be used fute-ball, golfe, or other such unprofitable sportes'.

It was an old popular custom in Scotland on Candlemas Day to hold a football match. Shrove Tuesday was another day for the football, but these games had only a loose connection with the modern form. A writer at the end of the 18th century described thus the Shrovetide match in the ancient village of Scone.

'The men of the parish assembled at the Cross, the married on one side and the bachelors on the other. When the ball was thrown up the game carried on from two o'clock to sunset. The game was this: he who at any time got the ball into his hands ran with it until overtaken by the opposite party and then, if he could shake himself loose from those on the opposite side who seized him, he ran on. If not, he threw the ball from him, unless it was wrested from him by the other party.

'The object of the married men was to hang it, or put it three times into a small hole on the Moor, which was the dool, or limit, on the one hand; that of the bachelors was to drown it or dip it three times in a deep place in the river, the limit on the other. The party who could effect either of these objects won the game.'

This match was typical of those before the first rules were drawn up at Cambridge.

Many of these crude games with a ball are recorded and sometimes there was more to them than running and kicking. It is noted in the history of the Scottish Borders that the gathering of raiders was often disguised under the pretence of a football match. Sir Robert Carey, who was Warden of the East Marches in the middle of the 16th century, mentioned in his memoirs that he was particularly vigilant when he heard that a football match had to be played.

Sir John Carmichael was murdered after a football match at Raeswood near

Lochmaben on June 16, 1860, but the last notable match of the old order was that between the men of Ettrick backed by Sir Walter Scott and the men of Yarrow backed by the Earl of Home. Sir Walter, a football enthusiast afterwards wrote, in commemoration, the song 'Lifting the Banner of the House of Buccleuch'.

The old crude form of the game still persists in the annual Ba' Game in Jedburgh but in the main the old ways were but old men's tales by the time that the S.F.A. in the Annual in 1877–78 were congratulating themselves, 'on wiping out that form in which the crowds took part, regaling themselves from time to time with ale and pancakes and in which windows had to be barricaded'.

They had become partial to sophistication and they were happy at having substituted 'the fine excitement of the noble run in a field where you must meet and play an opponent face to face, where the goal must be forced skilfully and where law and order give justice and fair play for all'.

They drew a genteel picture of an important match that season on a bracing day in the outskirts of Glasgow. We were invited to imagine 'a field where ten thousand people of various ages and degrees were assembled. A large stand, rising tier upon tier at one end, was filled with hundreds of spectators and round the other three sides of a roped-in enclosure congregated the rest of the vast multitude. In this enclosure stood the well-known goal with the upright posts and a horizontal bar.'

There was eager expectation on faces, players with quick bounding step and attired in light graceful costumes. There was the line up in battle array, forwards, quick of eye and lithe of limb, dexterously dribbling the ball and backs, strong and resolute, and the ball being propelled or followed by those untiring forms and for an hour and a half those players struggled with unfailing energy and dauntless courage and the utmost coolness and good temper.

But soon there were the stern realities of competition, the pressure of professionalism and, as they described it then, the greed of gate money. The Scottish Football Association had to develop a new phraseology, a less emotional and idealistic one, a humble one.

The English had already rescued the game from chaos in their territory by codifying a set of rules and making the play conform to the name, football. They barred handling. They also brought sense to it by decreeing that, since the goal was there anyway, a score should be marked for kicking the ball into it instead of into a space outside it as practised by the handlers.

In 1848 the first set of rules had been pinned on a tree in Parker's Piece, a playing field at Cambridge University. The Football Association had been formed in London in 1863 and their rules had inspired some young men in Glasgow to form Queen's Park in 1867. The F.A. Cup was instituted in 1871 to inspire the start of the Scottish Cup two years later. The game in its present form came from England. Even in Scotland that has to be admitted.

Although the Scots did follow England's lead in the game it was not long until they had mastered its arts at least to their own satisfaction and developed that strange arrogance which has persisted over the first century. Even in official circles the

'Wha's like us' attitude flourished but maybe then with more justification than at some later periods.

The *S.F.A. Report* for the season 1878–79 carried a curt paragraph, 'The International matches brought us, as we may say, the usual honours'. The *S.F.A. Handbook* proclaimed, 'It is with great pleasure your committee have to report that another season has passed without a single defeat to mar our brilliant record. It is now six years since an international was lost.'

Strength in depth and contempt for the opposition was shown in 1885–86 when, for the three internationals played, thirty-three separate individuals were used. No match was lost.

There was some flag waving in 1886–87 when the annual report declared, 'For seven years it has fallen to the lot of past committees to report that the standard of Scotland still waved triumphantly over the football world and it was with feelings akin to fear that this season's international battles were looked forward to. It is therefore all the more pleasing to chronicle that Scotland still stands where she did.'

One could detect a note of trepidation in that paragraph and the authoritative writer of the day, Forward, in the *Umpire*, confirmed it when he wrote at the end of that season, 'The narrow squeaks that Scotchmen have had in the last two or three internationals have convinced me that English football is now quite on a par with Scots'. That was a terrible admission to have to make.

It is a matter for Scottish regret that when football did settle down the S.F.A. had seldom further opportunity for reproducing that stirring language about brilliant records and the standard of Scotland waving triumphantly over the football world, and the line – Scotland still stands where she did – had little except a geographical significance.

2

The Game takes Shape

Football played on a rectangular field with goalposts and rules and the ball being kicked rather than thrown originated in England but the skills were first developed in Scotland. There the dribbling game was practised. Attacks were pressed with ten players and skill and artistry were first brought to the game. The Scotch play was admired throughout Britain and copied, but not for a long time matched. England could win only two of the first sixteen international matches played against Scotland and those two were at home.

This is strange for the writings of the day describe playing conditions which were far from suitable for close work on the ball. Indeed an article in the *S.F.A. Handbook* of 1880–81 suggests that football took over from cricket because the game could be played on less flat surfaces.

The writer described how the flat ground in Glasgow was swallowed up by the builders and houses and railway stations and churches and public works stood where many a cricket match had been played. Football could be played in the streets or on a big free coup and only the best aspired to a field where a farmer grazed his cows and sheep and for which the rent was but a trifle.

He asked, 'What did they care about ridges or furrows or that it was a difficult matter to see the lower goal posts when you were at the other end.' It must have been on such a ground that Queen's Park played East Kilbride. The *North British Daily Mail* of Monday, February 24, 1873 described the event.

'A match was played on Saturday between these clubs on the ground of the latter at East Kilbride. The field was rather narrow for the game and had been symmetrically divided, with an incorruptible fidelity to proportion, into 15 foot furrows, which, by introducing alternate hill and dale, no doubt lent a charm to the landscape, but while giving the place a poetic beauty, rather spoilt it for the stern prose of football. On Saturday last, probably for the first time in the history of this planet steeplechasing and football were combined.'

There was some trouble with a hedge which was too low and not much good in a cross wind for keeping the ball out of the next field.

There was another report of a Queen's Park journey, with them walking to Glasgow Green to play Eastern and the match being ended prematurely when the crowd 'broke' on to the field and some of the Queen's Park players developed well-grounded suspicions when spectators got too close to where their garments were piled.

The *Scottish Athletic Journal* reported on September 15, 1882 a Scottish Cup tie in which Rangers beat Jordanhill by 4–0.

'The Rangers were highly amused on their arrival at the outlying village to see the preparations being made for them. The field was a new one and anything but a bowling green and no touch line had been marked off. But the Jordanhill quickly discovered a method of remedying this defect and borrowing a horse and plough from a neighbouring farmer turned up a furrow and formed the necessary parallelogram with it. The furrow, however, was very dangerous, some of the Rangers getting nasty wrenches.' Later Rangers might not have been so amused.

There was now and again trouble from spectators but, it is hoped, not often such as was described in the *Scottish Athletic Journal* of October 13, 1882. The game was at Annbank.

'Not more than five hundred people were on the field and a slovenly looking, petticoated and extremely vulgar section of the crowd had answered to the courteous invitation, "Ladies free". The language which came from the lips of these ladies was sickening to listen to. The men behaved moderately well, and, in respect of them, it may be as well to forgive the fair sex in the hope that in future matches they will stay at home.'

Against that the Scottish Umpire was pleading on August 21, 1884, 'Is it reasonable or desirable that a man should be prevented from taking a female relative or friend to witness a match on account of filthy remarks?'

There were paragraphs which could have been written yesterday such as this one in a column headed, 'Things worth knowing'. 'That Association football is becoming notorious for scenes and disgraceful exhibitions of ruffianism. That the rabble will soon make it impossible for law abiding citizens to attend matches.' That was published in the *Scottish Athletic Journal* on September 27, 1887.

The game then was very physical and the definition of rough play which the S.F.A. ordered to be posted in all grounds in 1887 indicated what had been taking place.

The notice read, 'Rough play as specified in Rule 10 is, tripping, ducking, hacking, jumping at a player, pushing and charging from behind.' Charging was still allowed and exactly what that meant can be gathered from a paragraph in the *Scottish Athletic Journal* on October 20, 1882.

'This Ross seems to be a sturdy fellow. Rumour has it that he attends to training to a ridiculous degree. A run in the early morning is good for any man but practising charging against railway trucks is completely out of it.' And to think that at the end of the Second World War they were hailing Billy Houliston as the king of 'Rummel 'em Up.'

And then came the tactics. The basic formation in the 'seventies was two backs, two half-backs, and six forwards. They were deployed as two right-forwards, two centre-forwards, and two left-forwards. The goalkeeper acted as captain. Everybody was an attacker and in the *Scottish Athletic Journal* of November 24, 1882 a writer was lamenting that some country clubs were holding two backs static 20 yards from goal, 'to keep the goalkeeper in chat', he added scornfully.

He complained that two men were thus thrown out of the play so that the battle was carried on with eight men against ten and they should see that they were silly not to back up the front division. Lugar Boswell were slated for attacking with only nine men. What would he have thought of Sir Alf Ramsey's 4–3–3 formation that won the World Cup. The international team of 1888–89 was the first to be named with two backs, three half-backs, and five forwards.

The *Scottish Umpire* of August 21, 1884 was asking if the game had improved and stating, 'Take any club that has come to the front and the onward strides will be found to date from the hour when the rough and tumble gave place to swift accurate passing and attending to the leather rather than the degraded desire merely to coup an opponent.' That paragraph is timeless.

And there was the cynical view in the *Umpire* on October 2, 1884, 'Tell it not in Gath. Publish it not in Askelon. Strategy can never take the place of eleven good pairs of nimble legs.' That is the ageless get out of the pedestrian.

Aften ten years of organised football in Scotland the S.F.A. took stock. They reported that they had 133 clubs in membership and that one of them was from Newfoundland. There were eleven provincial associations and all had become affiliated. They were, Glasgow, Edinburgh, Renfrewshire, Stirlingshire, Lanarkshire, Southern Counties, Dumbartonshire, Ayrshire, Buteshire, Forfarshire, and Fifeshire.

There was satisfaction that England, Ireland, and Wales had again been defeated and only the 'unmitigated evil' of professionalism clouded the prospect. Of the 133 clubs at the end of the first ten years, nineteen were still active in the Scottish League at the end of the first hundred years. They were listed thus in the early S.F.A. records:

Clyde, formed 1877. Ground, Barrowfield Park, Bridgeton, five mins. from Bridgeton Cross. Colours, white.

Partick Thistle, formed 1875. 80 members. Ground, Muirpark, Partick. Colours, navy blue jersey, blue knickers, and red hose.

Queen's Park, formed 1867. 400 members. Ground, Hampden Park, Mount Florida. Colours, Jersey and hose black and white one-inch-striped and white knickers.

Rangers, formed 1872. 180 members. Ground, Kinning Park off Paisley Road, $\frac{1}{4}$ mile from car terminus. Colours, royal blue jersey, white knickers.

Kilmarnock, formed 1869. 100 members. Ground, Rugby Park, Dundonald Road. Colours, Oxford blue jersey with badge and hose, white knickers.

Dumbarton, formed 1872. 261 members. Ground, private, Boghead Park. Colours, blue jersey, white knickers, and red hose.

Dunfermline, formed 1874. 120 members. Ground, Lady's Mill, South Side of Dunfermline. Colours, blue and white jersey and hose, and blue knickers.

Heart of Midlothian, formed 1875. 220 members. Ground, Tynecastle Park, Dalry, Edinburgh. Colours, maroon jersey, white knickers, blue hose.

Hibernian, formed 1875. 200 members. Ground, Hibernian Park, Easter Road. Colours, green jersey and hose, blue knickers.

Airdrieonians, formed 1877. 100 members. Ground, Mavisbank Park. Colours, blue and white.

Albion Rovers, formed 1882. 30 members. Ground, Meadow Park. Colours, light blue jersey, white knickers.

Hamilton Academicals, formed 1875. 100 members. Ground, South Haugh, Hamilton. Colours, red and white stripes.

Morton, formed 1876. 90 members. Ground, Cappielow Park. Colours, two-inch blue-and-white-striped jersey, blue knickers, and red hose.

St Mirren, formed 1877. 300 members. Ground, Westmarch. Ground, off Greenhill Road, Paisley. Colours, black and white jersey and hose.

East Stirlingshire, formed 1880. 175 members. Ground, Bainsford, Falkirk. Colours, one-inch striped white and black jersey, and blue knickers.

Falkirk, formed 1877. 115 members. Ground at Hope Street. Dressing Rooms at Crown Hotel. Colours, navy blue jersey and white knickers.

Stenhousemuir, formed 1881. 40 members. Ground, South Broomage, Larbert. Colours, black and white jersey and hose and blue knickers.

Aberdeen, formed 1881. 30 members. Ground, Holburn C.C. Ground. Colours, Maroon jersey and navy blue knickers.

Arbroath, formed 1876. 50 members. Ground, Gayfield Park. Colours, maroon jersey and white knickers.

And with football prospering at the end of the first decade there were dreams of what was ahead. Glenavon, writing in the *S.F.A. Annual*, imagined the football international after the turn of the new century in which Scotland played America. It was possible for space had been annihilated and the Atlantic bridged with the 'electrics' once called steamers.

They were going from Glasgow to New York in less than twenty-four hours, 110 knots, and no vibration. The blessed electrics had been introduced not a moment too soon for the coal supplies were becoming exhausted.

There was a great crowd at the ground in Glasgow and *frae a the airts* for train travel was fast and cheap by the turn of the century. The Americans offered to bet evens but this was not taken, for by then, betting on football had been voted 'low and unmanly' and even degrading. The course language of which our forefathers had complained had disappeared and one could take a wife or sweetheart to a match. As for professionalism no such thing had been heard of for years, no club wanted anything to do with professional football players. Something must have gone wrong along the way to make the visionary look so foolish.

There was reason to have hope for an American international for the *S.F.A. Handbook* of 1887 carried an optimistic report from the American Football Association. It read, 'The American Association is now in its fourth year and the association game has now become one of the principal games here.

'Even in the warm summer months you will find a party of lovers of the game chasing the leather. The boys are quick at picking the game up and in a short time we will have native players who will take a lot of beating. Clubs are starting up all over the country. In the season 1887–88 we will have five or six new clubs from the New England states making a total of fifteen or sixteen clubs and we would have four times that number were it not for the distances between the headquarters and some of the states. The play is becoming more scientific and less rough. We have had no one hurt to any extent more than the barking of shins.'

Scotland had the missionaries out fine and early but the word seems to have fallen on the stoney ground of the gridiron or been lost on the wide open spaces.

3

The First Champions

The first Scottish club had been formed in 1867 by some members of the Glasgow Y.M.C.A. who used to meet in the South Side Park to enjoy a kick about. One of the originals writing thirteen years later in the *S.F.A. Handbook* of 1880–81 described the kicking as vigorous, if not exact, and the enjoyment true if not scientific. The game had no shape, the players no discipline.

The writer was one of the thirteen who formed the Queen's Park Football Club in 1867. He described how when a number of gentlemen met in the night of July 9, 1867 the difficulty was in drawing up rules for their club and for their game because they were the first. The secretary was instructed to communicate with the editors of *Cassell's Paper* and *Sporting Life* as they found themselves incompetent to form rules without the assistance of a treatise on the game.

The rules were formulated and printed and then there was conflict over 'the right of private interpretation' but play soon shaped the game and made the rules familiar. They had some resemblance to the modern game. The quaint difference in the Queen's Park rules was that bar or tape had no place in the game. A sky kick if admittedly between an imaginary line drawn upward from each post was a goal. That was a bit hard on goalkeepers.

Ends were changed after every goal and the touchdown was still part of the game but soon discarded when players chose to make sure of the touch instead of risking going for the goal. Hands were used and the ball might be caught on the bound or off another player but might not be lifted or carried. They played from fifteen to twenty a side.

Queen's Park sought games by encouraging other groups to form clubs and failing these they divided and played among themselves, Captain *v.* President, Captain *v.* Secretary, Clerks *v.* Field, Light Weights *v.* Heavy Weights, North *v.* South which was eventually North or South of Eglinton Toll. These matches were contested as sternly as any Cup-tie.

The writer described the enjoyable game of moonlight dribbling, that was before floodlighting, and his having played a practice match at 6 a.m. Then there was the excitement of the negotiations for the first match to be played on May 1, 1868 against Thistle won by Queen's Park by 2–0.

He described the original uniform: 'At first a simple varying badge worn on the right arm to distinguish opposing sides at practice. This was followed by the blue jersey, which is still the international colour, and a reversible blue and red cowl more like a winter night cap than anything else. Only shortly before the Cup contests began was this uniform discarded in favour of the now famous black and white strip.' Since Queen's Park represented Scotland in the first international match against England the blue, which was their colour then, became the blue of Scotland.

There was fun in the game. The original member described how the Queen's Park ground was opposite the Deaf and Dumb Institution. He went on, 'It was here some of our members learned the art of talking with their fingers. The boys of the institution had lessons in the game and taught their "Speech" in return. It was no easy thing to get an Institution boy told that he was off-side or had fouled especially if he did not want to be told.'

Queen's Park took possession of the first private football ground in October 1873 and had a strange trouble in wording the advertisement for the first match in it. They could not say where the match would be played for the field had no name. To save trouble the name of the nearest block of buildings was put down and so did Hampden Park get its name.

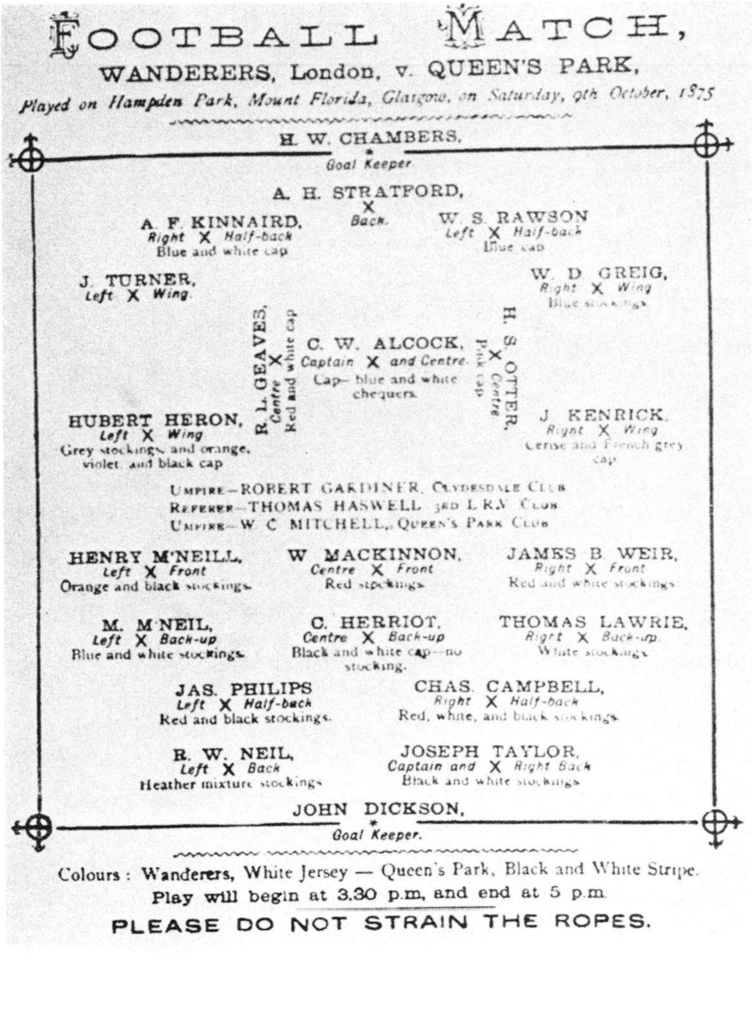

FOOTBALL MATCH,

WANDERERS, London, v. QUEEN'S PARK,

Played on Hampden Park, Mount Florida, Glasgow, on Saturday, 9th October, 1875

H. W. CHAMBERS,
Goal Keeper

A. H. STRATFORD,
Back.

A. F. KINNAIRD,
Right X Half-back
Blue and white cap

W. S. RAWSON
Left X Half-back
Blue cap

J. TURNER,
Left X Wing

W. D. GREIG,
Right X Wing
Blue stockings

R. L. GEAVES,
Centre X
Red and white cap

C. W. ALCOCK,
Captain X and Centre
Cap—blue and white chequers

H. S. OTTER,
Centre X
Pink cap

HUBERT HERON,
Left X Wing
Grey stockings and orange, violet and black cap

J. KENRICK,
Right X Wing
Cerise and French grey cap

UMPIRE—ROBERT GARDINER, CLYDESDALE CLUB
REFEREE—THOMAS HASWELL, 3RD L.R.V. CLUB
UMPIRE—W. C. MITCHELL, QUEEN'S PARK CLUB

HENRY M'NEILL,
Left X Front
Orange and black stockings

W. MACKINNON,
Centre X Front
Red stockings

JAMES B. WEIR,
Right X Front
Red and white stockings

M. M'NEIL,
Left X Back-up
Blue and white stockings

C. HERRIOT,
Centre X Back-up
Black and white cap—no stocking.

THOMAS LAWRIE,
Right X Back-up
White stockings

JAS. PHILIPS
Left X Half-back
Red and black stockings.

CHAS. CAMPBELL,
Right X Half-back
Red, white, and black stockings.

R. W. NEIL,
Left X Back
Heather mixture stockings

JOSEPH TAYLOR,
Captain and X Right Back
Black and white stockings

JOHN DICKSON,
Goal Keeper.

Colours: Wanderers, White Jersey — Queen's Park, Black and White Stripe.
Play will begin at 3.30 p.m. and end at 5 p.m.

PLEASE DO NOT STRAIN THE ROPES.

Wanderers *v.* Queen's Park, 1875. The teams played different formations. The players wore distinguishing hose and caps.

In 1870 the English Association played what they called international matches in London, but the teams were selected in London and were resident there and the old Queen's Park player recalled how one friend of his was chosen for Scotland because his name had a Scottish ring about it.

When the English Cup was started Queen's Park subscribed for the trophy and entered the first competition. They were generously allowed byes until only three other clubs were left in. The Cup rules required that the Final and the immediately preceding ties should be played in London. Queen's Park tried to arrange to play the Wanderers in the semi-final on a Saturday so that they might play the winners of the other tie on the Monday. They could not afford the double journey to London.

The team travelled to London played Wanderers and drew. Their plans thus fell through for want of money. They returned to Scotland and scratched. This was the first London trip ever taken by a Scottish club. The history of Queen's Park is the history of Scottish football until the Scottish Football Association was established.

Before the English Cup was instituted Mr Alcock, Secretary of the Wanderers club in London, challenged any eleven Scotchmen north of the Tweed. This was taken up by Mr H. N. Smith, described as an attached and enthusiastic member of the Queen's Park club. He carried on a long correspondence with Mr Alcock and eventually the match was arranged and played on the West of Scotland Cricket Club ground, Partick, on November 30, 1872 and was drawn. All the Scotch players were members of the Queen's Park club.

The Glasgow Academicals, the leading club in the opposition game, had offered their ground free for the match which was an indication of the friendliness then between the two codes. The match gave the game the impetus it needed and this resulted the following year in the formation of the S.F.A.

By 1880 there were others greater than Queen's Park and that proud old player from the original team was writing, 'Queen's Park has long since done its educating work and it must now fight for its place against its equals. This is no matter for regret. Rather let us rejoice. Now we dare not count victories till they are won. It is not so long since, playing both elevens, the club took 21 goals from the Alexandra Athletic. But this is trifling, not football. The days of 21 goals are for ever gone and we do not wish to see them again. Old folk grow older and young ones grow up. Then the young ones add their own experience to that of their teachers and two to one wins.'

And Queen's Park's educating work having been so fruitful – and the match against England at Hamilton Crescent having sent enthusiasm galloping – new clubs sprouted throughout the country. The Association was formed and the growth of interest can be seen in the advertisements of the day.

Forsyths were advertising the full range of football gear by 1876: jerseys 4*s.* 6*d.*, hose 2*s.*, caps and cowls 1*s.*, belts 2*s.*, knickerbockers from 7*s.* 6*d.* John Stuart of Buchanan Street in Glasgow let the world know that the new 'Rapid Dry Process' enabled him successfully to photograph football team groups. Robert Sorley of

Buchanan Street offered new designs in badges for football clubs. The Royal Hotel, George Street, offered to cater for visiting football parties, and Hay and Nisbet would print match posters at a day's notice. Commercial interests were quickly on the bandwagon.

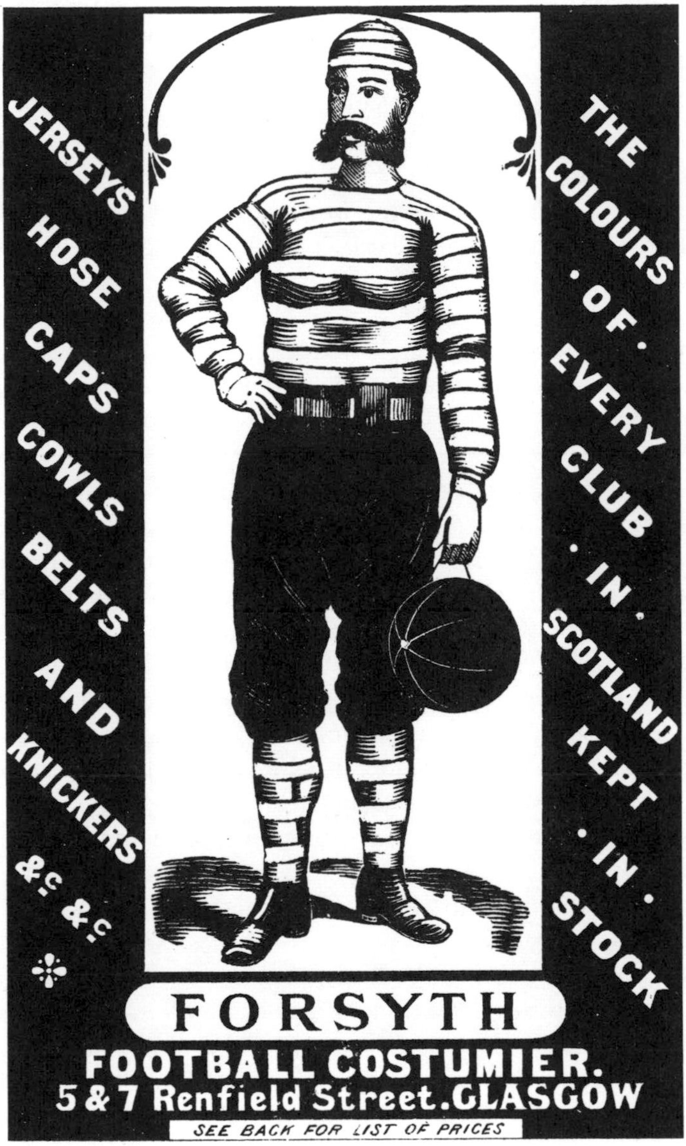
JERSEYS HOSE CAPS COWLS BELTS AND KNICKERS &c &c
THE COLOURS OF EVERY CLUB IN SCOTLAND KEPT IN STOCK
FORSYTH
FOOTBALL COSTUMIER.
5 & 7 Renfield Street. GLASGOW
SEE BACK FOR LIST OF PRICES

The well-equipped football player of 1876. The first distinguishing badge was a coloured armlet. Later a reversible, coloured cowl was worn before jerseys became standard. The buttonless ball came later.

Footballs ranged from 5*s*. to 12*s*. They were of good hide with vulcanised rubber insides, but unsatisfactory by modern standards for they were formed of long panels, running with the lacing slit, and caught at the common join with a button.

Not until 1887 did Thomlinsons delight the football world with a patent buttonless ball which sold from 8*s*. 6*d*. and 9*s*. 6*d*.

There were sixteen clubs at the end of the first season and fifty clubs in 1875 when the Scottish Football Association published its first Football Annual. The foreword to this annual gives some idea of the speed at which football matters were moving. The secretary, Mr William Dick wrote, 'The publication of this little Annual was only decided on a week ago.' He still managed to make sixty-four pages and sell six pages of advertisements.

Nobody could have forecast the effect which that first match against England, limited though its scope might have been, would have on the Scottish sporting public. The tickets had been put on sale at a shilling each in the shops in Argyle Street of Mr Millar the hatter and Mr Keay the hosier and they were bought by 2,500 spectators. But this was as nothing to the furore two years later when an estimated 10,000 crowded into Hamilton Crescent and brought such stir to the streets of Glasgow as had never before been seen.

A writer described the occasion: 'The match was the topic of conversation at every luncheon bar. Speculation was rife as to which team would win. England were favoured chiefly on account of their being reported to be a stone heavier on the average.

'The match was timed to commence at 3.30 and business in the city being then, as usual on Saturday afternoons, almost entirely suspended in legal offices and shipping and commercial houses, there was a great demand about that time for means of locomotion to Partick. Every tramcar which reached Jamaica Street en route for Whiteinch was besieged at that point by a crowd of young men. The outside seats were crammed in a second and the patience of the guards sorely tried in preventing more than the statutory number from gaining access to their vehicles.

'But the tramcars carried a very small proportion of the intending spectators. Cabs – two-and four-wheelers – along with numerous private carriages occupied the main thoroughfare while a stream of pedestrians hurried along the pavements. By three o'clock the ground at Hamilton Crescent was much crowded and on all four sides the ropes were strained by the masses. Soon the roads and streets were crammed by those wishing to gain admission and the windows overlooking the scene were full.'

During the next hundred years Scottish football followers were to learn much about the troubles of travel. For the first match at Wembley Stadium eleven special trains took them to London for a 25*s*. 6*d*. fare. In 1934, 52 trains took 23,000 followers to London and the conditions on these travelling drinking booths were shown in the strange goings on during the journey of the 9.30 out of Glasgow Central bound for the 1949 Wembley. Two men fell from that train and were killed, another was found astride a buffer, and yet another clinging to a running board.

Near the end of the hundred years, travel was more sophisticated and aeroplanes were finally shown to have been accepted when the inevitable extrovert organiser went round with the hat for the driver.

4

The Game Spreads

In the last year of the first century of Scottish football The United Arab Emirates Association applied for membership of F.I.F.A., the controlling body for world football. In the bulletin which announced their application a gentleman, Ydnekatchew Tessema of Addis Ababa, Ethiopia, was named as president of the African Football Association. There was mention, too, of Gabon, Yemen, Ceylon, and Kuwait. Football clearly has spread far from Britain where it started, and spread fast.

Yet the speed of spread has been as the lighting of a fire with two sticks compared with the spontaneous combustion after those eight clubs met to start the Scottish Football Association a hundred years ago. The conditions for the fast spread of an idea were not right for communications were slow. There were no television or radio to bring the game to the people. Newspapers only noted it with a paragraph or two reporting results under the racing programmes and information.

Yet the game spread with the speed of a grass fire in a dry summer and just two years after the S.F.A. was formed, puffs of smoke could be seen in Ayrshire, Dumbartonshire, Edinburgh, and Lanarkshire with the main blaze centred in Glasgow. In those 2 years the 8 clubs had multiplied to 50. There were 26 in Glasgow and the Suburbs, 6 in Ayrshire, 9 in Dumbartonshire, 3 in Edinburgh, and 6 in Lanarkshire.

The following year Glasgow had 35 clubs registered with the S.F.A., Ayrshire 15, Dumbartonshire 10, Lanarkshire 10, and Edinburgh had linked with the East and had 10 clubs including Dunfermline, Grasshoppers, Bonnybridge, Lenzie, and Dundee.

Before the first decade had ended football power had swung from Queen's Park to the Vale of Leven, that strip that straggles pleasantly from Loch Lomond to the Clyde. The Vale had three clubs, Vale of Leven, Dumbarton, and Renton. They were all formidable clubs and early Cup winners and Renton were to win acclaim as champions of the world. The *Scottish Referee* wrote, 'No greater ecomium could be passed on a football player than to say that he was one of Renton's great championship team of 1887–88.'

They were alleged to derive their strength from drinking chicken bree. In 1877–88 they beat all Scottish opposition and then, when challenged by England's best, West Bromwich Albion and Preston North End, they beat them, too, and were undisputed champions of the world. The team was built around a formidable half-back line, Kelso, Kelly, and McKechnie but after their championship year the team disintegrated.

James Kelly, the captain, and McCallum, a forward, went to join the new club, Celtic, which was being formed. James Kelly became Celtic's first centre-half, captain, and later chairman, and he was the father of Sir Robert Kelly later chairman himself.

The *Scottish Referee* on January 21, 1889 in an article on James Kelly commented, 'There are many people who believe that when Scotland adopted the centre-half-back position she sacrificed much of her power in the game. We do not share altogether that opinion and if the players who fill this position in other clubs were men of Mr Kelly's calibre then there would be no difference of opinion on the matter nor would we have cause to regret having followed England in adding to the defensive parts of our elevens'.

The position suited James Kelly and he was given it because he wanted to do everybody's work. In it he was always in the middle of the play. The writer made a good point on tactics and many were to echo him in later years as they lamented over the slavish following of English ideas to the detriment of the Scottish attacking game. The laments were relevant when the stopper centre-half was devised in England and copied in Scotland and later when Sir Alf Ramsey perpetrated a formation with only three forwards and won the World Cup to the dismay of those who were of the opinion that the thinking in football should be directed mainly towards scoring goals.

In 1887 Hibs became the first club to take the Scottish Cup out of the West of Scotland and there was relief that they did, for Edinburgh had been a big problem to the football pioneers because, there, players could not keep their hands off the ball. Hibs win was proof that at last the word had fallen on some good ground.

About football in the capital D. D. Bone in the *S.F.A. Handbook* of 1878–79 wrote: 'As far back as 15 years or so a union was formed in Edinburgh to draw up a code of rules to encourage the game of football. These rules were a combination of the present Association and Rugby, dribbling being largely indulged in but the goal posts were similar to those now in use under the latter code of rules, and a goal could not be scored unless the ball went over the posts. Matches were played between schools and other clubs. This game was vigorously promoted by scholastic clubs and young men attending college.

'Some years later when the number of young men sent over from England to be educated in Scotland, particularly Edinburgh, began to increase, these old rules were subjected to considerable alteration and eventually assimilated to those of the English Rugby Union.

'Eventually, however, new clubs springing into existence in the West did not care to play these rules and following the example of similar clubs in England adhered to what they considered an improvement on the old system of football and joined the English Association which had been formed in 1863.'

The first missionary expedition to Edinburgh was reported in the *Glasgow News* on Monday, December 29, 1873. It read: 'On Saturday last two teams, picked from Association clubs in the West of Scotland, played a friendly match at Edinburgh with a view of showing how the Association game is played, as in the East country only the rugby style of the play is known.'

That must have been the only occasion when Edinburgh citizens were happy to have Glaswegians show them how the game of football should be played. According to the *Scottish Athletic News* of December 22, 1882 the game under Association rules had been taken up in Edinburgh in 1874 by two clubs, The Thistle and the 3rd Edinburgh Rifles Volunteer Corps. For some years previously a bastard set of rules had been played in summer by three clubs, the Blue Bonnets, the Southern, and the Thistle.

The Blue Bonnets disbanded in 1873 but Thistle adopted the new rules and were alone in this for a year until 3rd E.R.V. Corps joined them. The following year, 1875, Heart of Midlothian, who had played for a short time as White Star, the Hanover, and the Hibernian came into existence. Some of the original Hibs members played with White Star but joined the new club at its inception so it could be said that both Hearts and Hibs sprang from the same root.

Hibernian were started by Irishmen in Edinburgh and consequently controversy set in early. The Edinburgh Association was formed in September 1875 but when Hibs applied for admission they were refused. It was said that they played rough and affiliated clubs were asked not to play them. They applied for admission to the Scottish Football Association but their entry money was returned.

Hibs continued to play but by the following year they presented a petition, signed by all the prominent players in the Edinburgh District, supporting their application for admission to the S.F.A. and they were admitted reluctantly. They were not allowed to play in the Scottish Cup competition that season.

It took some little time to tame the footballers of Edinburgh and the *S.F.A. Handbook* of 1877–78 had a report of the East of Scotland final, '1500 watched Hibs and Heart of Midlothian. To those accustomed to such matches in the West the play was decidedly poor not to say almost savage in the roughness of the often unnecessary charging.'

The struggle for the expansion of the game in Edinburgh was perhaps more difficult than elsewhere. The problems can be seen in a meeting of influential people reported in the *Scottish Athletic News* of December 1882. Those meeting requested the Commissioners of Woods and Forests to grant permission for football to be played from September 1 to April 1 each year on land between Holyrood Palace and Meadowbank.

Mr Watt, the secretary of the Edinburgh Association, reported that there were fourteen clubs in his Association and twenty clubs outside. They were responsible for good order and for permits to play. The Corporation sent word they would sanction football on the East Meadow. Stockbridge Park had already been opened.

A class struggle seems to have developed in Edinburgh, with Rugby the Establishment game. It was stated at the meeting that the game was being discouraged by the municipal authorities who put obstacles in the way of clubs seeking ground and that another discouragement, which had to be faced, was that the game was played only by the artisan classes. None of the upper or the middle class even tried the game except Edinburgh University. They formed a club in 1878.

St Bernard's was formed in 1879 and in the following year, the first of the East of Scotland Challenge Shield, went to the final but were beaten by Hibs 4–2. Edinburgh then had three formidable clubs Hibernian, Heart of Midlothian, and St Bernard's and maybe that was why the Edinburgh Association had the confidence to ask for an inter-city game with Glasgow and stick up for their rights over terms.

Mr John McDowall, the S.F.A. secretary, answered Mr F. G. Watt's request for a match by offering to organise one as a national team trial but, as Edinburgh was an association subordinate to the S.F.A., the main association should be responsible for the match and should keep the drawings.

Edinburgh's pride was hurt and they proudly answered that the Edinburgh Football Association was an independent association and in no way subordinate to the S.F.A. and rounded off the affair with the observation that Edinburgh was of the opinion that the S.F.A. just wanted to collar the swag.

A lot of plain speaking showed that the S.F.A. was equating itself with Glasgow. Administration was rationalised when the Glasgow Association was formed on March 21, 1884. The rivalry between the cities flourished, comically.

By the time that the Glasgow Cup competition was agreed to at the Annual Meeting on May 17, 1887 Glasgow was modestly describing their success as phenomenal and humbly claiming that the past season had been quite in keeping with the traditions of so historical a football centre. The report of that year recorded egotistically: 'It is not egotistic to say that no minor association in Great Britain has so many first class clubs under one jurisdiction.'

That season they passed off a defeat by Edinburgh with, 'A fairly representative team opposed Edinburgh on Powderhall grounds and after a close and even game Glasgow had to put up with a second defeat by 3 goals to 2. It is an ill wind that blows nobody good and this result will doubtless enhance the interest next season of the return in Glasgow.'

Before the tenth birthday of the S.F.A. their handbook was recording astonishing progress away from Queen's Park, Rangers, Third Lanark and the clubs from the Vale of Leven. The county associations reported enthusiastically.

The Ayrshire Association had been constituted in May 1877 with the Earl of Eglinton and Winton as Hon. President. They then had a total of forty-six clubs competing for their cup. They came from Cunningham, Kyle and Carrick. Lugar Boswell and Mauchline had been champions but that year the town of Kilmarnock was strongest and Kilmarnock Portland beat Kilmarnock in the association final by 4–2. They won the Ayrshire Kilmarnock Charity and Burns Cups that season. In that season from August 20 to June 3, they played thirty-four matches.

The Buteshire Association had been formed in February 1881 and had five clubs competing for their cup. Cumbrae beat Bute Rovers in the final that season. The ties took place in the spring of the year for Cumbrae, from Millport, found sea travelling difficult in the winter.

The Lanarkshire Association reported their most successful season both as regards unanimity and finance. They were not so successful with the timing of matches. Twice protests were upheld over first round ties between Clarkston and the Glendowan. The games finished in darkness and had to be replayed.

Hamilton Academicals beat Cambuslang by 3–2 in the final to take the Lanarkshire Cup, then the association took great pride in beating the Renfrewshire Association by 7–2 and humbly proclaimed that they had never thought they could beat a county with such teams as Arthurlie, Cartvale, and Abercorn.

A report from the Southern Counties lamented that most were far from football centres but declared that such love had the people of Moffat for the game that they would rather want their dinner than miss a good match. The club in Moffat had been started by the Rev W. H. Churchill a former Association captain of Cambridge University.

Mr Churchill while showing himself an enthusiastic lover of outdoor sports likewise endeavoured to instil in the young men a love for intellectual pleasures and to show them that if they desired to be respected and useful they must first learn to command themselves. He put them on two months hard training and they drew their first match, against Annan. His was a philosophy which did not take on.

Mr Churchill took his team to play the oldest club of the south, Queen of the South Wanderers, at Dumfries. They again drew but soon he had to leave for Reigate but not before he, his wife, and his sister donated a cup named after himself to be played for by an association combining Dumfriesshire, Kircudbrightshire, and Wigtownshire. The Southern Counties Association was formed in Dumfries on November 9, 1881.

5

Missionary Work

The Scottish Football Association excited with the explosion of the game at home and inspired with commendable missionary zeal went out to teach all nations while still but infants in the game themselves. They had remarkable results in winning converts from the paganism of Rugby. They planted the seed of football in the United States and Canada and as far away as Australia and it was not their fault that their teaching was not followed through.

Belfast was a stronghold of Rugby but on October 24, 1878 a select of Queen's Park and Caledonian played an exhibition match in Belfast on the ground of the Ulster Cricket Club. It is remarkable that there was such co-operation between cricket and football in those days. The first international between Scotland and England was played on a cricket pitch at Partick.

The results of this exhibition were reported to the S.F.A. in 1882 by Mr J. M. McAlery, Hon. Secretary of the Irish Football Association. He wrote: 'The statistics of football in Ireland show that the "noxious Scotch weed", as some of our rugby friends are inclined to describe it, has taken root deep in the soil and is spreading rapidly.'

That season, in addition to an Ayrshire Association Select, teams from Queen's Park, Abercorn of Paisley, and Johnstone Rovers had gone over to play and the Irish Cup was won by a team almost all of whom were Scottish. They formed the Queen's Island Club whose president was E. J. Harland of the shipbuilding firm of Harland and Wolff and on whose sideboard rested the trophy. His name was substantial backing for the game there.

Scotland at that time had sent the game to Canada and it flourished especially in the West. In the 1882–83 *S.F.A. Handbook* the Hon. Secretary of the Western Association, Mr D. Forsyth, B.A., reported that the twenty-four-club membership of the previous season had risen to thirty-nine. He was roused to wild optimism about the prospects but unfortunately he was a poor prophet.

There was similar enthusiasm in the States but unfortunately this too was misplaced. In 1886 Mr Joseph Walden, secretary of the American Football Association, reported to the S.F.A., from Newark, N.J.: 'The Association has now entered its third year and rapid strides have been made since birth not only in the numerical force of the clubs, but in the general excellence of the play. The game has entered the hearts of young Americans and captivated them with its many opportunities for a display of skill and daring and many are every year joining the clubs and learning the mysteries of football from their English and Scotch cousins.'

Distance inhibited progress and the following year the secretary was reporting sending a team 500 miles to play the Canadians and individual clubs sending teams on an all-night sail to play matches. Had transport been speeded before football was introduced to the United States then that country's position in world sports might have been so different and there would not have been the disturbing anomaly of one of the greatest sporting nations in the world being out of contention in the greatest of all world sports.

It has recently been established that the first athletics meetings in the United States were the Highland Games staged nostalgically by the Caledonian clubs and that the hammer throw was introduced to the States by them. Those early Scots settlers gave the States athletics, it is just a pity that their efforts on the football field had not been so successful.

When William Dick, secretary of the Scottish Football Association died on March 28, 1880 he was described as being respected, where football was played, not only in this country but in America and elsewhere. It is extraordinary to remember that the game had only been organised in 1873 yet seven years later a Scottish official was known all over the world.

At a conference in 1882 it was thought advisable to undertake an Antipodean Tour. That became a firm conviction two years later when there appeared in *The Scottish Umpire* a report of football in Australia. Something had to be done.

The report read: 'Victoria football is rotten. There is not one redeeming feature in it. It is more handball than anything else and is a mixture of rugby, handball, hacking, and wrestling. There are twenty players in each side and three umpires, two goal and one central umpire. The game is rough in the extreme and one club last year had to pay no less than £90 for doctors' expenses for attendance on injured players.' That was a fine state of affairs.

The Australian Association was established in 1884 but soon they were appealing for help from Scotland. 'We have had a very uphill struggle to introduce the Association game into Melbourne as the Melbourne people are so prejudiced in favour of the Australian game. We have come to the conclusion that we must in a systematic way look for recruits from home.'

Scotland spread its influences in England too and in 1887 no less than seven Scottish clubs took part in the F.A. Cup, Queen's Park, Renton, Rangers, 3rd Lanark R.V., Cowlairs, Partick Thistle, and Hearts. Both Queen's Park and Renton were beaten by Preston North End and 3rd Lanark lost to Bolton Wanderers. Rangers reached the semi-final but were beaten by the ultimate winners, Aston Villa.

6

Law and Order

Previous to the introduction of railways when matches, other than local, were seldom thought of there were different forms of the game throughout Britain. Each district, isolated and playing within its own bounds, had drifted into some peculiar style of play which, confirmed and developed by years of practice, had become characteristic of the place. Thus, in the middle of the last century, what was enforced in one place was forbidden in another.

Even in the great English schools, where the first laws of the game were developed, Eton, Harrow, Rugby, Winchester, Marlborough, Shrewsbury all differed in more or less important points of the game. When the railways were built to facilitate travel and community was able to play against community standardisation of the laws became essential.

Yet differences persisted after the first laws were codified and even after the Scottish Football Association was formed. Charging was banned in Ayrshire, they handled in Edinburgh and kicked the ball over the bar, and in Sheffield they had no offside.

The Football Association was formed in London in 1863 but the object of the Association was not merely to establish a uniformity of play. They insisted on the principle that the hands would only be used by the goalkeeper and that, as a writer at the time declared, the barbarous customs of hacking and collaring, conspicuous in certain other modes of play, should be condemned and eliminated.

He wrote: 'The present style of football, although considerably modified of late, still allows the use of the hands to such an extent that very often an entire stranger to the game would be more apt to call it Handball Maul than Football.'

He admitted: 'Accidents will sometimes happen in football but these arise from the nature of the game and to eliminate every chance of danger is as impossible as to change old age to youth. The game that requires neither courage nor endurance, that affords no physical contest to develop the bones and the sinews of youth may be a game devoid of danger but it is manifestly unfitted for a high spirited race such as ours. On the other hand there is no need to add by laws and the style of play to the chances of injury.'

By the end of the 'seventies there were eleven associations in Great Britain and the colonies, The Football Association (founded 1863), The Sheffield (1871), The Derbyshire (1871), The Scottish (1873), The Birmingham and District (1875), The Welsh (1876), The Edinburgh (1877), The Ayrshire (1877), The Canadian (1877), The Renfrewshire (1878), The Lancashire (1878).

The South of England, Scotland, and Wales early adopted the Association code but argued much before they saw eye-to-eye over the throw-in. Scotland held to the rugby style throw-in with the ball going in at right angles to the touchline. England allowed the throw in any direction but the ball was not to be played until it touched the ground.

Those wanting change in Scotland argued that the rugby style throw-in did not impose any penalty for a kicking out, time-killing, defensive tactic. They wanted a fifteen-yard penalty with the ball thrown in any direction. There was much heated argument and predictable accusations of following England slavishly.

Tempers rose when a National Football Conference was called for Manchester on December 5, 1882 with all football associations invited to be represented. There was a hectic meeting of the Scottish Football Association which declined the invitation and the *Scottish Athletic Journal* reported:

'Through the inability of the chairman to control the meeting the rowdy element, as is always the case when discipline is relaxed, asserted itself and the more respectable of those present, rather than be contaminated and brought to the level of the rougher, kept silent seeing that any argument with reason in it would be a mere waste of words. The meeting was packed for a purpose and the purpose was gained and at the expense of lowering the association in the estimation of all right thinking men.

'The resolution was proposed by an irresponsible individual and carried by the meeting and when only a very few were present, the majority having gone in search of much needed refreshment after participating in a stormy discussion which had lasted over four hours. Before the absentees returned the thing was done.

'Had anyone present proposed that the Association itself be dissolved we have no hesitation in saying that it would have been carried unanimously and with as little thought to the consequences as the resolution not to attend the conference.' The obvious lack of objectivity in the writer indicated how severe were the differences. S.F.A. meetings became more dignified over the years.

The English found a quick answer and held up the arrangements for the match against Scotland until the S.F.A. explained why they were sending no delegate to the rules conference. The S.F.A. committee worried by thoughts of loss of revenue diplomatically found a loophole and sent delegates to what they called a supplementary conference.

Uniformity was established at that conference. Scotland and England compromised over the throw-in. The ball could be thrown in any direction but with both hands and was in play as soon as it was thrown. Offside was agreed and a player could not play the ball unless three of the opposing players were nearer goal. Football was on its way nationally.

The Scots got their way over goalkeepers. They were permitted to step aside from a charge. Previously they were not allowed to carry the ball but it was accepted that taking a step or two aside could not be considered running. It was still not allowed to score a goal from a free-kick, and corner-kicks as well as the kick-off were termed free-kicks.

The adjudicating over breaches of laws was still left to the umpires. There were two of them along with a referee and all scores as well as fouls had to be claimed. The umpire showed agreement with the appeal by raising a stick, the referee by blowing a whistle.

In June 1887 the first steps were taken to control the wider field of the game. The International Board was formed at a meeting of the home associations, which were all there were in the world at the time. They formed rules which stipulated that the Board would be formed from two representatives from each of the four national associations, that they meet each June, and that resolutions could not be adopted unless agreed to by three-quarters of those present, but in the case of alterations to the laws of the game a unanimous agreement should be necessary.

The International Board took charge of the game with a resolution that 'Decisions of this Board shall be at once binding on all the associations and no alterations in the laws of the game made by any association shall be valid until accepted by this Board.'

Dundee's Scottish Cup winning team of 1910. Dundee beat Clyde at Ibrox by 2–1 after drawn games, 2–2 and 0–0. *Back row:* Neal, Langlands, Bellamy, W. Wallace (Secretary and Manager), Dainty, Hall. *Middle Row:* D. McEwan (Director), McEwan, Comrie, W. Longair (Trainer), Frazer, Chaplin, G. Walker (Director), Crumley, *Seated:* J. Cameron (Director), Hunter, ex-Bailie Robertson (Chairman), Lee (Captain), A. Williamson (Director), Macfarlane, A. Spalding (Director), Lawson, McCann.

Aberdeen with the Scottish Qualifying Cup after the 1905 Final in which they beat Renton at Dundee by 2–0.

In 1890 the penalty-kick was introduced at the suggestion of the Irish F.A. The following year the umpires were replaced by linesmen. In 1894 the referee was given complete control and it was no longer necessary to appeal. In 1912 the goal-keeper was forbidden to handle the ball outside his own penalty-area. In 1920 it was decreed that players cannot be offside at a throw-in. In 1924 they were allowed to score direct from a corner-kick. In 1925 there was a momentous change and a player could not be offside when two players instead of three were between him and the goal. This was on the proposal of the S.F.A.

In 1929 the goalkeeper was compelled to stand still on his goal-line when a penalty-kick was being taken and in 1931 he was permitted to carry the ball for four steps instead of two and, instead of a free kick for a foul throw-in, the throw reverted to the opposing side. In 1951 obstruction became one of the offences punishable by an indirect free-kick.

The pioneers did their work well in framing the Laws of the Game and only two major changes have been found necessary this century. There was the change in the offside law and latterly the provisions for substitutes which have had a far-reaching effect both in providing better spectating and in allowing for greater freedom in tactics. It is doubtful if ever again there will be another major change in the laws except, perhaps, to have a no offside area across the field 18 yards from goal.

7

A League and Professionalism

A curt letter from Mr Thomas Lawrie, secretary of the Queen's Park Football Club, dated December 7, 1875 showed the need for established and binding fixtures for clubs in the expanding game of football. Queen's had agreed to play Vale of Leven and the fixture had been used as a selling point for season tickets. They called off and Vale of Leven were annoyed. There was an exchange of excessively polite letters each with a barb in it.

Finally Mr Lawrie wrote: 'Your letter of yesterday's date is received. Unless drawn against you for the cup my club decline to play you at all. The correspondence has of course been private but you will not probably consider this a sufficient reason for withholding the letters from publication. I have nothing to add to former communications to which I refer you. Yours etc. Thomas Lawrie.' Gentlemen had fallen out.

There were continuing complaints from the provinces about city clubs failing to honour return engagements after they had benefited from the country clubs playing in the cities. The Association Challenge Cup did not provide a dependable match pattern. Some wanted one in league form but others did not and their objections was bound up with the inordinate fear of professionalism. For fifteen years the matter was debated before there was reluctant acceptance of a plan to form a Scottish League. This is not really long when it is remembered that the Scottish Rugby Union starting at the same time took 100 years to arrive at the same decision and against similar arguments.

In the early 'eighties professionalism had become established in the North West of England. Touts invaded Scotland seeking to entice players to England to play for money. Such was the feeling against them that many had to come in disguise for if they were discovered they were beaten up.

Some sort of a class struggle seemed to have been involved. The game in Scotland was originally a middle-class game and it was feared that professionalism would lower the status of it. This came through in a comment in *Scottish Sport*: 'The feeling is strong in those who have the best interest of football at heart, that the way to maintain the tone of the game is not to make it a trade.'

Accrington were to discover that Scottish football players were not paupers when they wrote to Frank Shaw, the internationalist right-wing of Pollokshields Athletic, offering him £120 per annum to play for them. Shaw's reply was: 'Dear Sir, On my return from a fortnight's cruise amongst the Western Islands, on my yacht, I found your letter . . .'. There was no need to read further.

Professionalism had been legalised in England in 1885 and the Football League founded in 1888 by a Scot, William McGregor, but in the committee of the S.F.A. there was strong resistance to following once again, the English lead.

The S.F.A. report on season 1884–85 noted that 'Mr McKillop, our esteemed president, has laboured indefatigably to have this evil suppressed in England and prevent it getting a resting place in our midst'. The Scottish Football Association sent a delegate to protest at the meeting in London at which the F.A. legalised professionalism.

There were repeated witch hunts in Scottish football seeking out those who surreptitiously paid players. Hearts were protested against by Dunfermline in 1884 on the ground that two of Hearts players, McNee and Maxwell, were being paid. McNee admitted that he had not wrought since he went to Edinburgh and Maxwell, that he had told another player that he could get him 26*s*. per week in Edinburgh.

It transpired that McNee had given up a good job in Busby when he had been offered 26*s*. a week by Hearts. Maxwell received a similar sum and Hearts were found guilty of employing them and were expelled from the Scottish Football Association. That is the skeleton in the cupboard of the modern Hearts.

Hearts, backed by the Edinburgh Association, applied for re-admission six weeks later and when it was shown that they had sacked McNee and Maxwell and elected an entirely new committee and a new set of office bearers they were allowed back to the fold of snow white lambs.

The pressure for change became heavy when the English faced realities and followed the legalising of professionalism with a league and especially when Celtic quickly became politically strong after joining the S.F.A. in 1888. They were the first club to be run on shrewd business lines, the first to become a limited liability company.

Leading up to league football was the proposal for the Qualifying Cup which would separate the big clubs from the small in the S.F.A. It was condemned by *Scottish Sport* the great defenders of amateurism. It claimed that 'The Qualifying Cup would set up an invidious distinction between the clubs forming the S.F.A.'. The notion that all clubs are equal has persisted among the small ones over the century.

Scottish Sport also declared loftily: 'True sporting spirit aims at elevating the game to a higher platform than pounds, shillings, and pence; it seeks to purify and enoble it and to rear and produce, not procure and pay'. That was a nice play of words on the twin worries of transfers and payments but as Mr J. H. McLaughlin of Celtic said when proposing the formation of the league, 'You might as well try to stop the flow of Niagara with a kitchen chair than endeavour to stem the tide of professionalism'.

And so it was. There was a meeting in Glasgow and twelve of the fourteen clubs who were invited committed themselves to a league claiming that an absolute fixity of fixtures was the central principle of their constitution.

There was the predictable criticism that they were obsessed by self-interest and were ready to embrace professionalism. 'Athlete', in the *Coatbridge Express* wrote: 'The prospect is dreary for the provincial clubs. The S.F.A. have been lax in not controlling fixtures and allowing strong clubs to play fast and loose with the weaker'.

The voice of the establishment, *Scottish Sport*, thundered on February 25, 1890: 'We believe the league projectors held a meeting in Glasgow during the week. What was done we cannot say for the matter evidently cannot either be discussed in public or reported upon. In its present position the scheme stands condemned by its very secrecy as a conspiracy against the present constitution of affairs and the present constitutional authority.' It feared League or no League would become Association or no Association.

When the rules of the League were made public *Scottish Sport* declared: 'Our first and last objection to them is that they exist. The entire rules stink of finance – money making and money grabbing.'

The Scottish League was formed in 1890 with Mr A. Lawrence of Dumbarton the first president, Mr J. H. McLaughlin of Celtic secretary, and Mr W. Wilton of Rangers treasurer. Celtic and Rangers were in early and deep and especially since Queen's Park refused to become involved. They remained strictly amateur.

The rules were a copy, more or less, of the English League rules. The bottom three clubs had to drop out but they were eligible for re-election. The gate receipts had to be divided two-thirds to the home club and one-third to the away club and there was a guarantee of £5 to the away club.

At this distance in time it seems that the Scottish Football Association might have seen the necessity of fixed fixtures and themselves formed a league and controlled league football but then, as now, the committee was too big and too wide with too many interests represented and clashing. Revolution was the only way to have anything radical done.

Eleven clubs joined: Abercorn, Cowlairs, Cambuslang, Dumbarton, Hearts, Rangers, St Mirren, Renton, Third Lanark, and Vale of Leven. Renton were found guilty of professionalism after five games and expelled. They had played against St Bernard's, whom the S.F.A. had already declared to be professional. Renton claimed that they had played a new club called Edinburgh Saints but the S.F.A. found that they and St Bernard's were one and the same club.

Clyde and Queen's Park had been invited to the discussions initiating the league but they had stayed out. They had misread the situation and soon they found their mistake.

The league competition was instantly successful. The first league handbook in the second season, 1891–92, listed a First Division of 12 clubs, an Alliance of 12 clubs, a Federation of a similar number, a Midland League of 10 clubs, a Northern league of 8 clubs, and an Ayrshire league of 10 clubs. They had 64 clubs organised and that was a formidable start.

Rangers and Dumbarton tied with twenty-nine points each for the first championship. The clubs played off for the title at Cathkin Park. Rangers led 2–0 at half-time. Dumbarton drew level in the second half and the clubs and the League Committee agreed to joint champions and each received a flag. In that first tournament 814 goals were scored in the 180 games and there was no game in which no goal was scored. They entertained.

Queen's Park were quickly to appreciate the hard facts of staying outside League football. Their secretary reported that they had had no application for home and away matches from Third Lanark, Vale of Leven, Rangers, or Dumbarton. On being asked why, the clubs each said that they regretted that owing to League fixtures they had no space for dates with Queen's. Few clubs had.

Since these were among Queen's Park's most lucrative fixtures this was serious for the old club who, besides, were not playing well and were losing much of their popularity and authority. Queen's Park had already had another source of income cut for the success of the English League deprived them of dates with the big English clubs.

As its sponsors had said, the League was exactly what Scottish football needed to extend its popularity and feed its crowds but, as its critics had asserted, it did lead to the legalising of professionalism in 1893, on the motion of Celtic.

Queen's Park watched the developments anxiously with the Scottish Cup ties their only certain means of income, and that precarious. When an opportunity arose to join they were quickly in. There was a quarrel between the First Division clubs and those of the Second Division when the two sections joined in 1899 and Queen's Park got in during the stramash and were admitted as members in May 1900.

A compromise was reached between the two divisions in which each division was to run its own affairs but that all matters which affected the league as a whole would be dealt with by the First Division.

Those who had feared that a Scottish League would be to the advantage of the big clubs had not long to wait until the all too familiar pattern was established with the well-endowed Celtic and Rangers having their winning cycles and the others trying to nose into the scene but only with sporadic success.

Rangers had been playing badly in the few seasons before the League was formed and indeed were near to the point of disintegration. They had opened Ibrox Stadium in 1899 after a season in which they had won but thirteen of the thirty-nine matches they played. In the show game to open the stadium they were five goals down to Preston North End at half time and losing 8–1 when the match was prematurely stopped to save them further unnecessary punishment, as a boxing referee would have said.

They reorganised their committee and the strength of the men who came in can be gauged by the fact that Willie McAndrew soon became Scottish League Secretary and Dugal McKenzie became president of the Scottish Football Association. Willie Wilton became match secretary and later a successful manager. Rangers were powerful in the establishment.

Celtic *v.* Rangers last century. Celtic then wore vertical green and white stripes.

And so Rangers, who had been criticised as a soft team, were hardened up for the start of the League, but their misfortune was that the astutely run Celtic with their new methods of dribbling and passing and their fine stadium had first run at success. They had come to football in 1888 with a ready-made team: Kelly of Renton, the Maley Brothers, and other established players from Hibs and Dumbarton. There were no apprentices.

Dumbarton shared the first championship with Rangers and then took the next but afterwards waned when the resources of the developing Glasgow, close by, became too overpowering for the peaceful Vale of Leven. Hearts butted in twice to prevent Celtic taking the next six championships.

That was a stirring period for Celtic, the club which was formed to provide soup kitchens for the poor of the East End of Glasgow and then quickly found themselves in big business in football with the best stadium in the world and enough imagination to exploit it.

In 1893 they played a game under 'the electric light' with lamps strung across the park hung from poles. They staged the world cycling championships. They experimented with anti-frost field coverings. Above all they had a sound, attractive team and staunch support.

Rangers had shown signs of developing strength by winning the Scottish Cup in 1904, their first success in the competition. They had previously been in the final against Vale of Leven but after a draw had refused to replay for they claimed they had wrongly been disallowed a winning goal.

Rangers made a historic gallop through season 1898–99. They played all their eighteen league matches without losing a point. They were not so good in the cups. They reached the finals of the Scottish Cup, the Glasgow, and Charity but lost them all. They were geared for the steady, consistent pace of league football and that team won four championships.

Hibs and Third Lanark each had a season as champions before an exciting Celtic team burst through in 1906 to alter all thinking about how the game should be played as radically as did the Hungarians in 1953. Almost unchanged, that Celtic team won six successive league championships and that was a record run that was not beaten until another Celtic team under Jock Stein won seven successive championships. To commemorate the earlier winning run Celtic were presented with a silver shield by the other clubs during the coming-of-age celebrations of the Scottish League.

That Celtic team was generally reckoned to be the best team to have played up to the First World War. They were managed by that stern character, Willie Maley, a member of the original Celtic team and later manager and secretary, a charitable man with fierce club partisanship and knowledgeable in football matters. He ruled his team from his office as also did the great Rangers manager, Bill Struth. The older players were left to decide the tactics and bring on the younger players.

A typical banner carried on the horse-drawn supporters' brakes at the start of the century. Supporting it are former Partick Thistle players Jimmy Davidson and Jackie Husband.

April 1933. Jimmy McGrory (Scotland and Celtic) chases yet another goal.

In those days players trained daily with interminable running on a track and exercises behind the goals. They were not allowed to walk on the grass of the football field far less train on it. They were not given a ball to practice with and the accepted reasoning was that if they did not kick the ball during the week then they would be all the more keen to have it on Saturdays.

Willie Maley believed that a football team should be built and not collected. He built the 1906 team round a formidable half-back line, Sunny Jim Young, Willie Loney, and Jimmy Hay. In front was a perfectly blended forward line, Alec Bennett, Jimmy McMenemy, 'Napoleon', the mighty Jimmy Quinn, Peter Somers, and Davie Hamilton. For that team Celtic changed to green and white hoops. Previously they had played in stripes.

Davie Adams was the goalkeeper, Alec McNair later came in at full-back and there was an interesting change on the right-wing which nowadays would be sensational. Alec Bennett left Celtic to join Rangers and was replaced by Willie Kivlichan who had been a couple of seasons on Rangers books and had played a few games for them. Policies were different then.

During those six seasons as champions Celtic played 192 league matches and lost only 23 games taking 305 of a possible 384 points. Their success was based on ball-playing, attacking football. Quinn, the sturdy centre, who could hold off the heaviest charge, had the strongest shot in football. The crafty play of Jimmy McMenemy was geared to making chances for his shooting. McMenemy himself never talked about shooting. He 'passed the ball inside the post'. It was said that in a game he should have a ball for himself and there should be another for the others.

While Celtic rebuilt at the end of that run, Rangers three times won the championship. Then Willie Maley was back with another great team with McMenemy still there but with Patsy Gallacher, another football immortal, beside him, and a popular defence, Charlie Shaw, Joe Dodds, and Alec McNair, then balding but still astute and capable of holding any flier.

There are handy divisions in the development of Scottish football since the Scottish Football Association 100 years ago brought order to a rowdy pastime. There were the years when the game took shape, when the rules were honed and the equipment standardised and some measure of skill put to use. Professionalism and League football rounded off that period and then the game had the proper shape.

Then came that Celtic team after the turn of the century to show that football was a team game. That team was abundantly rich in the skills of the game in personalities but above all they were a team and, the extent to which they were, brought a new concept to the game.

There was a pattern to their play and their individual skills were complementary. The neat wing play of Bennett and Hamilton, the tireless endeavour of Somers, the cute inventiveness of McMenemy, all were directed to opening the way for the dashing Quinn to score.

The phase was followed by one in which a re-organised Rangers set the standard, again with team work but adding the fitness of full-time training. They developed a style which was more simple and direct than the entertaining Celtic pattern and it set them on top of Scottish football with a heavy monopoly in the years between the wars.

In the years after the second world war there was a great boom in Scottish football. The people sought pleasure thirstily after the drought of the war years and a gay Hibs team, fitting the mood of the time, then Aberdeen, Hearts, Dundee, and Kilmarnock broke through the monopoly in contrast to the situation between the wars when only the superb Motherwell team of sophisticated forwards with that great left-wing, George Stevenson, and Bob Ferrier, were able to win the championship.

Like a Christmas rose bringing elegance and colour to a hard scene, a Motherwell team of style and talent broke the between-wars league monopoly of Rangers and Celtic. John Hunter, known throughout football as Sailor Hunter, fashioned the team to take advantage of the new offside law and score goals. They did that to perfection and the goalscoring records of Willie McFadyen and Bob Ferrier still stand.

The new offside law of 1925 gave the forwards the advantage of needing only two players, instead of three, nearer the goal. This was seen by some as encouraging defensive play but by Sailor Hunter, who was formerly an internationalist with Dundee, as an incentive to try for goals. The club had just previously had a reputation for goalscoring through Hugh Ferguson who, in the ten years after 1916, scored 238 goals for Motherwell before taking his total to 363 with Cardiff City and Derby County.

Sailor Hunter's thinking produced a specialist goalscorer, Willie McFadyen, who lay well up in the scoring area and had thoughts only for the goal. On either side of him were other perceptive footballers, George Stevenson, on the left, and John McMenemy, who could give McFadyen the running ball he liked on the right. On the wings were men who could send the ball over hard to McFadyen's head or have a shot themselves.

There were internationalists behind in the half-backs, Alan Craig and Willie Telfer, and the robust left-back, Ben Ellis, who played six times for Wales. Thus this attractive Motherwell had a great bank of sophisticated players making chances for two notable goalscorers, and the skill in the approach and the excitement of their finishing made them a popular team despite being provincials.

In every season from 1927 to 1934 they were in the top three of the First Division of the Scottish League and four times they were runners-up. Twice they reached the Final of the Scottish Cup. Theirs was an impressive record.

In season 1931–32 they won the Scottish League championship and won it decisively to delight everybody in football who valued skilful, effective football. They finished five points ahead of Rangers and 18 ahead of Celtic who were third. They lost only two matches that season and both away, to Rangers and Kilmarnock. They lost only one point at home, to Celtic.

They scored 119 goals in winning the championship and that was then a record. Willie McFadyen scored 52 of them and that is a record which still stands. They used to say that McFadyen could only score goals. Sailor Hunter agreed but he found it easy to tolerate such a limitation.

McFadyen's scoring was amply backed by the left-winger, Bobby Ferrier, the highest-scoring winger ever in Scotland, and one whose career lasted much longer than the explosive McFadyen. Ferrier played 626 games for Motherwell between 1919 and 1937. In season 1929–30 Bobby Ferrier scored, from the left-wing, 32 goals in 37 league matches and only Ken Dawson of Falkirk with 39 goals from 34 games on the wing has beaten that for quantity but his goals were scored in Second Division matches.

Ferrier's swerving shots, hit on the run, were memorable. He was English born and so not eligible for the Scotland international team. The Scottish League honoured him seven times but the Stevenson–Ferrier wing was international class.

Football had to be completely re-thought in Scotland when the Hungarian national team showed their skills in 1953. Even the very equipment had to be altered to the light-weight materials used by Puskas and the others and their ball skills sent Scottish footballers, and others elsewhere, to practise with a ball. It is a puzzling thought that although footballers in those days would agree that pianists should practise on a piano they themselves would not practise with a ball.

Those delightful Hungarians even changed the look of football players and it is amusing now to look at old pictures and see the players, of but a few years ago, with their heavy leather boots and their shins bulging from layers of cotton wool, bandaging and shinguards under their knitted woollen stockings.

The final phase was the one in which Jock Stein's Celtic, Scotland's greatest-ever team, not only proved themselves the best in Scotland but also in 1967 the best in Europe. The following year, but for an untypical lapse in discipline, they would have won the World Club Championship. They added sustained speed and tactical ingenuity to an adventurous attacking mentality and inordinate skill. As the first century ended they still were supreme after seven successive League Championships.

An unfortunate incident in which the Rangers manager, Willie Wilton, was drowned on May 2, 1920, had a significant influence on Scottish football. William Struth, a professional runner at one time, had joined Rangers from Clyde as trainer. When Willie Wilton died he was appointed manager and Rangers immediately moved into the most successful era in the history of the club.

In his first season the team was defeated only once in 42 matches and they took 76 points out of a possible 84. They won the League Championship by 10 points. They won it 16 times in the next 21 years and there was an arrogance, an inevitability about them, such as set them apart.

Bill Struth in his years as manager set out not only to make Rangers the best team in the land but always to think that they were. They were the best dressed. They had the best facilities. They were the best paid and the best treated. He instilled in them a tremendous conceit which eventually developed an arrogance in themselves and a sense of inferiority in most of the others. It was reckoned that Rangers reputation could usually be depended upon as worth a goal start.

Bill Struth was a hard little man in matters of discipline and on presenting a devastating front to the world but he interfered but little in the playing of the football. He stayed mainly in his expensively carpeted office at the head of the marble stairs, an office which contained a wardrobe and he would appear maybe in three changes of suit a day. He instituted and encouraged a sort of hierarchy in the club to control the players.

At the head were the established players and they dictated how games would be played. Beneath them were other groups which sorted themselves out according to experience. A player had to work through the groups but he had to be a long time in the first team before he was accepted by those select few centred round the captain.

Travelling fashions. Celtic leave to play Ajax, 1971. (*Insert*) Rangers leave on Anchor Line ship, 'California', for U.S.A. Tour in 1929. Sitting: Morton, Archibald Muirhead, and director Bowie. Seated on deck, Jimmy Kerr, trainer, and Bill Struth, manager.

It was a strict feudal system which worked and left Bill Struth free to build the business side of the club and establish an authority outside football. This he did with considerable success.

His first inspired move was to sign Alan Morton from Queen's Park and for a decade his teams were built round the little left-winger. He already was strong in defence with Jimmy Gordon and Bert Manderson at full-back and Willie McCandless replacing the formidable Gordon whom many reckon was the best all-rounder of all time.

Jimmy Bowie, Tommy Muirhead, and David Meiklejohn supplied class and strength at half-back and Andy Cunningham, Tommy Cairns, and George Henderson had power in attack but it needed the subtle skills of Alan Morton to make a team of them.

David Meiklejohn was the captain he selected to mould the new Rangers and an extraordinary player he was. There was a game in which Celtic led Rangers by three goals. Then the roused Meiklejohn took control and almost single-handed and with sheer football ability turned that situation round and Rangers won 4–3. The Glasgow Catholic newspaper, *The Observer*, at the time had a writer, 'Man in the Know', who was outrageously biased towards Celtic but not even he could

Willie Waddell (Scotland and Rangers) ploughs through the snow in a Cup-tie at Ibrox in 1954 and leaves Harrower (Third Lanark) stranded.

ignore Meiklejohn that day. He wrote, 'Meiklejohn, great enough to be a Celt'. He could think of no higher praise.

Rangers in those years of success were a wonderfully functional team. As great players moved on others came in. Bob McPhail, Dougie Gray, Tully Craig, Sandy Archibald, Jimmy Fleming – they kept the tradition going and added to an overpowering reputation of Rangers which was becoming fearsome to lesser clubs until it seemed that Scottish football was being controlled from the marble halls of Ibrox.

As the war years approached, Rangers had the new lords of the dressing room ready to continue their grip on Scottish football. George Young, a great captain in the making, was there, and Sammy Cox, a masterly all-rounder, had been plucked from Queen's Park.

There was a typical winger in Willie Waddell, all dash and strength and power and a cocky little inside man, Torry Gillick, of all the skills to set him running, and a lively centre-forward, Willie Thornton, to meet his crosses at the far post and score goals. It was said in over-simplification that Rangers' methods were no more than a long pass from George Young to send Waddell away and a cross to the far post for Thornton to head a goal. The style was simple but hardly as simple as that. They did not always leap the midfield.

When Rangers played a memorable match against Moscow Dynamo on November 28, 1945 it was the powerful tackling and the long positive passing of the left-half, Scot Symon, which earned Rangers a 2–2 draw. It was often overlooked that they had half-backs.

The quaintly-garbed Moscow Dynamo at Ibrox Stadium, 1945.

The scene outside Ibrox Stadium an hour and a half before Rangers played Moscow Dynamo in November, 1945.

8

International Target

The first international football match, between Scotland and England 100 years ago, was the impetus which rushed the new orderly form of the game into widespread popularity. It was therefore ironic that when the same two countries met 100 years later they should produce such a sordid, ill-mannered, vicious game with a cynical disregard for the spectators. Those responsible had turned the clock back 101 years and had given substance to the fears of those, who, in the 1880s, had fought so passionately in resisting the introduction of professionalism.

In those days long ago the big crowd, in the West of Scotland Cricket Ground at Hamilton Crescent, had appreciated that the new game they watched was a substantial one which could bring country against country.

They saw that, in its new form, stripped of the mauling and the scrambling of rugby, the new game had a better shape than the old and, since it was more open and easier of understanding, it made for better spectating. The opportunities the game gave for developing unsuspected ball-skills were quickly apparent. The game was manly without being crude and that fitted in with the mood of the period.

The leap back to crude football at Hampden Park was neither sudden nor unpredictable. There had been a steady, easily-traced regression in English football over the previous ten years. It showed in the ever-increasing destructiveness of football there and in the tolerance of the referees in permitting this until there was an obsession with fouling and players took pride, in a weird way, in only committing good fouls. Morality was being squeezed from the game. The trend has to be noted for Scotland was being nipped by the backlash.

The World Cup of 1966 did something to foster this spirit in an oblique way. Sir Alf Ramsey had been charged with the task of winning that World Cup for England on their own ground. He put commendable effort and organisation into the task but he was caught in a period when England were short of great attacking players and especially wingers.

He tried to form a near orthodox team with wingers using Connelly and Callaghan but discarded them and by circumstances was forced into a safe formation which compensated for the shortage of the attacking skills by a concentration in the midfield. There was a destructive aspect to the play, which because it was successful in that World Cup, projected itself into the play of the country as a whole.

Few commentators were happy with the methods that Sir Alf Ramsey had to adopt to win the competition but at least they were fair and he did win and he had to be given credit for making the best of unlikely material, the mark of a great manager. His methods should have been understood for what they were, an improvisation, and the fault was in copying them and then in introducing a violent destructive element into the midfield concentration.

The unfortunate part of the proceedings was that many of the Scotland players were competing in English league football. They had been indoctrinated in this heavy destructive football and they retaliated as part of the game and, some of them retaliated first. Scotland took little credit from the match.

Towards the end of the first century, professional football in Britain was getting too big and to the point of sickness. It had become to some a way of life instead of an embellishment of it and there was need for a brake on the hyperbole which had players and officials believing that football was a matter of cosmic importance rather than a game. To a background of diminishing gates, fees of £200,000 were being paid for a player. There was an air of extravagant show business but with unhealthy box office.

There was a need to appreciate again that the reality and the beauty of football lay in the fact that it was a game. Those who made it something more did it a disservice.

Hyperbole was the enemy. The English claimed that they had the most competitive league in the world as if that had any relevance to the quality of the football. An old-age pensioners' race at a church outing can be competitive without producing an Olympic winner.

That peculiar Scottishness came through in the oft-repeated claim that Scotland produced the greatest players, the most skilful players, that Sir Alf Ramsey was lucky to win the World Cup in 1966, that Scotland had they qualified would have won and all the time it was overlooked that Scotland did not qualify and that Sir Alf did win and came near winning again in Mexico while Scotland still failed to qualify.

The result of the exaggerations being believed was that in England competitiveness rather than quality became the obsession and it was a costly and bankrupting business keeping up with the Joneses. In Scotland, players who believed their own publicity and thought that they were the greatest wanted paying as such although the public were not accepting that rating and were not paying to see them. The game had moved into an era of unreality.

What gave some credence to the arrogant claims of greatness in Scotland was that some very fine players were indeed produced. Inevitably after England won the World Cup in 1966 there was talk that Scotland at the time had better players than England.

There was some justification for this sort of thinking for Scotland had available the extraordinary Jim Baxter, arguably as good a player as there had ever been and along with him, Pat Crerand, Bobby Murdoch, Billy Bremner, and John Greig, all of whom had played as half-backs in the World Cup qualifying matches. Billy McNeill and Ronnie McKinnon were available for centre-halves and the forwards were led by the tempestuous Denis Law, then in his prime, and available for places alongside him were Willie Henderson, Charlie Cooke, Alan Gilzean, Billy Johnston, and John Hughes.

In hindsight it does seem ridiculous that such players could be kept out of the World Cup finals and that view was confirmed the following season when they were brought together in some sort of order and beat the World Cup winning team by a comfortable 3–2 at Wembley Stadium, tormenting the opposition with that strange Scottish arrogance which delights in humiliating by showing off rather than by scoring goals.

9

Hampden Park

The annual match between Scotland and England is the oldest international fixture in the world for the simple reason that it was the first. It was always a popular match and before the First World War the first hundred-thousand crowd in the world had been drawn to it in Glasgow, at Hampden Park.

In those days the event was more firmly established in Scotland than in England for the match had a settled venue at Hampden Park. In England it was moved around the country to Birmingham, Liverpool, London, Newcastle, and Sheffield, but not until Wembley Stadium was opened in time for the 1924 Empire Exhibition did it move on the Hampden–Wembley axis thus starting the fanatical cult which persisted until more sophisticated travel than run-down railway carriages widened the speculating field and the pressures of club football put it in jeopardy in recent years.

Wembley was opened for the F.A. Cup-Final of 1923 and the stadium could not have had a more publicised introduction to the sporting world. The crowd appeal was pathetically misjudged and entry was on a 'pay at the gate' arrangement. Many thousands more than the stadium could hold arrived and too many crushed in when the gates were rushed. They spilled on to the field until it seemed that the contestants could put on their clothes and go home.

And then appeared that white horse, Billy, and his rider, P.C. George Albert Scorey, to coax the invaders off the field. Pictures of them doing so were sent all over the world and Wembley's opening had been spectacularly publicised.

The rise to national popularity of Hampden Park was more gradual. The present Hampden is the third one that Queen's Park have built, yet they never moved more than half a mile from where they first started to play the game.

Their first enclosed ground was a corporation field, across Cathcart Road from the Recreation Park, which they rented from Glasgow Corporation for £20 per annum. They moved to their second ground, and their own ground, in 1883 when Glasgow began to crowd into the South Side. Rents were raised in that area and Queen's Park's ground rent rose by 500 per cent. It did not help that the Cathcart Circle Railway line was scheduled to go through their park.

Queen's were for a season without a ground and again the affinity between football and cricket in those days was evident. They rented Titwood Park from the Clydesdale Cricket Club and on that field played an F.A. Cup-tie against Aston Villa. A special train was run from Birmingham for that match and that was the first football special to cross the border.

They had in the meantime leased another piece of ground and on it built two open stands and, with a cinder track thrown in, the stadium was by far the best in football. Yet what pleased the spectators of the day most was that for the first time there was a substantial rail of wood round the field instead of ropes and they rated the new simple amenity as 'just like Ayr Racecourse'.

This second Hampden was opened on Saturday, October 18, 1884 when Queen's Park played Dumbarton. The advertisements stressed that the kick-off would be at 3.30 prompt. The admission would be sixpence, with ladies free. The grandstand would be sixpence extra for each person.

Yet although Queen's Park were happy the Scottish Football Association were not. They wanted a settled ground and the best in the world for internationals, first, because they appreciated the popularity of them and secondly because they were the main source of income for the Association.

The second Hampden Park was used for the match against England until 1890. The following one was given to Rangers but then in 1894 the successful Celtic, just six years old, had completed the best ground yet in Britain and they staged the England match that year. They offered a capacity of 50,000 with stands.

Celtic rushed on with their ground to catch the internationals. The roof of the stand which had blown down in a storm was replaced, extra seating was built in and an impressive box was set aside for the press and the telegraph services. There was accommodation for 100 reporters, the first press facilities.

They re-turfed and drained the field and pushed the terracings, behind the goals, back to the barricades. A cycling track to accommodate the World Championships was built and banked to a height of seven feet and measured to give 18 laps to five miles. The ground was measured to hold 50,000.

Queen's Park did not give up the international date easily. They offered Hampden to the S.F.A. for the 1894 international for nothing if their members were admitted free. The game went on at Celtic Park and 46,000 crushed in. The takings were £2,650 which was then a British record and, of course, also a world record.

Celtic at that time were a shrewdly-run club on the business side and knowing that Rangers were their only real opposition for the internationals they came to an agreement with them in 1895 that neither club would let its ground for less than the total takings of the stands.

Celtic really worked on the 1896 international against England. They erected the first crush barriers and raised their terracings and stepped them. They made room for 57,000 and the gates had to be shut half an hour before the start of the match. There was an innovation in that they had on duty for crowd control 100 policemen and 150 soldiers from Maryhill Barracks.

The idea of using soldiers might have been persisted with. In the U.S.S.R. soldiers can be seen organising the queueing outside grounds and forming the first row of spectators round the ground to inhibit those who had thoughts of invading the field.

That match in 1896, just twenty-three years after the formation of the Scottish Football Association, gave another indication of how rapidly the game had spread and of how much interest newspapers had begun to take in it. A staff of twenty and a relay of messengers had to be employed to handle the 25,000 words that were telegraphed and the 800 press telegrams which were transmitted.

There were 60,000 at the Rosebery international in Celtic Park in 1900. The Scotland team wore the primrose and pink racing colours of Lord Rosebery, the Honorary President of the S.F.A. His horse, Lada, had won the Derby the previous year and Scotland marked the win and the new century by beating England 4–1.

Jimmy Brownlie (Third Lanark) Britain's oldest living internationalist on his eighty-eighth birthday. He played for Scotland in goal from 1909–14.

The pride of the premier club, Queen's Park, was hurt when the internationals were taken away from them. They organised themselves to buy a piece of ground and on it built the finest football stadium in the world. It was not enough that Glasgow already had that.

They negotiated for a piece of land measuring around 12 acres and got it for £800 an acre. The owner took £6,000 down and the remainder in £1,000 instalments. Queen's Park then had to worry about the Molls Myre Burn which ran through the field and about underground coal workings. The burn they bricked in and fortunately there has never been any subsidence from the mines.

The building of the new Hampden was facilitated by the fact that it was a natural amphitheatre but the Queen's Park committee took their time to be sure of getting it right. Even at that they erred. When the ground was opened in 1971 to re-lay a tired field it was discovered that they had failed to drain the ground.

The new Hampden established the practice of standing the spectators on solid earth terracings instead of on the wooden steps and scaffolding that had been previously used to raise them above ground level.

The new Hampden Park was opened on October 31, 1903 and Queen's Park's first opponents on it were, by arrangement, Celtic, despite the fact that the clubs were in rivalry for the internationals. Although not seeing eye to eye on occasions a strong friendship persisted between the clubs even until the present day and when the amateur club was worried financially in 1971 it was Celtic, who, unasked, donated them £10,000.

Rangers also had an interest, for the ground was opened by The Lord Provost of Glasgow, Sir John Ure Primrose, who was later chairman of Rangers.

The Celtic team which played that day was the basis of one of the most famous in the club's history and two seasons later they were to start a run of six successive League championships, which was only beaten by another Celtic team in 1972, yet Queen's Park won appropriately by the first goal scored on the ground and that by the inside-left, D. Wilson.

Hampden then had accommodation for 60,000 and it matched Celtic Park the biggest ground in Britain. Seventeen years later the capacity had been doubled. In its present state it has been measured to hold 183,570 but the crowds are restricted to 134,580 for the sake of safety.

The stadium stands on 16½ acres but Queen's Park own 33½ acres. The exterior grounds comprise an all-weather pitch which forms a car park on big match days, holding 1,500 cars. The East terracing is the bigger and a spectator standing on top of it is 60 feet above the playing field. He is 325 feet from the nearest goal and 685 feet from the West goal and 900 feet from the top of the West terracing.

The East terracing is measured to hold 62,000 spectators and the West, 41,000. The West terracing was covered in 1967. The enclosure in front of the North Stand which was built in 1935 holds 39,000 and the enclosure in front of the South Stand 5,600. The South Stand seats 10,054, the North Stand 4,476.

Hampden Park holds all the crowd records in British football and many of the records are European records. In 1937 the ground held 149,547 for the Scotland *v.* England match. Within a few weeks of that game it held 146,433 for the Scottish Cup-Final between Celtic and Aberdeen.

For a club match apart from a final the 143,570 who watched Rangers play Hibs on March 27, 1948 is a British record. The record aggregate is the 265,199 at the two matches in the Rangers *v.* Morton Scottish Cup-Final of 1947–48. The record European Cup-Final is the memorable Real Madrid *v.* Eintracht Final of 1960 and the record European Cup-tie gate is the 134,000 of the Celtic *v.* Leeds United tie at Hampden in 1969.

Scotland for long led the world in the size of its football crowds. In 1889 the £800 6*s.* 8*d.* plus £100 from the stand taken at the Celtic *v.* Third Lanark Scottish Cup Final at Hampden Park was a world record. As late as 1931 the 129,810 who watched the all Tartan Scotland team beat England by 2–0 was a world record crowd for any sporting event.

10

They Brightened the 'Twenties

The Scottish Football Association, to encourage Queen's Park to develop the ground, appropriately negotiated an agreement to stage all internationals against England there along with the Scottish Cup-Finals and this agreement was renewed in 1960 for fifteen years with the club receiving 25 per cent and 20 per cent of takings respectively for each match and the S.F.A. acquired the right of pre-emption should Queen's Park ever wish to sell the park.

With twin stages set up at Hampden Park and at Wembley Stadium in the 'twenties and an eager, swelling public recovered from the drab years of the war, the need was for stars to shine on those great stages, to adorn them, and to inspire pride in those who watched and identified with them. And the stars came out in one of the brightest eras of Scottish football and they were natural players of skill and personality, memorable players, and in abundance.

Such players needed no stage director. They could meet for the first time at lunch time on match day and produce in the afternoon well-ordered play, tactical play, exciting, satisfying play. They established the international cult which was to persist long after they were gone because they were men who had pride in their image. They cared about what the spectators thought of them. They cared for Scotland.

Attacking half-backs of stature and character crowded to get into the Scotland team. Jimmy McMullan and David Meiklejohn led them and there were, Peter Wilson, George Brown, and Alex Massie. What backing they were for forwards.

It was an era of spectacular wing play, the most exciting aspect of the game of football, and what wingers there were. Alan Morton and Alex Jackson, so different in temperament but so alike in effectiveness, the speedy Jimmy Crawford and the craftsman, Adam McLean, and to 'feed them', as they said in those days, the hard shooting inside-forwards Bob McPhail, Andy Cunningham, and Tommy Cairns; the more subtle George Stevenson and that genius in the long pants, Alex James.

Football then was simple and about scoring goals. The attitude started with the schoolboys. All wanted to score, none to defend, and the boy who owned the ball was the centre-forward or there was no game. They had two of Scotland's greatest ever centre-forwards to identify with. There was the bustling, courageous Jimmy McGrory, the greatest goalscorer of them all and the ill-fated Hughie Gallacher who tarnished football sophistication with irascibility. His was a story inspiring in its early passages, tragic in its ending.

The dashing mood of that happy period was exemplified in the Three Musketeers of the game, Alex Jackson, Alex James, and Hughie Gallacher, men whose skills were complementary, who played the game, with a twinkle lightening their determination, who could joke and argue and be a bit wild and be jealous of one another's publicity and with a laugh make their own. They were not always good for themselves but they were good for the game.

Alex Jackson came from Renton, that town in the Vale of Leven, where in the 'twenties the exploits of their world champions, who trained on the chicken bree, were still remembered. He first played senior for Dumbarton and when he was seventeen years old he had drawn the attention of many bigger clubs with the sparkle of his adventurous wing play. While still just seventeen he had made arrangements for a reunion of his Dumbarton team mates on the evening of the day he first played for Scotland. He never lacked confidence.

He had gone to the United States where lucrative jobs were being offered football players and when he, like others, returned, many clubs were waiting for him. That wily old character, Pat Travers of Aberdeen, and later, Clyde, outfoxed them all and signed him and his brother Wattie for less than £1,000. There could never have been any better bargain.

Of course he could not hold him for long. Alex Jackson was a long-standing, exciting right-winger who at the time was described as having laughter in his eyes and magic in his feet. He not only spread havoc on his own side of the field but he was deadly in meeting the cross coming from the far wing. He scored many spectacular goals and none better than the three for the Wembley Wizards in 1928.

From Aberdeen he went to Huddersfield Town for around £4,000 and then to Chelsea for £8,500. London suited his cavalier nature and he suited London and he became the highest earner in football.

He made appearances, at £5 a time, several times a week in the sports department of a big store. He was one of the first players to have his name used for advertising. He was on the payroll of a fashion hairdressers just to go in and have his morning shave. He was West London agent for a pools firm and he had a good going tavern in St Martin's Lane. Just before the war he went into partnership to take over the Queen's Hotel in Leicester Square.

He would have been a popular character with his bubbling, happy nature even had he not been a great player. On the field he was a thoroughbred, fast and graceful and exciting but his outside interests induced him to give up the game while there were two or three good years still in him. He was killed in Egypt during the war when a truck he was in crashed.

Alan Morton the cold professional, who was the foil to the dashing Alex Jackson on the other Scotland wing, was different in every possible way except effectiveness. No left-winger was ever better in his own day, and maybe no player, than Alan Morton.

He began his career in 1913 as A. L. Morton with Queen's Park and he was an internationalist before he joined Rangers in 1920 to become the first signing of Bill Struth. His two great inside partners with Rangers were Tommy Cairns and Bob

McPhail and they both defended his memory as the greatest winger of all time and even when Sir Stanley Matthews was at his peak.

Tommy Cairns comparing him with Matthews said, 'In the other arts, accuracy of the pass and the cross, dribbling and team sense he was Matthews' equal. In directness and goalscoring Morton was better.' Both he and McPhail insisted that they would rather play with Morton than Matthews for he never stopped the game the way Matthews did.

Bob McPhail said simply of him: 'He was always going in a straight line – for the goal. He could take the ball into the opponents penalty-area quicker than anybody I ever saw. He never pulled his tricks until a game was won and then he gave the crowd the entertainment they wanted.'

Alan Morton – 'The Wee Blue Devil'.

Alan Morton scorned anything that was even slightly ungentlemanly on the field and he was so far above all the others of his era in skill and field manners and in bearing off the field that when the Scottish Football Association held their Diamond Jubilee Dinner in 1933 he was the only player to be invited as a guest.

In his time he was feared as no other winger was and he was a big occasion man. He played many of his best games against England. They had to suffer him much for he played against them in every year from 1920 till 1932, except 1926, and that became known as 'The year Morton did not play'.

He was only 5 feet 4 inches tall but he had a deceptively long, floating stride which gave him smooth, unexpected speed and no back caught him once he had passed. When he was with Queen's Park the other winger was J. B. Bell, the Scottish furlong champion, and a measure of Morton's speed was that he could match him over 20 yards and give him a close race over the championship distance.

Alan L. Morton was born in the Jordanhill district of Glasgow. His father, a coal master, soon moved to Airdrie and steered his five sons into the mining industry. Alan became a mining engineer, a profession he practised all during his football career.

He was naturally right-footed but as a boy in Airdrie practised interminably to develop the other. He worked at chipping the ball through a hole in the cellar door in his father's garden and by the time he came to play the game seriously he had developed tremendous skill and accuracy and a pivot from the hips which kept him behind the ball and gave him his extraordinary balance.

England tried every kind of full-back to stop him. They put out big ones and small ones, tough ones and clever ones and an expressive new word was coined to describe the English problem. He was 'un-get-at-able'. Ivan Sharpe, the noted English journalist, found another description, 'The Wee Blue Devil', and the nickname stuck.

He was famous for his lob, the undercut cross which had the ball hanging in the air above the goal-area, a worry to defenders. His crosses were wonderfully accurate and Alex Jackson scored his three goals in the Wizards game from Morton crosses.

Alan Morton played for Rangers until season 1932–33 but after playing in five League matches that season he announced his retirement and was immediately taken on to Rangers Board of Directors'. He was an active director until ill-health confined him to his home in 1968. He died three years later. He had played 495 games for Rangers and scored 115 goals. He never played in a Rangers reserve team during all those years.

Bob McPhail was brought into the Rangers team in 1927 to take Tommy Cairns' place as partner to Alan Morton. He became his partner also in the international team. He had come from the best Airdrie team of all time which terrified others with a forward line of Reid, Russell, Gallacher, McPhail, and Somerville.

Bob McPhail was the big, strong, hard-shooting inside-forward who could come in on the play like the modern midfield players. He was ideal for serving Morton and for running on to the winger's accurate cut-back passes. Rangers beat off much English opposition to sign him as Morton's partner and how right they were.

He won seven Scottish Cup medals, six with Rangers and one with Airdrie. Rangers had gone 25 years without winning the Cup before McPhail joined them. He played for 14 seasons with Rangers and was in nine League Championship sides.

He was the ideal partner for another great player, Jimmy McGrory of Celtic. They had famous partnerships against England in 1931 and 1933 when Scotland won by 2–0 and 2–1. McPhail and his Airdrie team-mate, Hughie Gallacher, were belatedly brought together in the Scotland team against England in 1935. Both were well past their best yet Scotland won 2–0.

Hughie Gallacher had signed for Airdrie when he was convalescing from double pneumonia. He was all Airdrie needed then to make a great team and how right judgment of the directors was shown to be when they won the Scottish Cup in 1923–24.

Hughie Gallacher, centre-forward of the Wembley Wizards, 1928.

He had been born in Bellshill, Hugh Kilpatrick Gallacher, on February 2, 1903, the second son of an Ulsterman, who made a modest living from farming. He was an outstanding player at school where one of his team mates was Alex James who was later to combine so successfully with him on the international field.

He worked on munitions during the war and then in the pits where he was toughened for the punishment he took in the penalty-areas in later years. His second sport was boxing and he trained with the British champions, Johnny Brown and Tommy Milligan. He had the right background for the pugnacious game he played.

He signed for Bellshill Athletic for a promised £10 which never did materialise and that was an omen of the ill luck that was to follow him around. He played as a Junior for Scotland and afterwards signed for Queen of the South for £6 a week. He was just seventeen years old.

Almost immediately he married in July 1920 but it was soon clear that both he and his wife were too young for such a step. They stayed together for only a year. A son was born but died before he was a year old. He and his wife parted permanently in 1923. He only had happiness when he was playing football.

The Airdrie team was one of exciting skill and inevitably they attracted English clubs with money to spend and the biggest attraction of all was Hughie Gallacher. There were demonstrations in Lanarkshire when it was learned that there had been transfer talks but it was as inevitable as the tides that he would go.

On a cold November night he was shaken from his own personal troubles by a call to meet the Newcastle United directors and he signed for them and played his first game for his new club on December 8, 1925. Airdrie were paid £6,500 and that for the best centre-forward in Europe.

He was a fast, elusive, jinky player very difficult to dispossess as he shielded the ball and worked towards goal. Close to goal he was sharp in taking a chance with foot or head, and slick in the short, cool pass to make the chance for others. He scored in threes and fours for Airdrie and in one spell scored thirty goals in five matches.

Newcastle supporters were at first not impressed by his unathletic looks. He stood only 5 feet 3 inches tall, but when he began scoring goals he was quickly king of Tyneside. He thrived on the adulation.

He strode regally round the Newcastle pubs and accepted, as of right, the favours of the ladies of the town. He set out to be the best-dressed young man in the north with well-cut suits and he affected white spats and sometimes a white hat and often a rolled umbrella. He was a dandy, living hard but training hard. He surprised many with the seriousness with which he treated the game and the tools of his trade, his feet and legs.

After the Scotland *v.* France match in 1930, when he had tried to storm the night life of Paris and had retired exhausted, Chelsea negotiated his transfer for a fee of £10,000. When he returned to Newcastle for the first time as a player there were over 68,000 in St James' Park to welcome him back and there was reckoned to be another 10,000 outside who could not get in.

Scotland *v*. France, 1930. *Back row:* Nelson, Thomson, Wilson, Walker, Hill, Crapnell.
Front row: Jackson, Cheyne, Gallacher, Stevenson, Connor.

He was seen at his best in what some would claim was the best Scotland forward line of all time, the 1928 Wizards, Jackson, Dunn, Gallacher, James, and Morton, and certainly they were the best of their times. Gallacher was a giant among good players.

But the other side of him too often showed. He fought indiscriminately and was often ordered off and suspended. During a tour of Hungary he was accused of being drunk and disorderly on the field of play. There was a F.A. inquiry but typically he had a ready explanation and was exonerated. He explained that it had been a very hot day and that he had washed out his mouth with whisky and water.

There was a quick deterioration. He was transferred from Chelsea to Derby County for £3,000 and then went on to Nottingham Forest, Grimsby Town, and Gateshead. As his football deteriorated his personal problems grew until not even his memories could sustain him.

He could tell of his great goals, of the one he scored against Wales at Tynecastle when he took the ball from his own half of the field past three defenders and lobbed it over the goalkeeper as he came out; of slipping the ball between the legs of Harry Hibbs the English international goalkeeper; of taking the ball three-quarters of the length of the field on another occasion and sending the goalkeeper to one side and walking the ball in the other.

He had scored 387 goals in 543 league matches and they were fine to remember, and 22 goals for Scotland in 19 matches, but on the night of June 11, 1957 these were far from his mind. He thought only of an unfortunate life, of a broken marriage and a dead son and a divorce and a story that he had accepted illegal payments. There was the more pressing worry that he had in the morning to face a charge of ill-treating his daughter.

He walked heavily towards Dead Man's Crossing at Low Fall near his home in Gateshead. He brushed against a passer-by and muttered, 'Sorry'. It was the last word he spoke. Deliberately he walked in front of the Edinburgh to York express as it thundered over the crossing. Life had only been tolerable when he was playing football.

Not often have two such great centre-forwards as Hughie Gallacher and Jimmy McGrory been contemporary. It was because they were contemporary that McGrory played only seven times for Scotland and four of his caps were against Ireland. That perhaps had something to do with his club being Celtic and the need to give regard to the gate for the Irish game.

All that need be written to establish the status of James Edward McGrory in a memorable era of Scottish football is that between January 20, 1923 when he first played for Celtic and October 16, 1937 when he played his last game for the club he scored 410 goals in the First Division of the Scottish League. His goals in internationals and in Cup-ties brought his total of goals scored in senior football to 550. In British football only Arthur Rowley, of many clubs, has scored more but many of his were scored in a lower grade of football.

McGrory, broad shouldered and deep chested, had that mental attitude towards goalscoring which is missing in many system-coached modern forwards. His mind was always on scoring, always he was putting himself in a position from which he could score. His was a complete dedication to goals.

He had the equipment to score. He had great courage which sent him chasing and lunging at the half chance. He could head a ball more powerfully than anybody before or since. He could shoot with strength and accuracy and especially he could hook the ball so that he was shooting early and before goalkeepers could get set.

Jimmy McGrory was born in the tough Garngad district of Glasgow but in character he stayed untouched by the hardness of his surroundings. He remained always, on and off the field, pleasant and gentlemanly. He joined Celtic from the local St Roch's and was envisaged as the long-sought successor to Celtic's other great goalscorer, Jimmy Quinn.

From the start he could head powerfully and accurately and he claimed he learned to do so in the school playground. He was fortunate in that he was brought in with forwards who could make chances in the air and on the ground.

On his right was that other Celtic legend, Patsy Gallacher, a slightly hunch-backed little man who never weighed more than eight stone but was arguably the best football player between the wars. Patsy, 'The Mighty Atom', was renowned for his trickery with the ball and there was no way of taking it from him, and hardly by kicking him down, for he had a knack of rolling back on to his feet and carrying on loose-limbed and gangling with his stop-go dribbling. He was a hard little man into the bargain and feared nobody.

Besides he was a crafty tactician and superbly accurate and subtle in his passing. Nowadays people ask if Patsy Gallacher was as good as the legend and the answer is unequivocally that he was.

Jimmy McGrory developed under Gallacher's influence and thrived on the hard-driving crosses of Paddy Connelly who raced on a strip of turf one yard wide along the right touchline. One of the most blood-stirring thrills in football was Jimmy McGrory leaping to put his forehead to a thundering Connelly cross.

It has been guessed that half of Jimmy McGrory's goals were scored with his head and half of those must have had the ball bouncing on the goal line for he had the gift of leaping high, early, to wait on the ball and head it downwards and that is the one no goalkeeper likes.

Yet when in a match against Dunfermline on January 14, 1928 he scored three goals in nine minutes and had totalled eight before the game ended, all of them were scored with his feet. Jimmy McGrory, Celtic's Public Relations Officer by then, was honoured by the club at the start of season 1971–72 on the 50th anniversary of his joining the club. He opened the new cantilever stand.

Jimmy McMullan, known as Paddy to some, besides being a masterly inventive half-back was the most authoritative captain of his day. He had been a distinguished left-half with Partick Thistle and then with Manchester City but inevitably he is remembered as captain of the Wembley Wizards of 1928.

Typical were his instructions in the 1929 game against England at Hampden Park. When Alex Jackson was hurt and had to leave the field, Scotland was in serious trouble. He told young Alex Cheyne who, like Jackson, played for Aberdeen at the time, that he must play out wide on the right-wing and attempt to hold the ball out there, 'where we can come to no harm'.

It was in obeying his instruction with long runs that Cheyne won a corner-kick with two minutes to go. Sensationally, he scored direct from it and Scotland won. Alex Cheyne had only come into the team two days previously when Tommy Muirhead injured his nose and withdrew.

And then there was the always impressive but sometimes rebellious Alex James who first was noted in the most publicised forward line Raith Rovers ever fielded. In the early 'twenties those five, Bell, Miller, Jennings, James, and Archibald were reckoned to be worth £50,000 and that was before the first £10,000 transfer.

They finished third in the Scottish League in season 1921–22 and Tom Jennings scored 22 goals but Alex James was transferred to Arsenal in 1926 to become their most distinguished player then and the man who, from the midfield, controlled their game. It was significant that Raith Rovers were relegated in the season after Alex James was transferred.

The great Raith Rovers team of the early 'twenties whose forward line excited rich English clubs. *Back row:* Jennings, Moyies, Inglis, Brown, Morris, Raeburn Collier, Willis. *Front row:* Bell, James, Bauld, Gilmour, Archibald.

He was listed as an inside-left but the tubby little man with the long body on short legs who affected pants three sizes too big for him was what is termed nowadays a midfield player and, like Jimmy McMullan, played football on the ground.

Players such as these coaxed Scottish football into an era in which country was big, an era in which the match against England was the climax of the season, a climax which was prepared for by spectators two years in advance. The highest honour any Scottish player could comprehend was to wear the blue jersey of Scotland against England. Football then was still confined mainly to these isles. The distractions of European and World competition had not been introduced and only film stars earned over £100 per week. Then, in the main, only three internationals were played per season and internationalists were an exclusive set. Now there are many internationals and every Tom, Dick, and Harry is an internationalist. The honour has been de-valued.

11

The Wembley Rites

The first England *v.* Scotland match at Wembley in 1924 was an undistinguished occasion. Only 60,000 spectators were there to watch a dull game. Appropriately it was drawn and there was no indication of the great excitement which was to build up during the next fifteen years.

When the selectors met to choose the team for the match the following season at Hampden Park there were positive indications of what was ahead. So rich was Scottish football, that year, in players of international class that only one player with an English club was considered for the team. There was a mild suggestion that Neil Harris of Newcastle United was better than Hughie Gallacher.

There were no political implications in the decision of the selectors to nominate a team of players all of whom were with Scottish League clubs. An all Tartan team, the writers called it, and it was the first such to represent Scotland since 1885 and they were chosen because they were, by far, better than any Scottish players outside the country.

The team which introduced so many distinguished players to international football was: Harper (Hibs); McStay (Celtic), McCloy (Ayr United); Meiklejohn (Rangers), Morris (Raith Rovers), McMullan (Partick Thistle); Jackson (Aberdeen), Russell (Airdrie), Gallacher (Airdrie), Cairns (Rangers), Morton (Rangers).

The all Tartan team in 1895 had been humiliated and beaten 3–0 in Liverpool on Everton's ground but the 1925 team might have won by six goals instead of the two which Hughie Gallacher scored. Scotland's wing play demoralised England.

Little Tommy Magee had been set to mark Alan Morton but he was no more than an attendant on him as he followed the slippery Rangers winger all over the field. On the other wing Alex Jackson, only nineteen years old, was scampering happily and even against the great Sam Wadsworth was the best player on the field. They gave him the ball at the end in recognition of that.

Willie Russell, from the East End of Glasgow and a junior with Benburb, was a fine partner for the dashing Jackson. He was a cool, ideas player and with Russell, Meiklejohn, and McMullan controlling the game and springing the attacks it was little wonder that England were made to look a poor team.

Scotland beat England at Old Trafford the following year but the match was brought back to Wembley in 1928 and that day, March 31, was to be Scotland's finest football day between the wars, a delirious day when all the Scots' great conceit in their football became reality.

Strangely, before the match there had been no great confidence in the team.

Jimmy McMullan leads out the Wembley Wizards. Alex Jackson, Hughie Gallacher, and Jack Harkness follow.

Hughie Gallacher, Jimmy McMullan, Alex Jackson, and Alex James had been transferred to English clubs. There was bitter talk in which the clubs were called transfer fiends and the general accusation was that the pursuit of English gold had left the home game featureless.

And then the selectors left out the massive full-backs Jock Hutton, of the billiards table legs, and Willie McStay, the 'Tank', and ruthlessly dropped David Meiklejohn in one shocking moment. Into the bargain Andy Cunningham, Bob McPhail, and Jimmy McGrory were passed over. In McGrory's case that was bitterly controversial for Hughie Gallacher, who was chosen, had not played for two months.

The team announcement which stunned to silence the crowd which assembled at the S.F.A. offices at Carlton Place was: Harkness (Queen's Park); Nelson (Cardiff City), Law (Chelsea); Gibson (Aston Villa), Bradshaw (Bury), McMullan (Manchester City); Jackson (Huddersfield), Dunn (Hibs), Gallacher (Newcastle United), James (Preston North End), Morton (Rangers).

Eight of those were playing in English football and a popular cartoon showed three forlorn looking characters, Jack Harkness and the two little fellows Tim Dunn and Alan Morton leaving by train for London and one saying, 'If we only had another we could have a game of solo'.

Yet the three did not travel alone. That Friday night eleven special trains left Glasgow for Wembley, every one packed. The excursion fare was 25*s.* 6*d.* There was additional and distinguished support in the ten surviving members of the Rosebery team of 1900 brought by R. S. McColl the captain, by then a successful businessman.

The arrangements for the team looked less than satisfactory. The players had been instructed to meet on the Friday evening in the Regent Palace Hotel at Piccadilly Circus. On international nights there was no busier hotel and a little corner in the lounge had to be cleared of supporters to accommodate the team.

There they sat among the excitement, the noise, and the drink until around ten o'clock. Mr Robert Campbell, of Perth, then president of the S.F.A., called over the captain Jimmy McMullan and told him, 'I think you'd better get the players upstairs and talk about the game'.

Jimmy McMullan gathered the players but stopped on the first landing and delivered his address before the fray, 'The President wants us to discuss football but you all know what's expected of you tomorrow. All I've to say is, go to your bed put your head on the pillow and pray for rain.'

They must have prayed well and maybe to St Jude, the patroness of hopeless causes for they were wakened the next morning by rain driving against their windows. The conditions were right for Scotland's little ball-playing forward line. Yet it had not been a peaceful night for the Scotland trainer Jimmy Kerr. Alex Jackson and Alex James were up to their tricks. Jackson slept in another bed and James started a rumour that he had gone out on the town and the poor trainer sat up during the night waiting on him coming in.

There was a significant happening while McMullan's men prayed on their pillows for rain. Bishop, of Leicester City, the England captain, became ill during the night. He had to be withdrawn from the team and replaced by Healless of Blackburn Rovers.

And while all this went on the football trains sped south, their tartan cargoes more bemused by the mile, soaking drink that defeated discomfort and fed their arrogance. By the time that the neat little boxes of Welwyn Garden City appeared through the misty windows the revelry was hoarse and maudlin except for those who sprawled, grotesquely, in corridors and on seats, relieved from it by sleep.

Those supporters, as they were to do for many years, travelled uncouthly with all the discomfort and dedication of pilgrims. The special trains were made up of old, out-of-date rolling stock providing only essentials in wheels and seats and toilets. There were no dining cars or buffets. The overnight travellers brought their own sustenance.

Food was not appropriate to the carnival occasion and they settled for abundant liquid fare. Few stumbled to the trains without that bulky brown paper bag they nursed from the pubs, the 'kerry oot'. They sang the night away and only flagged, wan faced, as they sped into the dawn.

There is a neat theory about hard-drinking Scottish football supporters. They never give trouble in London, the reasoning being that by the time they reach that city they have been weakened and tamed by tiredness. After a twelve-hour session they cannot stand. Significantly the trouble had been in such places as Leeds, Newcastle, and Wolverhampton, towns at such a distance as allows them to arrive fighting drunk.

But in Euston Station they arrived pale of face, hoarse, and uncomfortably damp from washing in flooded toilets. They tried to arouse defiance with songs that soon tapered off. They blinked into the London morning in weird tartan garb they would normally have been self conscious of at Halloween.

They looked for somewhere to shave and somewhere for breakfast. They walked and stared and waited for 'the doctor's' to open to provide them with a reviver. By noon the energy was back and the voice was softened and ambition was high as time was called to make for Wembley Stadium, that citadel they had come to take.

They crushed happily into the tube and left it at the head of Wembley Way and there it was before them, the twin towers, the flags, the hawkers, the stalls, the touts, and they surged on light and bright and confident and miraculously transformed from the miserable lethargy of the morning. And then they were inside and the man in white was conducting the singing. They were there.

They argued with good nature and that pre-match condescension the football Scot develops, when in heavy herds, and sang the community songs with tolerance. Then suddenly the band was playing what was to be their Wembley Anthem in the years to come, 'Scotland Bonnie Scotland – Forever' and the last word dragged out with affection and passion and they yelled in exultation and were only hushed when impressively, 'Abide With Me' was taken up in measured tones.

There was the tension before the teams appeared through the tunnel and the screams of welcome, acclamation, and then apprehension as it was seen how small were the Scottish forwards. The reassurance was that guid gear gangs in small bulk.

There were 80,868 present that day at Wembley and the rain poured down as the Duke of York and King Amanullah of Afghanistan were presented to the teams and then the National Anthem stilled them ready for the off. The Scots were soon chilled and clutching arms in shock.

Smith, the Huddersfield winger, sped past Nelson, hardly noticing him in the passing. He strode in on Jack Harkness, strong and menacing, and hit his shot in mid stride. The goalkeeper was beaten and 'Goal' burst from English throats. But Scotland had luck with that shot as they had with the rain. The ball struck the base of a post and rebounded into play.

Then Jimmy McMullan had it and was holding it, sauntering coolly with it, letting taut nerves settle. Over it went to Alex James and he, too, nursed it and soon there was a string of composing passes sent around which found Alan Morton prowling on the left. He loped forward, slipped past the full-back on the outside and that long stride of his soon had him at the bye line.

There was a little stop-and-start shuffle along that line as he watched a blue-clad figure race for the far post. Precisely, he paced a neat pass in front of that forehead and Alex Jackson had not to break stride as he headed the ball past the perplexed English goalkeeper. That was cold, efficient striking and Scotland led after three minutes.

The little contemptibles had given their team the start they needed but the game was still far from won. The lead might have been quickly lost but Jack Harkness, the amateur goalkeeper from Queen's Park, made a daring save at the feet of three rushing English forwards.

And then the half-backs took over. As the rain came down Jimmy McMullan and Jimmy Gibson, both at one time with Partick Thistle, developed a confident liaison in the middle of the field and as the backs dug in they controlled the game with authority.

Alex Jackson was sent charging gaily on the right. Alan Morton tripped tantalisingly on the left and the English defence was kept wide chasing them. Little Tim Dunn found the space he needed in the middle as Hughie Gallacher kept the centre-half occupied and behind them the shuffling Alex James wrought his depredation.

There was football of such skill and trickery as those far travelled Scots had not dared hope for and then ecstasy as two minutes from half time Alex James struck a firm shot that was a scorer from the instant it left his in-step. The interval was alive with Scottish revelry.

England saw no fun in the situation and for twenty minutes in the second half they pressed persistently. The giant Bradshaw controlled Dixie Dean and the backs, Nelson and Law, who had settled so comfortably, held the others and soon Jimmy McMullan, when the English fire was spent, turned the game and with such spectacular Scottish forward play as had never previously been seen had the English chasing and turning and almost cracking.

Every one of those little forwards was a master of technique. They embellished their play with cheek and trickery and artistry. In the sixty-fifth minute another precise cross from Morton left Jackson to score with astonishing composure.

It was a Scottish fiesta as those little men feinted and jinked and Alex James scored another goal and Alex Jackson scored his third and Scotland led by 5–0.

It did not matter that Kelly got a belated goal for England from a free-kick.

The mood in Scottish football was ridiculously wild and the *Glasgow Herald* tried to soothe it with cold words: 'The success of the Scots was primarily another demonstration that Scottish skill, science, and trickery will still prevail against the less attractive and simpler methods of the English style in which speed is relied on as the main factor.'

Euston station had never known such scenes as the weary supporters made for their trains. There was a jazz band and dancing on the concourse and one Scot fell from the platform and lay unconscious on the track. He was taken to hospital.

And as the jollifications went on nobody seemed to remember that earlier in the season Scotland had lost to Ireland and that the Scottish League had been beaten by the English League at Ibrox by 6 goals to 2, the goals difference at Wembley.

The Wembley Wizards. What else could they have called that team which, 'Gave an exhibition of scientific football that was a revelation', as one English critic wrote. It was a result and an alliterative title such as the Scots love to remember. The victory did not need explaining for what the Wizards had done was what those tartan followers always knew Scotland could do.

There had been times, many of them, when the hopes of splendour had not worked out but there was always an excuse and anyway the lost games were irrelevancies. All they waited for was 1930 and they would show the English what football was all about and London what celebrating meant when giants were unleashed. Wembley clubs were started and their members began saving up for the next assault on London. The Wembley cult was established.

And then came in sobering anti-climax, the Wembley Follies, the Wembley Strugglers, the Wembley Unfortunates to assail the glorious memory of the

The famous Tommy Walker penalty-kick.

Wizards. In 1930 that flash on the right-wing, Sammy Crooks, was in for England along with David Jack and Scotland were beaten 5–2. Soon Cliff Bastin was adding his skills to theirs and bringing misery to the Scots but down they went to Wembley in ever greater numbers. The fun later was the attraction.

In 1932 there were 90,000 present and half of them were Scots. England won 3–0. In 1934 no less than 52 trains carried 23,000 passengers and Scotland lost 3–0. In 1936 Scotland found a new hero the youthful Tommy Walker. Camsell had scored for England and they led by that goal until Johnny Crum the Celtic centre was fouled painfully as he bore in on goal. It was clearly a penalty-kick and Crum had to be carried behind a goal for attention before it could be taken.

Tommy Walker, then just nineteen years old, had been deputed to take penalty-kicks and he went up to take this vital one although he had not been having a good game. It was a windy day. He placed the ball on the spot and stepped back. It was blown off. He replaced it and as he moved to take the kick it was blown off again. The crowd were silent, guessing that one so young must be at breaking point.

Again the ball was placed, firmly driven into the ground and it stayed. Tommy Walker shot the equalising goal as if it were a practice match. He later explained his reactions.

'I cannot even remember at what end of the ground the penalty-kick was given but I do remember vaguely the ball rolling off the spot. I just replaced it and hit it.' One of the great legends in Scottish football has persisted over the years because it was assumed that the young player must have been tortured by the distractions of the moving ball and all the time it had hardly recorded with him.

Tommy Walker was a remarkable international player in that when he did have a poor game, by his own standards of course, he still managed to score a vital goal. After the penalty-kick in 1936 he scored the winner in 1938 again when he had not been conspicuous.

Scotland *v*. England, 1929. Alec Cheyne's late winning goal direct from a corner-kick. Hughie Gallacher is ready to acclaim it.

12

After the Wizards

In the years between the miserable Wembleys the Scottish supporters had annual fortifying injections of hope at Hampden. Scotland beat England in five successive matches there, up till 1939 and the war, and that was inspiration enough to send the throngs to London hoping for more than the fun.

Hampden Park in that stretch held such crowds as astonished the whole sporting world and every second year a record was established.

In 1929 the wind blew and that and a light ball made a poor game but there were 110,512 there and they paid £6,102. They were hushed by a national disaster when Alex Jackson collided with that hard full-back Blenkinsop and was taken to the Victoria Infirmary with a dislocated elbow.

Young players found impressive stature in the emergency. Jimmy Crapnell of Airdrie in his first international was cheeky from the start, ordering more experienced men around. Joe Nibloe, fresh from Kimarnock's Scottish Cup-Final win over Rangers, matched him and that surprise choice, Jock Buchanan of Rangers, who had been ordered off in the Cup-Final broke up the English midfield play while Jimmy McMullan did the thinking.

Tommy Muirhead had damaged his nose in the Cup-Final and had to withdraw on the Thursday before the match. Alex Cheyne took his place and it was he who scored that goal direct from a corner-kick two minutes from the end which gave Scotland a plucky win and earned him immortality.

In 1931 there were 129,810 at Hampden for the England match and that was a record for any sporting event until then. 1933 was the year of the depression and the admission charge was reduced to 1*s.* 6*d.* There were 134,710 present. Crowd scenes in 1935 hastened the introduction of tickets; 129,693 got into the ground but it was reckoned that 200,000 turned up, and many had come from great distances. There was a stampede outside the ground. The walls were climbed and 320 casualties were treated.

Those abominations, tickets, were first introduced in 1937. It was the first all-ticket match and all the 150,000 tickets were sold, although only 149,547 checked through the turnstiles. Hampden had been extended and the new North Stand opened. The gate receipts were £20,000. The players were paid £6.

The 1931 team had been picked with a background of resentment. The English league had passed a rule debarring clubs releasing players for internationals on the day that they had a League fixture, except for their own association. Troubles over the release of players with English clubs is not a modern irritation.

Scotland that year had the satisfaction of the last laugh, at least the selectors had. They nominated a first eleven and a second team and all twenty-two players were with Scottish League clubs. That should have satisfied all national pride. They named: Thomson (Celtic); Blair (Clyde), Nibloe (Kilmarnock); McNab (Dundee), Meiklejohn (Rangers), Miller (St Mirren); Archibald (Rangers), Stevenson (Motherwell), McGrory (Celtic), McPhail (Rangers), Morton (Rangers).

Instead of acclaim no team was ever more harshly criticised. Traffic was stopped in Carlton Place by the crowd awaiting the announcement of the team. Crowds thronging outside the offices of the Scottish Football Association used to be a healthy indication of the public interest in the international team. It is a long time since anybody has waited to hear who has been chosen. The announcement was more specific and interesting in those days when a team was announced and not a pool of players.

The crowd that day condemned the half-back line as crazy. Colin McNab the red head was a good club man but a flop in representative games. Big John Miller of St Mirren was having his first international match. And then there were the forwards.

George Stevenson, the elegant one, was a good inside-left but who said he could play at inside-right? Sandy Archibald's selection was the end. He had joined Rangers in 1917 and had last been capped in 1924 seven years previously. It was an all tartan team said the fans but a team of panic.

That team which had been so pitied and despised was introduced to the Prime Minister, Ramsay Macdonald, and then they quickly and surprisingly took control of the game. They won the right to play with the wind and John Miller played the big South African, Hodgson, out of the game while Danny Blair took care of the other wing.

Even facing the swirling wind in the second half Scotland was confident and then exhilarating as Jimmy McGrory inspired them and roused the crowd with a spectacular run and shot. In twenty minutes of thrilling football, fit to match that of the Wizards, England were devastated.

Those unfortunates in white shirts could do nothing with Alan Morton. The lively Jimmy McGrory had them worried and the cold elegance of George Stevenson disguised his menace. It was Stevenson who leapt in to score when Hibbs could only parry Sandy Archibald's thundering shot. It was Jimmy McGrory who leapt to beat Hibbs as Morton's tantalising lob hung in the air. The powerful Bob McPhail kept the attacks going relentlessly.

There was an England fight back and Hodgson's shot struck Meiklejohn and was deflected as John Thomson, playing his first game against England, leapt. The ball seemed pushed beyond his reach but somehow, in mid air, as only he could do, he stretched the extra inches finding thrust from his own muscles and got a hand to the ball. Most who were there reckoned that they had never seen a better save.

David Meiklejohn, maybe Scotland's greatest-ever captain, was everywhere with foot and head as England fought to save face but a great Scottish team were not to be hustled. At the end Mr C. F. Sutcliffe of the English League said, 'I'm surprised that Scotland should go to England for players. There's no need for it'

W. D. Cocker marked the occasion in rhyme.

> 'And when the second goal was scored,
> Gosh! hoo the hale o' Hampden roared.
> The very polis loup and cheer,
> Nane look mair prood than the premier.
> For Ramsay lauchin gey jocosely
> Could maist hae shaken hands wi' Mosley.'

Glasgow was a city possessed that night. It was wild, and forgotten were the criticisms of the team. The Scottish supporters are great each-way punters. They criticise the team before it plays, adopt it when it wins.

There was more availability trouble in 1933. Alex James was chosen to play but called off on the Tuesday before the match saying that he was unfit. He played however for Arsenal on the Saturday and made himself an outcast. He had let the colours down. There was an Arsenal player in the match, the 'Highbury Express', Joe Hulme.

The interesting player, however, was that majestic centre-half, Bob Gillespie, who had retired from Queen's Park, became the club secretary, and then returned to the team to take them out of trouble. He was called into the Scotland team and made captain when David Meiklejohn called off three days before the match.

The sprinter, Jimmy Crawford, was already in the team and that was the first time that two amateurs had played for Scotland since Alex Christie and Bob McCole, thirty-four years previously. None has played since.

That Scotland team was the right one for the depression years. Two dashing goals by Jimmy McGrory, a left-foot shot which beat Hibbs by its speed and a typical dash and shot from McPhail's running pass sent the crowd into ecstacies and the Hampden Roar was awesome. At the end the English said, 'The crowd won the match'.

For the 1935 match the team met as usual at St Enoch's Hotel in Glasgow at noon on the day of the match. There was just time for a light meal before making off through the record crowd for the stadium. It was no inconvenience not being able to discuss the game for the England forward line turned out to be the poorest anybody could remember.

A new star was George Cumming, a clever composed full-back, whom Donald Turner had signed for Partick Thistle from Grange Rovers. He swept the opposing winger aside with nonchalance and took time to look around and place his passes. He started a new conception of constructive full-back play.

There was a new look also to the half-back line. Big Jimmy Simpson was in as a static, stopper centre-half, the first for Scotland, and on his right was Alex Massie who learned his football with Ashfield, a lively nursery in North West Glasgow and had played for Bury and some American clubs before signing for Hearts. Massie was in because of his superb understanding with the youthful Tommy Walker, then the most exciting young player in Scotland.

George Brown also from Ashfield was on the other side of Simpson and he, with his late tackles and smooth passing, along with the stronger but no less accurate attacking work of Massie were to make up for anything constructive which was lost by having a stopper at centre-half. England held Scotland to two goals.

The English renewed their forward line for the all ticket match of 1937 and sent up Matthews, Carter, Steele, Starling, and Johnston. They were moving into an era of great forwards. Jimmy Simpson said of them: 'I had a sore day. The interchanging of these inside-forwards had me nearly out of my mind. I had to be more of a cat than a policeman.'

Scotland were in trouble that day and an English spokesman said afterwards: 'I cannot recall a game in which the more skilful side were beaten as England were. Their ball control was miles ahead of the Scots.' The Scottish crowd were not concerned with such considerations. They got ten minutes of great Scottish football and two goals and that was enough to be getting on with.

Bob McPhail and Tommy Walker had taken a long time to get going and big Frank O'Donnell was too busy surviving against the he-man tackles of Young of Huddersfield to add much to the play. The English forwards were spectacular but there was always a tackle to upset the rhythm.

O'Donnell who had gone to Preston North End from Celtic had the ball in the English net in the first half but the referee after signalling a goal consulted a linesman, who had his flag raised, and changed his decision to a free-kick.

When it seemed that Scotland must be beaten Tommy Walker, with a long solo run, started the action racing and in a brilliant ten minutes Scotland shattered what was one of the finest England teams that had been sent North. Bob McPhail scored two goals and O'Donnell the other and the dashing Jimmy Delaney was unlucky that he did not score.

When Andy Beattie had been selected the supporters had asked, 'Who's Beattie?' and had to be told that he had been brought up in Inverurie and that provoked the question, 'Where's that?' He had been born in Kintore and played cricket. They were later to know him as manager of Scotland.

There was however general agreement that the game had been Jerry Dawson's. Jerry, christened John, came from Falkirk and he played with the brilliance that had come to be expected of him in Rangers goal and had thrown in for good measure some uncanny saves and particularly one when Matthews shot and the ball was past him and going away. He twisted and got his right hand to it. A goal then would almost certainly have won the match for England. There was, too, a point-blank save from Steele which left the centre gaping in awe. Jerry, a great joker, was not kidding in that game.

13

The Scottish Cup

The end of a century of the Scottish Cup neared, in 1972, with the team of the century, Celtic, winning the Final by the highest score of the century. Indeed the 6–1 by which they beat Hibernian had only been equalled by Renton when they beat Cambuslang by an identical score in 1888.

Hampden Park by then was proud of bearing but run down and tattered. The amenities, once the finest in the football world, had long since ceased to be modern or even adequate. It was reckoned that it would take half-a-million pounds to bring it to a reasonable state of repair and then there would have to be extensive alterations to provide more sophisticated accommodation and amenities appropriate to the more comfortable way of life at the time.

The cost of the upkeep of the ground was, by then, far out with the resources of Queen's Park. They had started the century as the premier club in Scotland but their rigid adherence to amateurism had resulted in their becoming a very ordinary Second Division club, an anachronism in a commercial age when the word amateur in sport could more appropriately be equated with inefficient.

There was no longer any stigma attached to taking payment for a performance which the public paid money to view. Indeed amateur was an obsolete term and that had been recognised in such sports as cricket and tennis where the ideal used to be strong and bigotted.

Queen's Park's sentimental persistence in adhering to a code that was as old-fashioned as football knickerbockers had reduced their attraction so that they were seldom playing to more than a thousand spectators at their home games, and generally to three-figure crowds, and all the time maintenance of the ground gobbled up money and their overdraft increased alarmingly.

The Scottish Football Association worked to relieve their problems and tried to involve the Government and the City of Glasgow in financing Hampden Park as a national stadium and that was the principal task on hand as they approached their centenary.

And then on Saturday, May 7, 1972 Celtic brought to the shabby stadium, football of splendour and a crowd of 106,102 to thrill to it, and a 6–1 score was much to the liking of a manager, Jock Stein, who had said: 'A no-scoring draw might please the theorists but if goals have not been scored then things have not been happening to the liking of the spectators. You dare not forget about the fans. Success is not just winning cups. The game exists because of people and for people, and real success is in a packed stadium.'

The Scottish Cup.

The Celtic team that day seemed to be vulnerable. Stein had been coaxing it through the transition period and only four of the players who had won the European Cup were in the side. Hibs were a team being reorganised by a new manager, Eddie Turnbull, and beginning to show heartening signs that his way was effective.

The vital incident which had a decisive effect on the outcome took place in Celtic Park around two months before the Final. Celtic then were winning consistently but not always convincingly. They had not consistent authority in midfield and that was because Bobby Murdoch, one of the few world-class players in Scotland, was unfit.

His main concern was a long-standing weight problem. He had dieted over the years and attended health clinics and the unwanted weight came off. Then it was back on and Stein nursed his frustration as he sought a midfield player of authority and every day saw one there before him but too heavy and sluggish to do himself justice.

Then came the day when he called Murdoch to his office and told him, 'Get it off or get out'. And as Bobby looked aghast he remembered his team-mates from the memorable Lisbon Final who had moved out of the club and he was stunned at the thought of his having to go.

He shed eighteen pounds in twelve days of furious work and then started to build up his strength and seek match fitness. The Celtic trainers, Neil Mochan and Bob Rooney, produced him on Cup-Final day glowing with health and fitness and again a great player. It was only his fifth game of the season.

With Murdoch available for the ball from the backs and directing the play from the middle with long passes of wondrous accuracy and subtlety and short neat ones to link the running attackers, Celtic were roused to the confidence which Stein had known only Murdoch could inspire, and flair and panache were unloosed on the unfortunate Hibs.

Perhaps in the following season they might have been able to handle this surging Celtic but in the process of finding themselves they were overwhelmed in midfield where one of the great team-men of the century, Pat Stanton, had been left unaided.

Goals came freely after the captain Billy McNeill, in his ninth Cup-Final, had scored in the second minute and Alan Gordon had equalised for Hibs in the twelfth. Dixie Deans, recently transferred to Celtic from Motherwell for a modest £20,000 and bringing with him an embarrassing record of field indiscretion, showed his new outlook with a happy, disciplined display which produced three goals, an unusual crop for a Cup-Final. Lou Macari got the other two goals for a score that was hard on Hibs.

The only joy that Hibs could take from the occasion was that the game ruthlessly exposed the extent to which Eddie Turnbull had to reconstruct although, for sure, he would have preferred to have had the lesson on a less public occasion.

If there could be criticism of the Scottish Cup-Final it would be that with other distractions and with the general depression it had not been possible, in the post-

Billy McNeill the Celtic captain scores a typical goal.

war years, to make it a carnival climax to a national competition, a show game, a festive occasion in which the football was the important thing.

Too often the attitude had been that the Final was just another game and club managers have been known to talk that way. The Scottish Cup-Final is not just another game and it was never meant to be. The dangerous trend as European football developed was that the Scottish Cup was becoming a qualifying competition for the European Cup Winners' Cup just as the Scottish League Championship tended to be a qualifying competition for the European Champion Clubs' Cup. If that attitude is allowed to dominate Scottish football then the domestic game will be devalued in a way which would have shocked those proud pioneers who nearly 100 years ago with exciting vision, established the Scottish Cup competition.

In the first year of its existence, the Scottish Football Association showed a credit balance of £1 11*s.* 4*d.*, not enough to finance the Scotch Cup for which they were established. They sought donations from the various clubs that had sprung up and were able to spend £56 12*s.* 11*d.* for a Cup and eleven silver gilt and gold badges. The same Cup is being played for to this day and the Association never made a better bargain.

If the complaint is valid that the occasion of the Cup is being allowed to become too humdrum it certainly was not so in the early seasons of the competition. The Scottish Cup in that first season, 1873–74, was instrumental in standardising the rules. This is evident in a report of the first Scottish Cup-tie to be played.

The *Glasgow Evening News* reported in October 1873: 'The first tie for the Association Challenge Cup was commenced on Saturday when the Kilmarnock club met the Renton on the ground of the Queen's Park club at Crosshill, Glasgow. The ball was kicked off at ten minutes to three o'clock and for 40 minutes a well-contested, but not by any means scientific, game ensued. The Kilmarnock club were at a disadvantage through not being thoroughly conversant with Association rules, having formerly played the Rugby game and also from being a man short.

'On account of this the Renton club kept the ball well up to the goal posts of their opponents, as they received several free-kicks in succession through some of the Auld Killie's men persistently using their hands which is not allowed according to Association rules.' Renton won 3–0.

The primitive form of the game was demonstrated by the number of protests which plagued the Scottish Cup competition in its early years. Before the start of each season the S.F.A. pleaded with the clubs not to protest on trivial grounds. Most were based on the crowds spilling on to the field and interrupting play. This was predictable for they were only held back by ropes and not until Hampden Park was built had they a wooden fence.

A serious protest was the one in 1879 which gave Vale of Leven a walk over in the Scottish Cup-Final replay. After a 1–1 draw, Rangers 'protested against the decision of umpires and referee respecting a second goal which was taken by Rangers but disallowed on the unanimous decision of both umpires'. The committee decided against the protest because it was on a matter of fact connected with the play. Rangers were still dissatisfied and appealed but the appeal was dismissed.

So on Saturday, April 26, Vale of Leven turned up at Hampden Park for the Cup-Final, along with the referee and the umpires, and lined up on the field in accordance with the instructions of the committee. Rangers had not turned up at kick-off time and the Vale took the ball up the field and sent it through the unguarded goal and so were the Cup winners.

Queen's Park also took the Cup in 1884 without a final contest. On Tuesday, February 1, 1884, Vale of Leven sent a telegram to the committee informing them that they could not play in the Cup-Final on the following Saturday owing to the death of Mr J. Forbes, one of their backs. This was allowed.

There was another telegram the following Wednesday stating that two of their players, McLintock and Gillies, were unwell and also that their reserves, Brown, McLeish, and Struthers, were indisposed. They hoped that the committee would grant an additional opportunity for playing the match but this plea was dismissed. Queen's Park claimed the Cup when the Vale refused to play and they pleaded the Vale's match against Rangers as a precedent. The committee, with the chairman claiming to have a sense of strict, conscientious impartiality, found in Queen's favour and gave them the Cup.

There were amusing protests such as in 1886 when St Andrews protested against Pollokshields Athletic on the grounds that the goal-line was several feet behind the posts. That seemed a good defensive tactic. In February 1888 Arbroath protested about Abercorn's method of collecting the gate money. The committee found that it had been collected according to use and that the treasurer did not leave the gate with the drawings until accompanied by an Arbroath official. The conduct of the Arbroath club was judged to be reprehensible and they were made to apologise.

Hearts lodged a protest after being beaten by Vale of Leven 'on account of utter incapacity of referee owing to a physical infirmity of defective eyesight'. The referee produced a medical certificate from an eye specialist and Hearts were made to apologise.

Rangers protested in 1884, that Arbroath's ground was two feet too narrow. A telegram sent to the Scottish F.A. by Rangers said: 'Beaten on a backyard.' The referee said that, measured along the goal-line, the field was over the minimum but measured at right angles it was 49 yards 1 foot. Arbroath were ordered to make their field square.

The first Scottish Cup-Final on March 21, 1874 was played in a drizzle of rain before a crowd estimated at between two and three thousand and it produced the first 'was it a goal?' controversy. Letters appeared in the newspapers debating the issue.

The *Glasgow Evening News* of Monday, March 23, 1874 reported the incident: 'After playing for about 20 minutes a shot at goal was made by the Clydesdale forwards and the ball being caught by Dickson, who was the Queen's Park goalkeeper, seemed to slip from his fingers and was sufficiently far under the tape to have secured the fortress. One of the umpires gave it as a goal but the referee agreed with the other that it was not, so it was not allowed. There was no scoring till half-time but Queens won by 2–0. They took the Cup, predictably, in the first three years.'

The competition soon became unwieldy because of the extraordinary spread of the game. In the fourth year of its existence the S.F.A. had 91 clubs in membership with 4,470 registered members and 81 clubs entered for the Scottish Cup.

The numbers grew sensationally every year until in 1879 the Secretary was declaring proudly: 'Football is now our national game, not by tradition, but by the free choice of the nation'. In 1891 the committee had to make a divided entry, and the formation of the Scottish League pushed them to this. They seeded sixteen clubs, the semi-finalists of the previous year and twelve others considered next in merit.

The competition survived the legalising of professionalism and the popularity of League football and indeed these innovations which had been so much feared by the Scottish Football Association brought good order to the competition.

Jimmy Delaney the dashing and exciting but brittle right-winger is the man who knows most about Cup football. He alone won national Cup medals in three countries. He started with Celtic in the Scottish Cup, then won an F.A. Cup medal with Manchester United, and an Irish Cup medal with Derry City.

He said of Cup football that a team inspiration to bring out the bit extra which is needed in the sudden death atmosphere of a Cup tie. Then, when there is a side fitted for Cup fighting, they need luck – luck in the draw, luck to escape injury, luck in the play. He nominated injuries as the greatest worry and talked of how in the later stages of the tournament when the tension is mounting the players become injury conscious and hold back in tackles. That is when knocks are most likely.

He instanced as luck in play a tie he watched from the stands, because of injury, between Celtic and Stenhousemuir. Celtic led and then Stenhousemuir equalised. He thought near the end that Stenhousemuir should have been given a penalty-kick but their appeal was refused. Celtic won the replay and went on to win the Cup and Delaney won his first Scottish Cup medal.

An inspiration could have been the mighty Jimmy Quinn who scored three goals in the Final against Rangers in 1904. Another inspiration was Jimmy McMenemy who had joined Partick Thistle from Celtic to finish off a long career and then found himself in the Final against Rangers in 1921. It was a Rangers team which had lost only to Celtic that year and were to amass the record points total of seventy-six.

McMenemy nursed the erratic Thistle in 1921 and then, when Jimmy Bowie had to leave the field for a few minutes for attention, the Thistle right-winger, Blair, scored and that was luck. Thistle had the Cup and that team gave to Scottish football, Willie Salisbury, a left-winger with a touch of eccentricity and he was entertainment.

Inspiration was back in 1928 in the person of David Meiklejohn and if ever Rangers needed it that was that day. They had not won the Scottish Cup for twenty-five years and their failure in that tournament while winning all else was a music hall joke. They survived an early incident which might have shattered their hopes. Paddy Connolly, the Celtic right-winger shot strongly, and it seemed a score until Tom Hamilton dived and saved spectacularly.

Then came one of the most momentous incidents of Scottish Cup history. Alan Morton from the left lobbed the ball into the goalmouth. Jimmy Fleming volleyed and it was going into the net beyond John Thomson when Willie McStay leapt and punched the ball clear. It was a penalty-kick.

David Meiklejohn faced up to the kick with the memory of twenty-five unsuccessful years behind him and the best goalkeeper in the world in front of him. He placed the ball carefully, stepped back, and wiped the toe of his shooting boot on the back of a stocking. Then he drove the ball firmly past John Thomson and everybody knew then that a bogey had been killed. Rangers who had not won for twenty-five years then ran up the highest final score, 4–0, in twenty years.

There was joy supreme in Ayrshire when Jock Aitken and Jimmy Williamson scored the two goals for Kilmarnock which beat Rangers but Ibrox pleas of misfortune when Tully Craig missed a penalty-kick. There was inspiration again the following year when Partick Thistle held Rangers to a draw and Rangers brought Alan Morton back for the replay in place of Willie Nicholson. There was misfortune for Thistle when Jaikey Jackson went up for Tully Craig's lob but was blinded by the sun and missed it. That goal cost Thistle the cup.

There was luck, too, in the 1922 Final when Willie Robb, the Rangers goalkeeper, handled outside the penalty-area and Morton, from the Tail of the Bank, won the Cup when Jimmy Gourlay scored from the free-kick. Morton had never previously won a Cup tie against Rangers and in the previous six games Rangers had scored twenty-four goals against their four.

Hibs had not lost a goal in the 1923 competition until Celtic's Joe Cassidy, in the Final, headed the ball over Willie Harper as he came out and that was disappointment.

The inspiration of the little wonder, Patsy Gallacher, won the 1925 Final. Dave McLean had scored for Dundee and they led by that goal with seven minutes to play. Then Gallacher set off from the edge of his own penalty-area in that peculiar stop, start, meandering way of his and beat man after man. When he was close to goal, where Jock Britton waited, the left-back Thomson brought him down with a heavy tackle and as the Celtic supporters shouted, 'Penalty' he somersaulted backwards with the ball held between his feet and carried it to the net. He had to be disentangled from the net. It was the weirdest Hampden goal.

Jimmy McGrory then rose above everybody to head a winning goal from 'Jean' McFarlane's free-kick with two minutes to go but, with seconds left, Dave Halliday's shot went desperately close and that was ill luck.

East Fife shocked Celtic in the 1927 Final when Jock Wood, a centre they had taken from St Mirren, scored, but Celtic with John McMenemy, son of the famous Jimmy, scored three goals. McMenemy, considered by most to be too young for the Final, was told by Willie Maley in the dressing room for the first time that he was

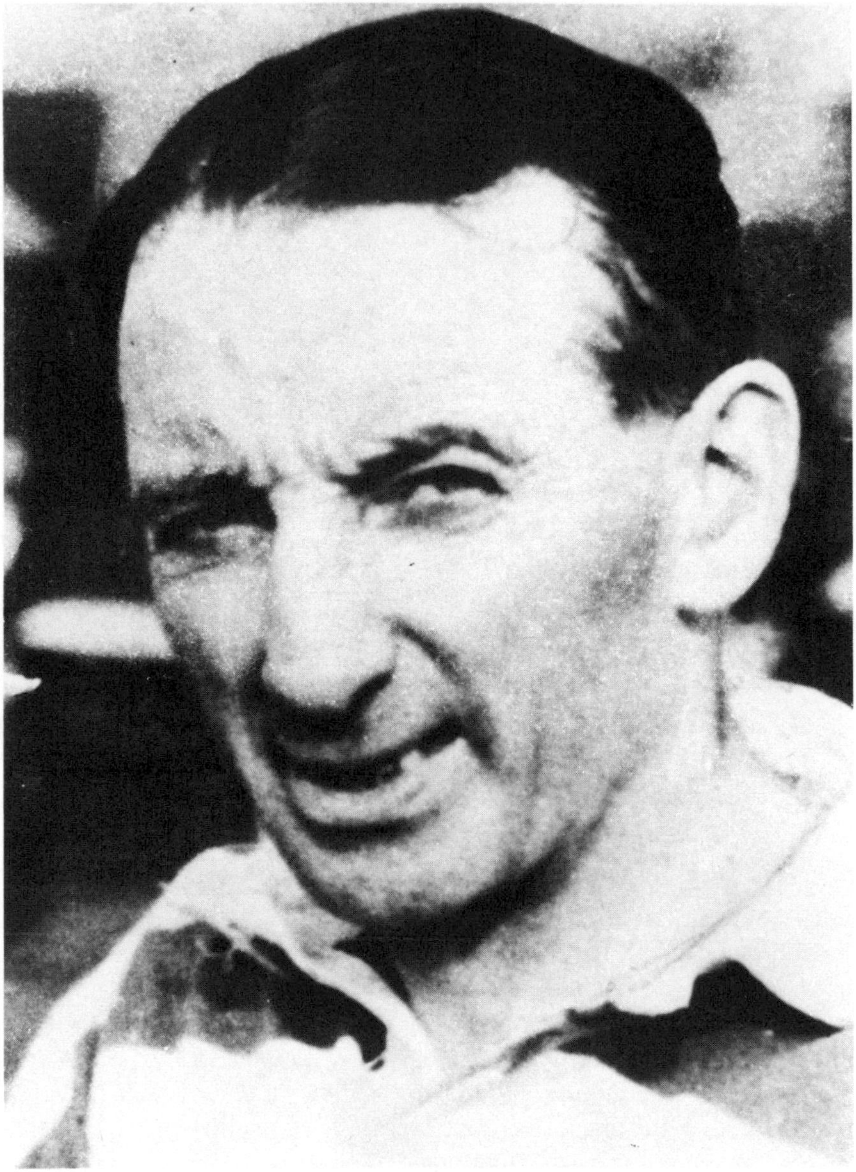

Patsy Gallacher – 'The Mighty Atom'.

playing. He had not wanted to worry him. That was psychology.

There seemed a happy ending in the making in the 1931 Final for that elegant Motherwell team, which was the only one to break the league monopoly of Rangers and Celtic between the wars. They led Celtic by two goals with but eight minutes to go. It looked hopeless for Celtic even when Charlie Napier lined up a free kick near goal and surveyed the wall of defenders in front of him.

The football manager of the 'thirties. Tommy Muirhead with his St Johnstone players: (*left to right*) Clark, Stewart, Campbell, Smith, Fulton, and Davidson.

He was a notable blaster of powerful free kicks but as the defenders braced themselves he chipped the ball to Jimmy McGrory, who had been left unmarked. The ball was quickly in the back of the net and McGrory was chasing it in and retrieving it and shrugging off congratulations as he hurried to place it on the centre spot and have the game restarted.

And then as the last minute was noted on the watches which had appeared anxiously in hands all round the ground Bertie Thomson, the cheeky little Celtic right-winger, was slipping past Hunter and racing to the touch-line. Thousands willed him to cross the ball but instead he doubled back and took the ball to his left foot. He sent an awkward in-swinger between goal and defenders. Somebody shouted, 'It's yours Alan!' But there were two Alans in the Motherwell defence, Alan McClory, the goalkeeper, and Alan Craig, the centre-half, and the wrong one went for it.

Alan Craig, already apprehensive about the dashing McGrory, put his forehead to the ball and, in maybe the most tragic moment of the Scottish Cup, knocked the ball past his own goalkeeper. He knelt and beat the turf in anguish and there was nobody who had not sympathy for him.

November 1937, before managers wore tracksuits. Pat Travers, Clyde's new manager, talks to players, Beaton, Hughes, and Kirk. Watching in shirt sleeves is that great character, Mattha Gemmell, the Clyde trainer, who offered to take a training job with another club on condition he was allowed off on Saturday afternoons to watch Clyde.

There were 100,000 at the replay on the following Wednesday even although it was clear that Motherwell had lost their chance. Celtic had never lost a Cup replay. Motherwell were beaten by 4–2 and many regretted that that fine footballing team had not earned the glory their attractive play deserved. They were compensated the following season with the League Championship.

1937 was the year of the big crowd when 146,333 watched Celtic beat Aberdeen by 2–1 and it was reckoned that there were another 30,000 outside waiting and judging how the game was running by the shouting. The following year was for the romantics.

The only Second Division team to win the Scottish Cup. East Fife in 1938. *Back row:* Russell, Laird, Tait, Milton, Harvey, Herd. *Front row:* Adams, Miller, McCartney, Sneddon, McLeod, McKerrell.

East Fife, the Second Division club who had lost to Celtic in the 1927 Final were in another Final against Kilmarnock. Dave McLean, who was later to manage Hearts, had taken them over a hard road to Hampden. They had beaten Airdrie, Dundee United, Aberdeen, Raith Rovers and all away except Dundee United and Aberdeen and Raith after replays. Then they needed three games at Tynecastle Park to eliminate St Bernards in the semi-final.

The Final was a tense game and finished in a 2–2 draw. When they replayed the following Wednesday they were still drawing after ninety minutes but East Fife scored twice in extra time and so became the only Second Division club ever to win the Scottish Cup and almost certainly they will still be carrying that honour at the end of the next century of Scottish football.

There were, that year, the usual human stories of the Cup, as they are called. David Herd was injured in the first Final match and was out of the replay. John Harvey was transferred from Hearts, whom he was later to manage, and played in the replay and so won a Scottish Cup medal in his first game for East Fife.

The East Fife club were extraordinary Cup fighters. While still in the Second Division they were back at Hampden in 1948 against Falkirk in the League Cup-Final and after a no-scoring draw won the replay by 4–1.

In that season they were managed by Scot Symon, a successful player with Rangers and later to be their successful manager, and under his direction they returned to the First Division of the Scottish League with 53 points out of a possible 60. Scot Symon had East Fife three times at Hampden in a year which is something of a record for a small provincial club. They lost to Rangers in a Scottish Cup semi-final, beat them in a League Cup semi-final, and then beat Dunfermline in the League Cup-Final.

They were third in the Scottish League Championship of 1951–52 and were formidable opposition. They had great players, wee Tommy Adams of the caliper legs, George Aitken, Charlie 'Legs' Fleming, of the thundering shot, and the steady Alan Brown. There was sadness for them to end the 1949 season. Charlie Fleming had just scored one of Hampden's greatest-ever goals when Mr John McArthur, chairman of the club, collapsed in the directors' box and died.

The Scottish Cup competition had been halted for seven seasons during the Second World War just as it had been for the five seasons of the first one. But there was a difference for, while the game resumed much as it had left off in 1919, momentous changes were near when a new start was made in 1946–47. There were to be changes in the scope of the game as it spread into Europe and indeed the whole world. The incentives were increased to match those of more glamorous public entertainers and so there was to be a change in the spirit in which the game was played.

There might have been some omens of change in that the Laws of the Game were rewritten in 1938 and there had been the first six-figure league attendance in Europe when 118,577 watched Rangers play Celtic on New Year's Day, 1939, and in the same year players were first numbered.

14

The War Years

Grim words from Mr Neville Chamberlain in September 1939 informed the people of Great Britain that they were at war with Germany. There was understandable consternation and apprehension. Football was halted for a brief period while the shocked civilians waited for immediate attacks from the air and in that mood crowds could not be allowed to assemble in such a ready target as a football ground. There was no panic, just apprehension.

The Government were aware, however, that the public needed distractions from the cares of war and that there was none better than football. Permission was given quickly for football matches to be played. Within a month a hasty shape was fashioned with Regional Leagues in the East and in the West and each with sixteen clubs. Six clubs suffered exclusion.

These plans did not work out. A severe winter closed some grounds for a long period and clubs lost considerable money. Cowdenbeath closed after six months of war-time football and others talked about similar action. By May 1940 eight of the thirty-eight pre-war League clubs were not operating and a fund to help them was started by imposing a five per cent levy on all League matches.

There had been so little action on the war front that there was a complacent proposal to revive the First and Second Divisions of the Scottish League to rectify the financial position but before the League meeting to discuss the proposal could be called France and the Low Countries were ablaze from German aggression. The Scottish League suspended its competitions and gave permission for local leagues to be formed.

In the summer of 1940 the Southern League was formed with sixteen clubs: Airdrie, Albion Rovers, Celtic, Clyde, Dumbarton, Falkirk, Hamilton Accies, Hearts, Hibs, Morton, Motherwell, Partick Thistle, Queen's Park, Rangers, St Mirren, and Third Lanark.

There was an attempt to form a North Eastern League but this was delayed for a year because St Johnstone and Dundee were reluctant to join. Meanwhile there was a Southern League Cup and a Summer Cup carried through bravely although the clubs did not know from week to week who would be available for the matches. Crowds were small but the game even as a talking point did serve the purpose of providing an escape from the cares of the times.

Professional football became near-amateur for the League match guarantee was fixed at £50 and the players wages at £2 per week. Yet much that was useful came from the war years and particularly the idea for the Scottish League Cup. The competition followed the close of the League programme with the sixteen clubs formed into Leagues of four each with a home and an away match against the other three clubs and the winners of the sections meeting in the semi-finals. The idea was extended after the war to produce the present Scottish League Cup with all clubs from both divisions taking part.

The major inconvenience of war-time football was that clubs could not be sure of a settled team. Players were involved in the Services and in war work and so, without warning (for there was much secrecy about movements), they could become unavailable for their clubs. A system of guesting was used and many famous players turned up in the most unlikely places.

Matt Busby became available to Hibs and with them was first recognised as a great player. For a brief period he fitted into a group of young players who became in the years immediately after the war one of the greatest teams seen till then. A lively little impish man, Harry Swan, who, for thirty years until 1963 was chairman of the club and president of the Scottish Football Association for five eventful years, supplied the imagination and cunning behind the most famous of Hibernian teams.

He was often called a visionary because of his advocating League reform, floodlight football, European football, sponsored football, while others with shocking conservatism did not want to know of such imminent advances like conservationists who oppose the building of adequate roads hoping, it seems, that if the motor car is ignored it will go away.

Harry Swan did no more than recognise that there was the electric light and that aeroplanes had brought Europe as near in time as Aberdeen used to be to Central Scotland clubs, and that commercial businesses had money which they wanted to spend on popularising their name. He was a realist rather than a visionary and believed that since floodlights, aeroplanes, and sponsors' money were there they should be put to the use of football.

His misfortune was that he was preaching in an age when those who controlled Scottish club football were insular and distressingly lacking in courage. They had become complacent rather than excited when an inevitable phase, brought on by reaction to the dull life of war time, sent people out to spend money and enjoy themselves and football got more than its share of support.

Attendances soared and football was good but most shrank from innovation that might have developed the enthusiasm and extended it. They drew back, like gauche country boys from the glittering plates and cutlery of a sophisticated restaurant, when competition against Europe or the world was mentioned. Scotland was to suffer much humiliation before that period was over.

And while legislators dithered, Hibernian, a team of all the attacking graces, developed in Edinburgh and even in Glasgow there was admiration and envy of their forward line. There had been many famous Scottish club forward lines to slip off the tongue over the years.

There were the Celtic five before the First World War, Bennett, McMenemy,

Hibs Famous Five return to Easter Road for a club presentation to Jimmy McColl who had been with Hibs for half a century. They were joined by Johnny Halligan, a colleague of McColl's in the 'twenties. *Left to right:* Gordon Smith, Bobby Johnstone, Jimmy McColl, Lawrie Reilly, Johnny Halligan, Willie Ormond.

Quinn, Somers, and Hamilton and the Raith Rovers line Bell, Miller, Jennings, James, and Archibald. Rangers had Archibald, Cunningham, Henderson, Cairns, and Morton but none of them outshone Smith, Johnstone, Reilly, Turnbull, and Ormond.

The Hibs famous five began to form around 1946. The elegant Gordon Smith was the first to find a permanent place and then there were the powerful Eddie Turnbull and the smooth left-winger, Willie Ormond. At centre-forward then was Alex Linwood, enormously skilful and masterly in the air. Between Smith and Linwood was Bobby Combe, a strong worker, who latterly moved to the half-back line to support the line when Lawrie Reilly and Bobby Johnstone moved in.

These five were immediately successful and they brought a new concept to Scottish football for they did not stick rigidly to set positions. At that time a full-back played on the flank of the defence marking a winger who stayed on the wing, and he would be a reckless full-back who would stray beyond the centre line, a rash winger who would go inside.

Hibs altered that thinking and maybe because they had an inspiring and thoughtful manager whose influence is too often overlooked. Willie McCartney was a big, laughing, happy man who would have looked naked without a flower in his button hole. He had a magnificent presence which hid his special knowledge of football. His father had been manager of Hearts and so had he before changing to Hibs.

He gave official sanction to the switching of Hibs forwards. He had Gordon Smith in his office one day to ask him why he had not stayed on his wing the previous Saturday. Smith told him that when he took the ball across field to the left wing he left a space for somebody to move into and that others in the forward line were prepared to do that and introduce an element of surprise.

Gordon Smith said of him: 'Mr McCartney was a big man but he was always prepared to listen. At other times he could shatter us without saying a word and just by his personality and presence. If things were not going well with us he would come down from the Directors' Box and stand in the middle of the tunnel, where he knew we would see him. I would say to myself, "Oh, my God! We'll have to do something", and we generally did.'

Willie McCartney had the knack of switching players and although his team selections did at times look ridiculous they usually came off and he had spectacular results with switches during a match. He was a much underrated manager.

Gordon Smith remembers a train journey after a match in 1947 when Hibs were challenging for the League Championship. There were but a few players in the compartment along with Willie McCartney and Harry Swan. The manager was silent for a while then broke from his reverie to say, 'I'd love to win this League Championship. If we could win this League I would give every player a hundred pounds.' Such a sum was a lot of money at that time and Harry Swan quickly dissociated himself from such reckless enthusiasm.

The sad upshot was that Hibs did win the League Championship, in April 1948, but Willie McCartney had died in February. He did not live to enjoy the team he built to bring pleasure to so many others. The team which became famous were all signed by McCartney and, when his players went, decline set in.

Harry Swan too was at his best when he had Willie McCartney keeping him in order. The manager was boss at Easter Road and at a time when it was not common to bar directors from the dressing room there was something awe inspiring in Willie McCartney saying in the dressing room before a match, 'And now Mr Chairman will you leave us'.

'The Famous Five', as the Hibs forward line came to be known, had their excellence recognised with 130 Scotland and Scottish League selections among them.

They scored 1,500 goals. Hibs, with them, won the Scottish League Championship in 1948, 1951, and 1952 but they could not win the Scottish Cup.

There was a theory about that. It was said that this best of all Hibs teams did not have a defence to match the forward brilliance and so they were vulnerable in Cup ties. Defenders were quickly forgotten as the names of the Famous Five lived on.

In fact during the formative years the forwards were raised to greatness by the men behind them. First there was Matt Busby, but for a little while, and then most important of all Willie Finnegan and Sammy Kean, both marvellously creative. They were perfect feeds in temperament and ability for the showmen forwards. Yet the defence never was thoroughly satisfactory and Willie Ormond tells a story of the sharp-tongued Laurie Reilly standing with hands on hips after the defence had lost a goal and shouting at them, 'Have we got to score four again today'. The greatness of those Hibs was that they could score four when they were needed.

It is a matter for regret that those five forwards never did play together in a Scotland team. On one occasion four were chosen. Turnbull was left out and the others confessed to feeling 'terrible'. The five had merited selection and it would have been fitting and a popular honour to have them all in a Scotland team.

Gordon Smith established a unique record when he left Hibs to play with Hearts and Dundee. He was in their League Championship sides. Thus he played for three clubs in the European Champions' Cup and that was a formidable achievement.

15

Manager of Scotland

Football boomed in Scotland in the years immediately after the war. The crowds were big. The play was spectacular and the players ambitious but the club men did not match their spirit. They developed a sense of inferiority as had not previously been noticed. They shrank from competition against the world. They would not risk defeat. It was a depressing period in the management of Scottish football, a period when world status was lost.

The Four Associations of Great Britain had withdrawn from the world controlling body, F.I.F.A., in the late 'twenties on the question of sham-amateurism. After the war they were enticed back. F.I.F.A. officials travelled to London and asked Britain to give them the benefit of their experience. It was a flattering request and when they were promised a vice presidency and a member of the executive they rejoined.

In 1950 Scotland was invited to match its football against the world but the Scottish Football Association wriggled out of the challenge. F.I.F.A. offered places in the Finals of the World Cup in Brazil to the winners and the runners-up in the British Home Championship. Scotland decided they would go only as champions of Great Britain.

Scotland and England played at Hampden Park in a deciding match for the Championship but, while England had already won and accepted a place in Brazil, Scotland needed a win to compete as champions. England beat them by one goal to nil and Scotland declined to travel as second best. F.I.F.A. pleaded with them to reconsider their decision but they insisted that a bargain had been made and that they would stick to it. Thus started an era of half-heartedness in international football.

The attitude was exemplified in the story of the Scotland team managers starting with the appointment of the first one, Andy Beattie, in February 1954. He claimed that he had been appointed without direction, preparation, or backing. His was a reluctant appointment.

The reason was that the idea of a manager with full control of the team was not in keeping with the thinking of the club men who formed the S.F.A. There were few managers then with full control of club teams and the club men could see no necessity for changing club practice for the national side. Even such a powerful manager as Scot Symon of Rangers had to submit his team selections to his board of directors and, on one memorable occasion in a European Cup tie in Milan, his selection was altered. Club men were convinced they could run an international team as they ran a club team.

In 1954 managers were, in the main, desk men and going on the practice ground with the players was something which foreigners did. At any rate Beattie resigned, disillusioned, during the 1954 World Cup and there were three years spent arguing about a replacement. Finally in January 1958 the father figure, Matt Busby of Manchester United, was appointed Scotland manager but in February of the same year he was seriously injured when the Manchester United plane crashed at Munich Airport.

The team trainer Dawson Walker was in charge of the Scotland team in the

Andy Beattie, Scotland's first manager, 1954.

Matt Busby, the Scotland manager, with the selection committee of the Scottish Football Association. *Left to right:* Haig Gordon, Hugh Nelson, Willie Palmer, John Park, Willie Waters (Secretary), Willie Allan, Matt Busby, Tom Reid, Willie Dunn (Assistant Secretary), Ernie Walker.

World Cup of 1958 in Sweden and Scotland was eliminated. In September 1958 Matt Busby reported that he had recovered and he took over the team again but he was over-optimistic and he had to give up in December of the same year.

The critical Andy Beattie was surprisingly given another chance and re-appointed in March 1959 but he was soon in trouble. He clashed with the Scotland captain, Bobby Evans, over tactics in Vienna. He shocked the S.F.A. with a letter in October 1960 in which he asked to be excused on the eve of the match against Wales at Cardiff. He watched his new club, Nottingham Forest, at Blackpool and missed the international match at Cardiff. He had to go, and he did, in the same month.

The S.F.A. were still not convinced that the team manager job should be a full-time one and in November 1960 Ian McColl, a Scottish internationalist, was appointed while still playing with Rangers reserves towards the end of a notable career. He was allowed to sit in with the Scotland selectors and advise on team selection.

After four-and-a-half years his authority with the players began to wane and, in May 1965 when he was staying with the players at Largs and preparing for World Cup matches against Poland and Finland, he was faced by an S.F.A. deputation and sacked. Jock Stein of Celtic took over the squad on a temporary basis but with defeat in Italy in December 1965 Stein's commitment ended and another manager had to be sought.

In January 1966 the job was advertised but in such terms as showed a reluctance to go the whole way. The advertisement described the job of Scotland manager as one, 'Which might suit those with other business interests'. Willie Waddell formerly of Rangers and then Eddie Turnbull manager of Aberdeen were offered the job but the terms did not suit them.

Finally in March 1966 John Prentice a former Hearts, Rangers, and Falkirk player and manager of Clyde accepted the post but immediately extreme incompatibility between him and the selection committee was apparent. Negotiations on the terms of his contract lasted from March to September and he was sacked in October. He was accused of seeking another job while still negotiating with the S.F.A.

When the linen had been washed and taken in and folded it was seen that Scotland were committed to a full-time team manager. It had taken a long, unpleasant thirteen years of controversy and failure to harden the official attitude which in February 1967 had Bobby Brown, former Queen's Park, Rangers, and Scotland goalkeeper and then manager of St Johnstone, appointed as full-time manager of Scotland.

Bobby Brown, extrovert and gregarious, had initial success. His career started brightly in February 1967 and glowed when his Scotland team beat Sir Alf Ramsey's World Cup-winning team with magnificent, arrogant Scottish football. There had been diminishing success but what little there was carried him through his first four years term. Failure in the World Cup qualifying matches and especially a failure in Hamburg in 1969 hastened his going and he was sacked from the job with still three years of his second term to go. He had been heavily criticised for the Hamburg defeat.

The following Spring, Bobby Brown was under heavy pressure from the Scotland supporters at Wembley when his team performed miserably against England. Unmercifully they chanted for his dismissal. The S.F.A. in July 1971 called him to account and dismissed him. He had produced only 1 win in the previous 10 internationals. He had charge of Scotland in 27 matches and only 9 had been won. Ten were lost and 8 drawn. He had started successful and inspiring but had lost the confidence of the players, the supporters, and his employers.

To replace him the Scottish Football Association appointed that most rumbustious of Scottish fanatics, Tommy Docherty, who had carried his nationalism through an international career which spanned the world. Full status had been given to the job by appointing a highly-qualified man and paying the rate for the job, and that's more than England paid Sir Alf Ramsey.

The free hand which Tommy Docherty was given with the national team was in sharp contrast to the conditions under which the first manager, Andy Beattie, had worked. Whereas Beattie took the players the selection committee of the S.F.A. gave him and was hampered in his preparation of them, Docherty chose his own and was sympathetically listened to in all matters concerning travel and training.

Tommy Docherty (*right*) watches Nat Lofthouse beat Harry Haddock to score for England against Scotland at Wembley Stadium in 1955.

The Wembley Scots of 1957. *Back row:* McNaight, Collins, Fernie, Younger, Hewie, Ring, McColl, *Front row:* Docherty, Reilly, Young, Mudie, Caldow.

Scotland at Wembley, 1957. George Young introduces Tommy Docherty to Lord Rosebery. Waiting are Tommy Ring, Bobby Collins, and Willie Fernie.

The one Jimmy Cowan missed in the 1949 match against England at Wembley. It was later known as Cowan's match.

'Last minute' Laurie Reilly beats Alf Ramsey and equalises with seconds to go against England 1953.

Great Britain's most capped players then, George Young and Billy Wright, lead their teams onto Wembley in 1957.

16

The World Cup

By the time the 1954 World Cup came round there was a strange mixture of enthusiasm and indifference for the tournament in the Scottish Football Association. The president, Harry Swan, was keen but the secretary, Sir George Graham, although a leading figure in European and World football affairs, was not excited and later described his attitude in a terse sentence, 'We hadn't the stuff'.

And so Scotland's first participation in the finals of the World Cup was an embarrassing affair, reluctantly conceived and ill-managed. Fortunately the mood of the S.F.A. changed after this competition and maybe the shambles of it helped. There was ever-increasing enthusiasm until, by the 'sixties, commitment was complete, entry automatic, and preparation thorough within the limitation of the availability of players with English clubs.

The 1954 affair had started with a great show of British independence. It was decided that each home country would stand on its own and that the British Championship, the oldest in the world, would not be reduced to a qualifying competition for the World Cup.

Scotland were drawn against Norway and Finland in a qualifying section. An inexplicable blunder was made in the manner of selecting the Scotland team for the qualifying matches and for the finals. Before the match against England at Hampden Park eighteen players were named and from them were to be chosen the team to play England, the teams to play Norway twice, and Finland once and, if a place in the finals were won, the party to travel to Switzerland. No room was left for changes should there be loss of form and in addition the selection committee would choose the teams and not the manager, Andy Beattie.

There was quickly a complication for there was no obvious captain for the team. George Young was the established Scotland captain but he had been unfit for the pool before the England game and although he was fit for the World Cup matches the selectors stuck to their previous decision and would not include him.

Scotland played the first match against Norway at Hampden on May 5, 1954 and played miserably in winning 1–0 and were jeered by the sparse 20,000 crowd. The team was: Martin (Aberdeen); Cunningham (Preston North End), Aird (Burnley); Docherty (Preston North End), Davidson (Partick Thistle), Evans (Celtic); Johnstone (Hibs), Hamilton (Aberdeen), Buckley (Aberdeen), Brown (Blackpool), Ormond (Hibs).

At least Scotland had won and that gave them a good start for Oslo and the return match. Before leaving for Oslo only twelve players turned up for the team training at Ayr. Docherty and Cunningham were on tour with Preston North End and they were flying direct. Johnstone and Ormond were with Hibs in Germany and were due to return for the training but instead stayed on and played against Bochum in Dusseldorf.

Such cynical disregard for the importance of the occasion had not been anticipated since Harry Swan, the president of the S.F.A., and Sir George Graham, the secretary, were in the party in Germany. The players arrived at Ayr while the others were packing to leave. 'I'll take the rap', said Harry Swan. 'I got the dates wrong'.

The selectors in charge, Tom Reid, George Carroll, and Andrew Beattie were urged to drop the missing players but the senior selector, Tom Reid, argued, 'Why punish the players and Scotland?' In the event the selectors dropped Bobby Evans, Willie Ormond, and Bobby Johnstone in Oslo. Doug Cowie (Dundee), John McKenzie (Partick Thistle), and Neil Mochan (Celtic) went in.

Scotland played depressingly but managed a 1–1 draw and then beat Finland 2–1 and so qualified for the finals in Switzerland. Then there was another astonishing decision. Beattie would take only thirteen players to the finals and two were goalkeepers. They went without Scotland training gear and to the embarrassment of many trained in their club jerseys. When the Austrians presented them with a pennant before the kick-off in the first match they had none with which to reciprocate.

The folly of such a small party was quickly evident when Bobby Johnstone was injured and had to be replaced. George Hamilton of Aberdeen was called up but he went reluctantly saying, 'I'd rather stay at home and play golf'. He had slowed considerably since his first cap seven years previously. He elaborated: 'It's unfair to ask the rest of the team to wait for me. When it's a fast game on a hard ground as in Switzerland you have to try and keep up. I lost seven pounds in Norway and I had hoped for a rest to put it on again.'

Hamilton made up the thirteen who went to Switzerland but did not play. Scotland first played Austria and lost 1–0 but might have had a penalty-kick when Neil Mochan slipped the ball between Happell's legs and was pushed when going round him to score. They had played well for an hour and then slumped.

In the match against the world champions, Uruguay, in Basle they were humiliated and devastated and beaten 7–1. Harry Swan said during the second half, 'I wish this game was over'. Tom Reid said afterwards, 'It was like me playing Joe Davis at snooker'. A half-hearted attempt had been appropriately punished.

Before the match there had been a strange atmosphere in the Scotland camp. The manager, Andy Beattie, with a weird sense of timing announced before the match that he was giving up his appointment as team manager. He had made up his mind before flying to Switzerland and had left details of his reasons before leaving Glasgow. Scotland's first efforts in the World Cup indeed had been puny. The improvement was gradual.

For the 1958 World Cup in Sweden Scotland had improved in attitude but had not yet learned the extent to which preparation was necessary. The national team was not even run on club lines for there was no manager. The trainer Dawson

Walker of Clyde was nominally manager but the captain, the goalkeeper Tommy Younger, took the team talks and carried out all negotiations with the selection committee.

It was strange in the first place to have a goalkeeper as captain and one of the sights of the tournament was to see the bulky goalkeeper toss the coin before a match and then hare back to his goal before play was started, worrying in case the kick-off should find him only half way there.

The qualifying matches were handled satisfactorily but finished on high controversy. Scotland had beaten Spain at Hampden Park and then planned the two away matches, with a friendly between, against West Germany.

Switzerland were beaten in Basle and so Scotland had almost qualified and that left the match in Madrid to be won. In Basle George Young was injured and this was to lead to unpleasant controversy. Young, the captain of Rangers, was also captain of Scotland and a formidable character. Some thought he was too formidable as is always when powerful personalities are concerned.

His ability as a player was never in question and neither was his inspiring influence and he had been Scotland's most-capped player when he went on that trip to Europe. His injury kept him out of the friendly match against West Germany. Then he announced that he was fit for the match in Madrid for which he and others had assumed he was an automatic choice.

The selection committee under Mr Willie Watters did not select him and instead announced that Bobby Evans of Celtic would be at centre-half. A furious Young announced that he would never play for Scotland again. Switzerland were beaten at Hampden Park to complete the qualification.

And so Scotland went to the finals in Sweden and were settled in Ekilstuna and that was something that had not been confidently expected when England had won 4–0 at Hampden Park. Another surprise was that Northern Ireland captained by Danny Blanchflower had eliminated Italy and were also through to the finals.

Scotland were in pool two along with Paraguay, Yugoslavia, and France who were then of such power as they have not since matched. They had three superb inside-forwards Fontaine, Kopa who had been playing with Real Madrid, and Piantoni. They were immediately threatening by beating Paraguay 7–3.

The first match for Scotland was against Yugoslavia and looked ominous for they had recently beaten England by 5–0. The Scotland team which was selected was: Younger; Caldow, Hewie; Turnbull, Evans, Cowie; Leggat, Murray, Mudie, Collins, Imlach. It was strong in the middle and Eddie Turnbull, then thirty-five years old, was remarkably powerful. Yugoslavia led after seven minutes but Scotland wore them down and Murray scored for a draw.

After that satisfactory start there was one of those astonishing errors of judgment which at the time plagued Scottish international football. Tommy Docherty and Archie Robertson, who were not needed for the match against France, were sent to Norrkoping to study Paraguay and France when they played. They came back with accurate information about Paraguay and principally to the effect that they were a strongly physical team. Little interest was shown in their information until they wondered why they had been sent.

Despite the report that Paraguay were, 'rough and fit and good' such delicate players as Mudie, Robertson, and Fernie were chosen for the forward line along with the little fellows, Leggat and Collins. Such powerful characters as Sammy Baird and Dave Mackay were left out. Scotland did well in the circumstances to hold Paraguay to a 3–2 result.

Scotland too late brought in the big men Baird and Mackay for the match against France which they had to at least draw to maintain an interest in the competition. Kopa and Fontaine had scored for France and Baird for Scotland when near the end Scotland were awarded a penalty-kick. John Hewie took it and struck a post and the ball rebounded almost to the centre of the field. Scotland had no luck in the competition.

In Sweden it was noticed how Scotland had been left behind in the matter of preparing for matches. It had not until then been fully appreciated that foreigners had mastered the old game and had brought sophistication to it. It was a lesson painfully learned for it is never easy for the masters to admit to being old-fashioned and to change their ways.

Scotland performed creditably in the qualifying matches for the 1962 tournament losing in a play-off to Czechoslovakia in Brussels after beating them at Hampden Park. The merit of that was shown when the Czechs went to the Final in Santiago and lost to a great Brazil side by 3–1 after holding them to a draw at half-time.

On a May evening in 1965 the secretary of the Scottish Football Association, Mr W. P. Allan, arrived at the hotel in Largs where the Scotland team were preparing under the manager, Ian McColl, for World Cup qualifying matches in Poland and Finland. He had gone to carry out the instructions of the Association and terminate the contract of the team manager. He had not given satisfaction with his handling of the team. It was then announced that Celtic had agreed to loan the S.F.A. their manager, Jock Stein, for the trip.

This drastic intervention at least proved the determination of the officials to try earnestly for a place in the finals although to change the manager a few days before such vital matches was less than prudent.

Stein's Celtic had just won the Scottish Cup and he took over the pool of players amid much enthusiasm. Finland had been beaten in the first qualifying match at Hampden and Stein's call to the team was to win the games in Poland and Finland and then there would only be two home games against Italy and Poland to be won at Hampden to ensure going to the finals. He did not want qualification resting on the final game. It was away to Italy.

The Scotland team for the Poland match stayed in a youth hostel in a depressing place in Silesia, Chorzow, a 200-mile train journey and then a bus run from Warsaw. On a miserable Sunday evening of heavy rain Scotland lost a goal in the seventh minute but then, playing well-ordered football, they got the game going their way and might have won but had to be content with a goal, scored by Denis Law, fourteen minutes from the end and a draw.

Stein altered the team for the second game. He wanted a high-scoring win to impress Italy and so he placed in the forward line, Denis Law, Neil Martin, and Willie Hamilton who among them had scored over eighty goals the previous season. With Willie Henderson and David Wilson on the wings, Pat Crerand switched to the right of the midfield immediately behind his club-mate at Manchester United, Denis Law, and John Greig beside him, there were hopes of an impressive total of goals in the Olympic Stadium in Helsinki.

Instead Scotland made a drab, tedious job of beating Finland's amateurs 2–1. Few players found their true form and only Law, Wilson, and Crerand played well. Afterwards Crerand was voted the best player in the match and awarded a trophy.

Three points from the two matches on the continent was satisfactory and when Scotland played Poland at Hampden on October 13, 1965 the happy prospect was that if they won, as they were entitled to expect, after drawing in Poland then they need beat Italy only once in two matches to earn at least a play-off with the Italians in a neutral country.

For this match, Willie Johnston of Rangers, a former pit boy in Fife, who had just six months previously played for the Scotland youth team, was preferred on the left-wing to John Hughes of Celtic, and Jim Baxter was left out as he was not deemed to be match fit. He was nearing the end of a controversial international career. Billy Bremner of Leeds United was given his place.

Scotland *v.* Brazil at Hampden Park, June 1966. Pele (10) asks for calm. Jim Baxter (*left*) is not so sure. Ron McKinnon, John Clark, and Billy Bremner look on.

Poland had been beaten by Finland in the previous month and panic measures were taken after that humiliation and five changes were made in the team from the first match. This all seemed to the benefit of Scotland and they went confidently into the vital match sure that they would adorn the World Cup final series when they were held the following year in England.

There were 107,500 at Hampden Park hoping to acclaim a Scotland victory and such seemed well on the way when in the fourteenth minute the centre-half, Billy McNeill, came up for Willie Henderson's corner-kick and the goalkeeper, Kornek, palmed the ball off Gilzean's head for it to drop in front of McNeill. He drove it hard to the roof of the net.

With Johnston exciting on the left and Denis Law menacing in the middle there was the satisfying prospect of more goals, but they did not come. Then in the second half there was anxiety as Scotland lost their grip on the midfield and there was some sloppy defending. Yet with six minutes to be played they still led by that early goal.

Then the Scottish goal was left gaping and Liberda scored. As the crowd showed irritation over the lead being lost the goal was exposed again a minute later and a bouncing shot by Sadek deceived Bill Brown and slipped into the net. The vital game was lost and the crowd demonstrated their anger noisily.

Stein re-organised the defence for the match against Italy at Hampden Park on November 9. The Rangers full-backs, Greig and Provan, replaced Hamilton and McCreadie. McKinnon was at centre-half instead of McNeill, and Baxter was back again along with Crerand in the midfield. Hughes was on the left-wing in place of the youthful Johnston.

Enthusiasm had been promised by Stein and he gave that 100,000 crowd just that. They gave Italy no choice of tactics but hammered them into defence. Yet goals were hard to score and there were only 100 seconds to go when Scotland at last scored with a goal which had been planned on the training field at Largs.

Willie Henderson had been told to race inside if Baxter veered to the right. He would take the Italian full-back with him and Greig would have space to run into. And so it happened. Baxter in that casual, masterly way of his was working the ball to the right. Henderson sprinted inside and the full-back, the great Facchetti, went with him. Greig raced down the unguarded wing and Baxter, with incomparable skill, swerved the ball round the centre-half and right into the path of the charging Greig. A spectacular shot flew past Negri and Scotland had won. Henderson got Stein's congratulations.

As the Scotland team satisfied the crowd with a dignified lap of honour it was being quickly worked out that a win in Italy on December 7 would earn qualification and a draw would result in a play-off.

And so to Italy and with tremendous backing for the team and an unprecedented order that all football involving World Cup players had to be postponed on the Saturday before the squad met for training. The apathy of the 'fifties had been conquered and the conviction substituted that Scotland must be represented on the football fields of the world to which Scots had helped to spread the game.

But soon there was disappointment and in unexpected places. Bill Shankly and Sir Matt Busby, reckoned to be the most fervent Scots in English football, announced that their clubs, Liverpool and Manchester United, were due their players' first allegiance and that they could not excuse important players from a Saturday game ten days before an international match. The nuisance of non-cooperation had struck again.

Liverpool's Billy Stevenson had suddenly become important when Jim Baxter became unfit and unavailable for the trip. Denis Law was the forward inspiration. They both played on that Saturday when the others in the pool rested and as luck would have it both were injured and had to withdraw.

Bill Brown the goalkeeper had also withdrawn and Jock Stein had to make a hurried trip to Burnley to inspect another goalkeeper, Adam Blacklaw. In Manchester on his journey home he heard the news of the withdrawal of Law and Stevenson and was miserable but he could not guess the full extent of his troubles.

During the following week Billy McNeill failed a fitness test and had to withdraw, while Willie Henderson was under treatment for a leg strain, a strain that was to prove vital to Scotland's chances.

The Italians, seizing every psychological advantage, took the match to Naples where a hysterical partisan atmosphere could be depended upon. When he arrived in Naples with the remnants of his squad, Stein tried his hand at psychology and declared, 'The disaster of the injuries will boost the morale of the rest of the team'. It might have but there was still another disaster.

At training on the day before the match Willie Henderson had a recurrence of the strain which had troubled him. The news was hidden from everybody and even the officials of the S.F.A. and when Henderson did not appear on the field with the others they were as astonished as everybody else.

Stein remembers now, 'When Willie Henderson's strain recurred and he had to call off we just had nothing left to win the game with. We had to play for a draw and a play-off.' This he did by naming Ron Yeats, the Liverpool centre-half, at centre-forward but in the event played him in the middle of the defence alongside Ronnie McKinnon.

Everything had gone well for the Italians as they trained at Coverciano near Florence and their trainer, Edmondo Fabbri, was so content that he gave them a day off on the Sunday to go and watch a match at Pisa, staying behind himself so as to allow them every freedom.

Italy arrived by train in Naples where the station throbbed with the excitement. A half-holiday was declared for the hysterical Neapolitans and it was being remembered that Italy under Dr Fabbri had never lost an international match at home. The record was to continue.

For a while the enforced makeshift Scotland team played well and held the Italians but then, in an unfortunate moment in the thirty-eighth minute, McCreadie mis-hit the ball in front of goal and Pascuttie scored. Scotland's well-ordered football crashed on that mis-kick.

Until then the cold Ronnie McKinnon had been spreading composure throughout the defence. Provan and McCreadie had been impressive full-backs. Bremner marked the renowned Rivera into obscurity, and Murdoch and Cooke worked skilfully in taking the ball out of defence, leaving the heavy defending to Greig. But there was no effective attack.

With that goal went Scotland's qualification and they were unfortunate that before a frustrating afternoon was over Italy scored two more goals. They did not deserve to be beaten by three goals. As Stein said at the time, 'Most roads are paved with good intentions but this one was littered with obstacles'.

And so Scotland was destined to wait another four years, but the mood had changed from 1950 and there was impatience for the next attempt. When it came there was to be more frustration and talk of what might have been but, at least, the attitude was right.

Malcolm MacDonald, the manager of Kilmarnock, was interim manager of Scotland after John Prentice was dismissed. Then in February 1967 Bobby Brown, former Rangers goalkeeper and then manager of St Johnstone, was appointed manager of Scotland, and commissioned to win a place in the finals of the 1970 World Cup in Mexico. He had spectacular initial success when his team beat the 1966 World Cup winning team of Sir Alf Ramsey.

He had started at the top but his fortune deteriorated progressively and partly because of that trouble of all Scotland's managers, obtaining the release of players from clubs who are highly committed in League football.

He was still on the heights of popularity when Scotland were drawn in a qualifying section along with Austria, Cyprus, and West Germany. The pattern was soon set when Scotland beat Austria at Hampden Park. Brown had promised a hard-working Scotland team and they needed to work hard after Austria scored in the third minute.

Cyprus did not give Scotland much bother although they almost surprised West Germany and only in injury time were they beaten. On a baked pitch of grey powder resembling crushed cement in Nicosia, Bobby Murdoch scored two goals, Alan Gilzean another two, and Colin Stein one. Those five goals were impressively scored and only one corner-kick was conceded.

The result of this section was clearly between Scotland and West Germany and they met on April 17, 1969 in Hampden Park. A familiar and distressing Scottish story was unfolded. There had been much attacking by Scotland, fierce in its intensity, brilliant in conception, and then they lost a goal.

Bobby Murdoch and Billy Bremner had dominated the midfield. They had kept the tricky Jimmy Johnstone and the speedy Bobby Lennox running on the wings and with the ball going high to the menacing heads of Denis Law and Alan Gilzean the West Germans were defending desperately. Such formidable attackers as Haller and Overath were restricted to defending.

Then in the thirty-ninth minute and at the height of the Scottish ascendancy, the Germans had a harmless looking free-kick. The ball was played to Gerd Muller as he stood back to goal and covered by McKinnon and Greig. He pushed and wriggled and turned between them and had a peep at goal and that was all he needed. West Germany led.

They led until five minutes from time. Then Charlie Cooke the master of the weaving run, who had been substituted for Lennox, swerved through the defence. He moved to send the defence one way and stroked the ball in front of Bobby Murdoch as he came through on the other side. A memorable shot hit on the run made a draw for Scotland. They had deserved better.

In the next game Scotland took eight goals from the unfortunate Cyprus and then came the decisive match against West Germany in Hamburg, in October. Scotland that night played maybe the best football they had played in any World Cup match yet they lost. The team had been well prepared yet finally were beaten by blunders.

After Jimmy Johnstone had given them the lead they settled to play with authority. Billy Bremner won the vital midfield battle by subduing Overath who was as formidable a midfield player as was to be found in the world. Beside him Peter Cormack found space enough in which to play the game of his life.

Eddie Gray was tormenting the German defence on the left and there was a smooth rhythm in the team and it was against the run of play when West Germany went ahead. Then Alan Gilzean put Scotland level again and the hunt was on for the goal that would take Scotland to Mexico.

Among the Scots there were prayers for team changes. It was noticed that Germany were playing no left-winger against Greig at right-back, but that they had

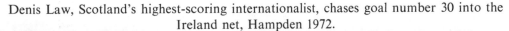

Denis Law, Scotland's highest-scoring internationalist, chases goal number 30 into the Ireland net, Hampden 1972.

a right-winger whom that natural attacker, Tommy Gemmell, had to cover. Gemmell was better than Greig at running into space and Greig was better at covering. It seemed obvious that the backs should be switched. But no switch was made by the manager.

It seemed too that the eager Charlie Cooke should be brought on to change the pattern midway through the second half. But no change was made and, as the Scots supporters worried, the German right-winger, Libuda, in a blind spot over Tommy Gemmell's shoulder got the ball, streaked away with it, and scored. Scotland lost and were out. Manager Bobby Brown was bombarded with heavy criticism and never did regain the popularity he lost that night.

He had a chance to recover in the European Championships of 1972 but disastrous matches against Belgium and Portugal sealed his fate. The crowd howled for his dismissal at Wembley when Scotland went down tamely to England and he went.

For a new century of Scottish football there was a new manager, Tommy Docherty, modern in his methods but agreeably old-fashioned in his belief that Scottish football, as it was at the start of the first century, was still the best in the world at the beginning of the second. It was a conviction not backed by the records but a stirring one to take to the World Cup of 1974. And immediately and typically the fond dream was disturbed. Docherty resigned to manage Manchester United and Willie Ormond, once of Hibs, was charged with leading Scotland into the new century.

17

The Scottish Football Association Promotes

The Scottish Football Association, after 100 years of buffeting, was a more complex body than its pioneers had intended. It was a conglomerate unique among the Football Associations of the world in that it carried no less than eight associations which had attached themselves over the century. There were the Army F.A. in 1900, the Scottish Amateur F.A. in 1909, the Scottish Churches F.A. in 1927, the Scottish Junior F.A. in 1886, the Scottish Juvenile F.A. in 1899, the Scottish Schools F.A. in 1904, the Scottish Secondary Juvenile F.A. in 1921, and the Scottish Welfare F.A. in 1919.

It was an arrangement which reflected the tremendous interest in the game in that various grades could sustain their own national body, but it was an untidy and uneconomical arrangement which did not appeal to those who like a smooth flow through logical grades.

There was an attempt in the early 'fifties to bring order to the organisation. There was a proposal to organise on an age basis, the unanswerable argument being that it must be wrong to have father and son playing together as was possible in the Junior grade.

The Association had grown without direction but when some tidying up was proposed the obstacle was that each grade was proud of its own independence and many who had little empires were not prepared to give them up and the perks which went with them. They insisted on keeping their own identities and the Scottish Football Association were thus trapped within an illogical system.

As at the start, the S.F.A. was run by a council but one which had grown over the years until it comprised forty-eight representatives, beyond question far too many. The numbers had been increased by giving seats to the Affiliated National Associations and by increasing under pressure the representation of the League Management Committee from two to nine and then to twelve.

This Council governs all grades of football in Scotland from Schools to International level and it is often overlooked that they have responsibilities far beyond the League clubs and the National team though no responsibility at all for the organisation of League football.

Indeed the scope, composition, and function of the Scottish Football Association has been much misunderstood. The Association is in fact the clubs. Any criticism of the Association is therefore criticism of the clubs. When clubs criticise the Association they are, in effect, criticising themselves and not some ghostly body out in space. The clubs get the sort of Association they deserve for they form it.

The Association has a duty to foster and develop the game in Scotland and the evidence is that since the war they have been more active in pursuing that object than at any other time. In the early 'fifties they set up a coaching scheme which was against the thinking of the time but in keeping with modern thought. There was a reluctance within the Association at first and resistance among League club managers. Coaching, at the time, was a dirty word to them.

The first coaching school was held in Ibrox Stadium and then moved to Jordanhill Training College where it survived the early resistance until, at the end of the century, the Association was scarcely able to provide sufficient places for all those who wished to take the annual residential course.

The School was finally based in the Inverclyde Recreation Centre at Largs and in 1972 an overflow course had to be held in Stirling University. No less than 150 students took the two-week residential course that year and sat examinations for the Preliminary Certificate and the Full Award. So much had the early resistance been overcome that more than half of the managers of the Scottish League clubs held certificates from the course.

The Scottish Football Association also pioneered a scheme for referees which is unique. It was started by the secretary of the Association, Sir George Graham, in 1946. In most countries the referees have an organisation independent of the national association. Sir George argued that more could be done if in some way the referees were linked with the national association.

He had adopted the principle of one association with branches. A scheme was set up with a number of supervisors who were formerly prominent referees to act as a liaison between the District Referees' Associations throughout the country. These supervisors were charged with supervising refereeing, conducting examinations, and supervising grading of referees.

As the system now works the supervisors go to matches, not to spy, but to look after the interests of referees and linesmen. They report on what they see and records are compiled from their reports so that the Association knows how the referees comport themselves in the eyes of the supervisors.

Then the Scottish League submit summaries of the reports on the referees received from the clubs. So to the views of the supervisors are added the views of the clubs. The supervisors assess the abilities of the referees at the end of each season and make recommendations which are normally approved by the Referee Committee of the S.F.A. Referees are thus judged objectively which did not happen before the scheme when a man was sometimes graded not according to show he refereed but according to who he knew.

When the Scottish Football Association along with the other home countries rejoined F.I.F.A. in 1946 they became important members in that they ran the football match in 1947 which revived the finances of F.I.F.A. The S.F.A. organised a match between Great Britain and the Rest of the World at Hampden Park which raised £30,000 for the international organisation and left it to pursue its post-war work without financial embarrassment.

In the circumstances F.I.F.A. might have felt some obligation to Scotland yet in the last century the membership of Scotland was being held in question. Uruguay had a proposal, which found favour in some quarters, that Great Britain should be one unit in F.I.F.A. and that the home countries would lose the separate identities they had held in football since the 1870s, before any other national association had been formed.

Mr W. P. Allan the secretary of the S.F.A. flew to South America to explain the special situation with regard to the pioneering home associations and had success in having the motion withdrawn. Yet it was disturbing that after the work that Scotland had put into developing the game from its rowdy beginnings, helping significantly in drawing up the Laws of the Game, and then raising the money to make F.I.F.A. a working body, there were those members who thought of reducing the country to but a part of a unit and with no direct voice or indeed participation in world affairs.

The Great Britain *v.* the Rest of Europe match had been a fine stimulus to the game after the war. The game took place at Hampden Park on May 10, 1947 and three Scots, the sturdy wing-half, Archie Macaulay of Arsenal, the sharp goal-scorer, Billy Steel of Dundee, and Liverpool's consistent left-winger, Billy Liddell.

The British team on that great Hampden occasion was Swift (England); Hardwick (England), Hughes (Wales); Macaulay (Scotland), Vernon (Ireland), Burgess (Wales); Matthews (England), Mannion (England), Lawton (England), Steel (Scotland), Liddell (Scotland).

The teams take the field for the G.B. *v.* Rest of Europe match at Hampden Park in 1947. In dark shirts, the G.B. team are led by George Hardwick. Johnny Carey leads Europe.

With one of the greatest centre-forwards of all time, Tommy Lawton, together with Stan Matthews and Wilf Mannion on one side, and Billy Steel and Billy Liddell on the other, it is little wonder that Britain scored six goals against the one scored by the Rest. Mannion had two, Lawton two, Steel one, and Parola was forced into putting the ball into his own goal.

The Scottish Football Association had powerful voices in the talks which led to the formation of the European Union of Football Associations, E.U.F.A. Sir George Graham who was secretary of the S.F.A. tells of how he and Bob Williamson, the treasurer of the S.F.A., attended a meeting of F.I.F.A. in 1952. After lunch there was talk that the European Associations should band together as those in South America had done.

Thus started the idea for the European Union and an unofficial committee was formed to explore the idea and this committee eventually drafted a constitution. This was sent around Europe and a final draft was made at a meeting in Copenhagen with Sir George Graham attending. Sir George was called from holiday in the South of France by the S.F.A. president, Harry Swan, to attend a meeting in Vienna on March 2, 1955 and in the afternoon session the European Union was formed.

A mark of Scotland's part in its formation was that Sir George Graham was made a member of the first committee and afterwards, when the European Cup was instituted, he became chairman of the committees which ran it. The European Cup was the brain child of the veteran French journalist Gabriel Hanot and his newspaper *L'Équipe*.

They asked the Union for permission to run a competition for champion clubs. The Union were not happy about this but after lunch decided that if E.U.F.A. organised the competition that would be different. A quick decision on rules resulted in a stipulation that no team would be allowed to play in the competition unless they were champions of a country. The other European Cups, the Cup Winners', and the E.U.F.A., were obvious followers on as air travel facilitated rapid movement around Europe.

The Scottish Football Association has been in enthusiastic co-operation with E.U.F.A. since its inception. Scotland has participated every season in the E.U.F.A. Youth tournament and in 1970 staged the tournament. There were sixteen nations competing and four centres were used, Largs, Aberdeen, Inverness, and Bridge of Allan. The Final between West Germany and Holland was played at Hampden Park and the match was drawn after extra-time. That most unsatisfactory tie-breaker, the toss of a coin, was in operation for the last time. West Germany guessed rightly and took the cup. They had lost it in the same fashion the previous season.

The Scottish Football Association's most successful co-operation with E.U.F.A. was in staging the European Cup-Final on May 18, 1960. Real Madrid, who had monopolised the competition since its formation in 1955, won their fifth successive Final by beating Eintracht Frankfurt by seven goals to three.

There were 127,621 at the Final, the biggest crowd ever at a European Cup tie. They paid 10*s*. for standing on the terracing, the first time such a high charge was made, and the receipts of £55,000 were a British record. That crowd saw what was the best game of football ever played until then and there will never be many better. They were moved to ecstatic appreciation. Never in Hampden have there been more emotional scenes than when Real Madrid, in their white, cavorted round Hampden's field in a lap of honour.

All the desirable football skills had been on view and those legendary characters Di Stefano, Puskas, and Gento, whom they had known about from television and from newspapers, came to life before them and larger than life.

During a game which beat out a steady rhythm of satisfaction for the full ninety minutes they thrilled to the haughty generalship of di Stefano, to the technical magnificence, cool ingenuity, and precise shooting of Puskas, to the flashing speed of Gento. Around them were the other great craftsmen, Del Sol, Canario, Santamaria, and the others. Above all there were ten goals, ten magnificent goals.

The credit which Eintracht took from the match was that they never ceased to be worthy opponents for the greatest of all club sides till then. They had toyed with Rangers in the semi-final, beating them by a 12–4 aggregate, and that was a measure of their worth among ordinary teams.

But Real Madrid were no ordinary team. They were a collector's team with treasures gathered from all the football world. Their problem was to select the eleven best from the best which they had accumulated in the world markets.

Eintracht almost shocked them in the early minutes of the match and Meier's swinging shot slapped against the crossbar. And then in the twentieth minute Eintracht did score to startle the lofty Real. They reacted predictably and equalised in the twenty-sixth minute. It was a goal of typical simplicity. Canario's cross eluded the defence and di Stefano with affected indifference struck it into the goal.

In another two minutes di Stefano was moving to the ball as it broke from the diving body of the goalkeeper and he had it in the net before anybody could move. And then he was strutting from penalty-area to penalty-area demanding the ball, using it with authority, seeking acknowledgment as the master.

Then, almost on the interval, the Hungarian 'Galloping Major', Ferenc Puskas, came on the scene with his strutting little strides, jockeyed for position, and, from ridiculously near the by-line, struck a cool shot over the head of the goalkeeper. Only he could have done that.

Then the flying Gento was pushed and the referee Jack Mowat gave a penalty-kick and it seemed a waste of time asking the greatest shot of them all, Puskas, to take it and the score was 4–1. Soon the blur that was Gento was clear and sending the ball into the middle and Puskas bowed benignly to nod it into the net. Again portly Puskas was pivoting in that startling way of his and shooting another goal and Real's magnificence was worth them all.

Stein got one for the gallant Eintracht but that only inspired one of Hampden's greatest goals. Di Stefano was back in his own penalty-area demanding the ball and then sprinting straight through the middle striking together a cluster of sharp passes before hitting a lordly shot into Eintracht's net. Stein got another for Eintracht and nobody grudged them the score.

The great Real Madrid team that day was: Dominguez; Marquitos, Pachin; Vidal, Santamaria, Zarraga; Canario, Del Sol, di Stefano, Puskas, Gento.

18

Disaster and Tragedy

Disaster and tragedy there had to be in those first 100 years of Scottish football. Huge crowds had been drawn to the games, intense emotions moved them, and there was no previous experience of the forces generated when roused crowds swayed and pushed. Twice at Ibrox Stadium these forces exceeded the predictable and there was death. At Hampden Park these emotions also produced a riot which caused a Scottish Cup to be withheld. One player was killed on the field of play, John Thomson, one of the greatest goalkeepers of the century and, in 1970, the most terrible disaster of all happened in a terracing stairway in Ibrox Stadium.

The first disaster at Ibrox Stadium was during the international match with England on April 5, 1902. It was the result of lack of experience of what was needed to raise a crowd above ground level.

The Rangers Football Club had gone to much expense in building a terracing to increase the capacity of the ground. It was thought at the time that a timber structure was the most suitable and this was erected and on a wooden framework the steps for the standing spectators were built.

Ibrox was packed for the England international that day and all was well until Bobby Templeton, the exciting winger then of Aston Villa and later of Kilmarnock, sprinted along the touchline and left the England defenders trailing. The crowd on the west terracing leaned forward to watch him and they swayed and slipped and part of the wooden structure gave way under the strain. Bodies went tumbling down through the struts.

When the tally was taken it was found that 25 spectators had died and that 24 were dangerously injured. Another 493 had to be treated, a heavy price to pay for the knowledge that only solid earth and concrete could be trusted to withstand the swaying of an excited crowd.

The riot in Hampden Park took place on the day that Celtic and Rangers supporters for the only time got together and shared a common cause, a common war cry, the same ammunition. The result of their coming together was maybe worse than the embarrassment in Scottish football of having to segregate them.

In Hampden Park that day they stirred such a hellish brew of hooliganism as has never since been seen. The riotous occasion was the replay of the Scottish Cup-Final in April 1909. There had been murmurings of discontent over the large number of drawn ties and consequent replays involving the clubs. The clubs were wildly accused in letters to the newspapers of playing for the money and that the draws were fixed. It was thought strange that there were no draws in charity cup matches in which the clubs took nothing from the gates. It was mob reasoning with no grounds in fact.

There had been an S.F.A. inquiry over the League match between Celtic and Rangers a month before the Cup-Final and the referee had been suspended for not taking sterner action over some incidents on the field. Against this background of rough play and distrust the Final was played and the draw was made by a sensational goal.

The Scotland team for the Ibrox disaster game, 1902. *Back row:* James Wilson (Rangers' Trainer), Bobby Walker (Hearts), Nick Smith (Rangers), Ned Doig (Sunderland), A. Kirkwood (S.F.A. President), Jock Drummond (Rangers), Alec Raisbeck (Liverpool), R. Dixon (S.F.A. Treasurer), Jacky Robertson (Rangers); *Front row:* Bobby Templeton (Aston Villa), Sandy Brown (Tottenham), Dadler Aitken (Newcastle United), Geordie Livingstone (Celtic), Alec Smith (Rangers). Jock Drummond always wore a cap.

Celtic had led and Rangers had overtaken them and were in front by a goal with three minutes to go. Then the Rangers' goalkeeper, Harry Rennie, had the ball in his hands, sensing that the mighty Jimmy Quinn was charging in on him, turned and carried the ball, still in his hands, over the line. The award of that goal by the referee J. B. Stark kept the arguments going till the following Saturday when the replay took place.

There were 60,000 there that day. Again Jimmy Quinn pulled back Rangers early lead and the teams were level after ninety minutes, no surprise to the cynics. Extra time was expected and there was fury when it was seen that the players were leaving the field and that the clubs intended having another replay. The crowd did not know or care that the S.F.A. rules at the time stipulated that there would only be extra time after the third game.

There were cries of 'Play on' but of course they were ignored and some jumped the barricade and crowded round the players' tunnel screaming, 'Play on'. A policeman, probably provoked, was seen to be rough with a demonstrator and the crowd went berserk.

The goalposts were torn up and paraded. There were ninety-seven policemen present but the officer in charge held them to protect the stand, surrendering the field to the rioters. Wooden barricades were torn up and a bonfire made of them. Mounted police were brought into action but the crowd retreated to the terracing and stoned them. There were baton charges which were repelled with stones.

The fire brigade were called out when the pay boxes were set on fire but their hoses were cut and there was a weird sight when police and firemen lined up to protect the hoses and stoned rioters to keep them away. Soon there were 300 police reinforcements called from all over the city.

Twelve doctors and a squad of nurses tended the injured including forty-five policemen. As they did so the destruction spread to property outside the park and damage scarred the route into the town. Peace at last settled on a shamed Hampden Park. On Monday morning one solitary rioter appeared in Govan Court and he was fined £5.

The clubs met and then announced that they would not replay the tie. The S.F.A. met and asked when clubs had started to run Scottish football. The S.F.A. decided that the Final would not be replayed and the Cup was withheld.

The death of John Thomson shocked Scottish Football as any fatal accident to a player but the shock of his death was worsened because of his own personal qualities which were appreciated even by his most bigoted opponents. He exemplified all that was graceful and good in the game. He was arguably the greatest Scottish goalkeeper of all time. He was a gentleman from the coal-fields of Fife who bore none of the ruggedness of the area.

He faced death at four o'clock in the afternoon of September 5, 1931. A dull game between Rangers and Celtic at Ibrox Stadium had gone into the fifth minute of the second half. In the making there was that situation described in Glasgow as 'A draw, nae fitba'. The teams seemed to be reconciled to the fact and had thoughts not for winning but for preventing defeat.

Then another Celtic attack had broken down and as they lost the ball it broke to the young medical student, Jimmy 'Doc' Marshall. He pushed it square to the captain, David Meiklejohn, and Rangers broke from defence. Jimmy Fleming raced up the right-wing, dodged a tackle by Willie McGonagle, a fervent Celtic back and, seeing Celtic's defence thin, pushed the ball through the middle and in front of that crinkly-haired Irishman, Sam English, at centre-forward.

English was new to the team and had only come in when he had passed a fitness test that morning. That was a cruel twist of fate for him. He stroked the ball ahead and bore in on goal where the lithe young goalkeeper in red jersey waited. The ball ran a little ahead of English as he approached the penalty-area and that was when John Thomson exploded into action. He dived forward, his body parallel to the ground, as Sam English drove his foot into the shot. Thomson's head struck the Ranger's knee and as the ball was deflected past a post he lay prone. Sam English turned to look at him and waved frantically for help.

He saw blood spurting and staining the turf and knew that the young keeper was badly injured. He was indeed. He died that night without regaining consciousness. He was but twenty-three years old.

There was a terrible sadness throughout football which turned to a torrent of emotionalism as preparations were made for the funeral. Life stood still in Glasgow and then John Thomson was laid to rest like a prince. There were 30,000 mourners at his funeral in Cardenden. Two special trains carried 2,000 mourners from Glasgow and 20,000 others were at Queen Street station to see the train away. Many more travelled by coach and car to Fife. In Glasgow there were memorial services and for many years afterwards there were pilgrimages to his grave.

Fortunately there have been few serious accidents and what there were bought experience. The crowds were held back from the field of play in the early days of football by ropes and latterly by containing walls. But the correct strength for these walls was not found until after an accident at Shawfield Park in 1957 when a wall collapsed under pressure, a boy was killed, and forty other spectators injured.

Modern ideas on safety methods when a crowd is leaving a ground were evolved after the terrible accident in Ibrox Stadium on Saturday, January 2, 1971 after a Rangers *v.* Celtic match.

It had been a depressing game for Rangers supporters and Celtic seemed to have won. But then as the crowd was moving away Rangers scored in the last few seconds and, in the enthusiasm on stairway 13, somebody stumbled and fell, others toppled, and body piled on body while others crushed in from behind.

When order was brought to the ghastly scene sixty-six people were dead, most of them smothered in the crush of bodies, and hundreds more were injured. Meanwhile many had gone home from the match unaware that anything out of the ordinary had happened. The accident had taken place over the brow of the terracing and away from the view of most spectators.

The extent of the shock was such that Celtic and Rangers supporters came together to aid those left in distress by the accident and they attended religious services in each others churches. It was a bond of sympathy which was soon forgotten.

19

The 'Fifties

Rangers, after the war, were more strongly challenged than before but they were still, by far, the most formidable club over a long stretch. Their resources ensured continuing strength, their reputation was inhibiting to most opponents, their mystique made them strong in the politics of the game and had many seeking their friendship.

The great Hibs team of the early 'fifties came and went; Aberdeen put together a team of sound, sensible football, won their first Scottish Cup in 1947, and were twice in successive finals in 1953 and 1954. A wise old man, David McLean, trained a new manager for Hearts, Tommy Walker, and he produced the team Edinburgh had dreamed about since they had first been taught, there, to keep their hands off the ball.

Then Bobby Ancell, who was a perfectionist almost to the point of being a crank, produced a sophisticated Motherwell team which charmed all in football with the delicacy and grace of their play while Bob Shankly led a much under-rated Dundee team to the League Championship and to the semi-final of the European Champions Clubs' Cup. With any luck they could have been the first British team to win the trophy.

Celtic had a revival in 1954 with a League and Cup double but always Rangers were there, the team to be beaten, the team with the big names. Yet in 1950–51, 1951–52, 1953–54, 1954–55, the years when Bill Struth was an ill man and nearing the end of his career as manager, they never won a major trophy. Only when Scot Symon, the former player and manager of Preston North End, succeeded Struth did they re-form and resume their winning ways.

They came out of the war with a team of formidable players but with a defensive complex because, strangely, the players with the most overpowering personalities were in defence. They had two centre-halves of tremendous stature, Willie Woodburn and George Young who for some years was at right-back for Rangers and in the Scotland team to allow Woodburn to play at centre-half.

Woodburn, an intense player, was often in trouble with opponents and with referees. In latter years, when he was on journalistic work, he was a dangerous man to sit next to in a press box as he still reacted vigorously to the play.

He had been brought up in Edinburgh and went to a rugby-playing school but he had great allegiance to Hearts. When they showed no interest in him he signed for Rangers, in 1937, resisting appeals from his school to remain in rugby and from his father to stay out of professional football. He came to Ibrox during a transition

Aberdeen win the Scottish Cup for the first time, 1947. The captain, Frank Dunlop, is carried by (*left to right*) Taylor, McCall, McKenna, Hamilton, McLaughlan, Williams, Harris, Waddell, and the chairman, Mr W. Mitchell. Final result: Aberdeen 2, Hibs 1.

The goal which brought the Scottish Cup to Aberdeen for the first time. Stan Williams beats Hibs goalkeeper, Kerr, in the 1947 Final.

period when the established players of the 'thirties, Bob McPhail, George Brown, and Jimmy Simpson were moving out, reluctantly. He was quickly established as Rangers' centre-half but then a gangling spindly-legged youngster, George Young, went to Rangers, from Kirkintilloch Rob Roy, as left-back. He seemed no threat to Woodburn.

But Woodburn badly damaged a knee playing against Hibs in a sensational game which Rangers lost by 8–1 and by the time he was fit, after a cartilage operation, Young was established and it took him five years to win his place back again.

Young moved to right-back to accommodate him and Rangers had a defence whose strength, efficiency, and assurance were so intimidating that a team who scored more than two goals against them felt entitled to a lap of honour. The term, 'Iron Curtain', was borrowed from European politics to describe them.

In goal in that defence was the athletic Bobby Brown who was mis-cast in that he brought with him the air of refinement of the amateur. He had played with Queen's Park. Elsewhere there was uncompromising professionalism among those who strove to keep the ball away from Brown.

George Young was a man of ungainly physique. He had huge high shoulders on a mighty torso tapering to coltish legs, and although opponents might fear his superb skill in tackling and shrewdness in tactics they never had to fear the unfair use of his weight. Willie Woodburn was maybe as good a player in the air as there has been in Scotland and on the other side of him was Jock Shaw whose style was typified by the severity of his haircut and the nickname which fell inevitably to him, 'Tiger'.

At right-half was Ian McColl who, like Bobby Brown, was later to be manager of Scotland. He was a long-striding player suited to going forward but inhibited by being shackled to cover in that defence in depth. The other wing-half, Sammy Cox, would have been a great player in any era either as a wing-half or a left-back where he eventually played for Rangers and Scotland.

He was a wiry little Ayrshire man, marvellously cool and perceptive in his play, the man who brought class to the defence. He like Woodburn was almost technically perfect in his position. These players had attacking ability which was neglected as George Young pulled them in around him to shut off the goal.

These defenders of forceful character and commanding presence put their defensive mark on the game in Scotland. They played to a style which was not to the liking of spectators in general but it produced results for Rangers and that was all that was asked for by their followers. It is rarely that a team has all its great men in defence and only Willie Waddell and Willie Thornton of an indifferent range of forwards matched them in their era. A common description of Rangers' simplified style of play at the time was a long punt out of defence, a run by Waddell on the right-wing, and a cross to the far post where that magnificent header of the ball, Willie Thornton, was lurking.

The first significant breach in the 'Iron-Curtain' defence of Rangers was made by the Referee Committee of the Scottish Football Association. They suspended

Willie Woodburn *sine die* in September 1954. He had reacted violently in a match against Stirling Albion in August of that year and had been ordered from the field once too often. He was thirty-four years old then but Rangers were looking for still another couple of years from him.

Scot Symon had taken over Rangers in June of that year; Bill Struth had retired, in April 1953, passing on the succession to Symon, a great Rangers wing-half who had turned the memorable game against Moscow Dynamo in November 1945 with his powerful tackling and firm passing. Almost his first job was to accompany Woodburn to the Referee Committee meeting.

He said afterwards: 'I was well aware of the extent of the job of rebuilding Rangers after a period of transition and I had one consolation. It was that I would have a masterful personality at centre-half at least for a couple of years around which to build my team. Woodburn's suspension threw me out of gear more than the loss of any other player I have had under my control.'

While Symon worked on Rangers, other interests were brought to bear in a period which was to revolutionise the thinking of the game and expand the sophisticated side of the play to a degree not hitherto considered. The expansion of the game in Europe and beyond had been ignored in the arrogant view that football was still a British game.

The Austrians had been to Hampden Park in 1950 and had won by 1–0, the first time that Scotland had been beaten at home by a foreign team. The occasion had been laughed off as an after-effect of the war. It was the year Scotland shunned the World Cup in Brazil, the year when Scottish football was still looking through the wrong end of a telescope.

And then in 1953 the Hungarians of Ferenc Puskas and the other greats came to Britain and the game could not laugh at them for those in it could not wipe astonishment off their faces. These visitors produced ball-control of a kind which had previously been seen only on a music hall stage.

They demonstrated a new conception of teamwork and tactics and even new lightweight equipment which was necessary for their gentle and subtle touch on the ball and the agility of their movements. The thinking on the game was altered almost overnight. Players wanted new lightweight boots instead of the stout, leather variety with which they used to bash the ball. They thought the secret of the Hungarians' virtuosity was in the equipment. And then they found it was in practice.

Work with the ball at training became fashionable for it was appreciated that only with practice could the proficiency of the Hungarians be matched. It had to be admitted that again something had been taken from Britain and significantly improved. There was no going back to the old ways and indeed Scotland did take an important part in consolidating the expanding continental game.

In the year after the Hungarians, a former French international player, Gabriel Hanot, then a journalist with the great Paris sports paper, *L'Équipe*, advocated the establishing of a European Cup for champion clubs of the various European countries. His paper were prepared to back the idea.

They invited sixteen clubs to compete, and included Hibs, but only after the invitations were out did they ask permission from the new European Union to organise the tournament. The Union were huffed and initially refused permission but after lunch a broader view was taken when feelings were better. The Union decided to take over the competition and named it the European Cup and only champions of member countries would compete.

Sir George Graham, secretary of the Scottish Football Association, was one of the conciliators and he became chairman of the organising committee which was set up. And so Scotland had to raise complacent eyes over the hedge at the bottom of the garden and notice that there was a world out there in which they kicked a ball and in a most sophisticated way. The development of the game moved into its last and finishing stage.

In the East End of Glasgow it was quickly noticed what was going on. The Celtic Football club had sent their players to study the Hungarians and the new trends and to have their standards brought up to date. The thinking of the players was stimulated and particularly that of the slim centre-half, Jock Stein, and that, some years afterwards, was to have a spectacular effect on Scottish football.

Jock Stein had been a centre-half with Albion Rovers, and Webber Lees, the manager, later remembered him as a great talker on the game. He was a pit worker but had caused no great excitement in football. After three seasons he had gone to play with the Welsh non-League club, Llanelli. He had been recommended to Kilmarnock by their former player Jimmy Williamson but they missed him by a few days.

He was floating unnoticed in a Welsh backwater when he became dispirited after the house he had maintained in Hamilton was twice burgled. He and his wife, Jean, decided that they would return home when the club was eliminated from the English Cup. When this came to pass he went to the ground on the Sunday morning to tell the manager and return to the Scottish pits.

Instead the manager told Stein that he was on his way to his house to tell him that Celtic wanted to talk with him and he had to leave immediately for Glasgow. Celtic engaged him to give experience and steadiness to the middle of the defence of a team of young reserve players which they had gathered at the instigation of the chairman. 'Kelly's Kids' were to be the basis of the Celtic of the new era.

Stein never did play in that reserve team. The two regular centre-halves were injured before the season started and Stein had to go into the first team. He was immediately successful and was a better player among good players. It seemed one of the great romantic stories of football that he had gone from the oblivion of a non-League club, just dodged the pits, became captain of Celtic, and led them to a League and Cup double. But as it turned out that was only the preface to the most successful success-story of any player in the 100 years of Scottish football.

Celtic had come out of the war badly and on a Saturday in April 1948 faced the most critical match in their history. They were due at Dundee where they had been soundly beaten on recent occasions. They had to take two points to preserve their status in the First Division of the Scottish League. A defeat or even a draw would entail an embarrassing wait as other teams tried to beat their points total.

The depths of Celtic's mediocrity then could be gauged from the fact that, in nine League matches played in the early months of 1948, they scored only three goals and two of these were from penalty-kicks. It is often forgotten that the greats can slump so badly so it should have been no surprise when some years later their great rivals, Rangers, suffered the mortification of ordinariness.

As well as being condemned to fighting relegation, Celtic that day suffered the penalty of failure, neglect, for the attention of football was focused on the Scottish Cup-Final between Rangers and Morton.

Bobby Evans, until then a forward, played his first game for Celtic as a half-back. John McPhail brought point to their play with cool passes to split the Dundee defence. Jock Weir a jovial, hectic attacker, newly signed, gave Celtic a lead which was lost when McKay scored twice to have Dundee ahead with half an hour to play. Weir scored again and then, with two minutes to go, scored his own and Celtic's third and they were saved.

Celtic's good name had been preserved and it was to be made use of in 1953 to help pull the crowds to the Coronation Cup which the S.F.A. had organised in Glasgow. They had since the war won only one trophy, the Scottish Cup in 1951, and that seemed slim reason for them being included in this prestige competition in which they joined Aberdeen, Hibs, and Rangers and the English clubs Arsenal, Manchester United, Newcastle United, and Tottenham Hotspur.

The only justification for Celtic being invited, apart from their ability to draw crowds, was the historical one that they had won the two previous competitions involving English clubs to be organised in Scotland. After the Ibrox disaster, Rangers had put up for competition in 1902 the Exhibition Cup they had won in 1901 to raise money for the disaster fund. Along with Celtic and Rangers, Everton and Sunderland competed and Celtic beat Rangers by 2–1 in the Final.

The Exhibition Cup played at Ibrox Stadium in the summer of 1938 was an attraction for the Exhibition held in the nearby Bellahouston Park. Aberdeen, Celtic, Hearts, and Rangers represented Scotland, and Brentford, Chelsea, Everton, and Sunderland came from England.

Celtic at that time were in better shape for they had just won the League Championship for the second time in three years and they had those well blended inside-forwards, Malcolm MacDonald, John Crum, and John Divers. They won the trophy when John Crum scored a goal against Everton in extra-time in a thrilling Final.

The 1953 Coronation Cup provided stout English opposition. Arsenal had just won the Championship, Manchester United and Spurs had been champions in the two previous years, and Newcastle United had won the F.A. Cup in 1951 and 1952. Rangers and Hibs were winners and runners-up in the Scottish League and Aberdeen had only lost the Scottish Cup-Final to Rangers by a single goal in a replay.

Neil Mochan, who had been newly signed by Celtic from Middlesbrough to bring shooting-power to a forward line with an excess of cleverness, had a special knowledge of the game besides his big shot. He led Celtic to a 1–0 win over Arsenal. There were 60,000 at the match. Manchester United beat Rangers by 2–1 and Aberdeen found Newcastle United in the mood and lost 4-0. Hibs had to go to extra-time to eliminate Spurs 2–1.

Celtic's joker, Charlie Tully, trying not to be funny. In the air with him Bob Milligan (Stirling Albion).

There were 73,000 at Hampden to see the subtleties and eccentricities of Charlie Tully disturb Manchester United and Celtic won by 2–1. Hibs' 'Famous Five' found their form and demolished Newcastle United 4–0, and so Hampden Park was set for a Final between two Scottish clubs. That was good for the flagging Scottish morale and equivalent to a win at Wembley, and maybe better, for the cream of English League clubs had been routed by Scottish clubs in serious competition.

The teams that day were, *Celtic*: Bonnar; Haughney, Rollo; Evans, Stein, McPhail; Collins, Walsh, Mochan, Peacock, Fernie. *Hibs*: Younger; Govan, Paterson; Buchanan, Howie, Combe; Smith, Johnstone, Reilly, Turnbull, Ormond. The Hibs team were just past their best; the Celtic team beginning to find a pattern.

Fernie, who had replaced the injured Charlie Tully on the left-wing, was initially a torment to Hibs as he strode past Govan. But soon this pressure made a chance for Mochan, and Tommy Younger with the sun in his eyes could hardly have seen his scoring shot. A minute from the interval there was a sign of what was to come when John Bonnar dived to save brilliantly from Reilly's header.

John Bonnar, generally criticised because of his lack of height and his inconsistency had so little inspired the Celtic directors that they had tried to sign the Scotland goalkeeper, Jimmy Cowan, from Morton. He found such form as held the elegant Hibs at bay during a second half in which their tremendous class was unloosed on Celtic. In that siege of Celtic's goal the worth of Jock Stein was established as was the potential of Bobby Evans at wing-half, but it was Bonnar's goalkeeping which beat Hibs.

Winning that Coronation Cup sent Celtic confidently into the following season sustained by a sound half-back line, Bobby Evans, Jock Stein, and Bertie Peacock. They lost what was generally thought to be a League decider to the emerging Hearts but recovered and went to the top of the League by beating St Mirren in February and eventually won by five points.

There was steady progress in the Scottish Cup and a crowd of 102,000 at Hampden to see them against the runaway leaders of the Second Division, Motherwell. A headed goal by Charlie Aitken forced a replay. There were 92,000 to see Celtic win the replay and qualify to meet in the Final Aberdeen who had beaten Rangers by 6–0.

The teams in the Final were, *Aberdeen*: Martin; Mitchell, Caldwell; Allister, Young, Glen; Leggat, Hamilton, Buckley, Clunie, Hather. *Celtic*: Bonnar; Haughney, Meechan; Evans, Stein, Peacock; Higgins, Fernie, Fallon, Tully, Mochan. Aberdeen had a smart forward line. Graham Leggat and Paddy Buckley were direct runners and between them was George Hamilton a studied player of tremendous skill and composure who could bring their speed to bear with accurate, running passes. 'Gentleman George', they called him and there was nothing disparaging in the name.

Celtic's strength was in their half-back line but the Irishman, Charlie Tully, who had been brought from Belfast in a thief's bargain, was unstoppable on his day. When he did hit form he lived up to the happy legend which had grown around him since the day when he demoralised a Rangers team with his hand signals and purposeful dribbling. He was the most highly-publicised player on the Scottish scene, a character, a joker, but also a great player.

Neil Mochan gave Celtic the lead when one of his tremendous shots was deflected into the goal off a defender. George Hamilton neatly made a goal for Paddy Buckley and the game was level through much of the second half. Then Willie Fernie swerved his way along the by-line and pushed the ball in front of Sean Fallon for him to shoot the goal which gave Celtic the double. They left immediately to study the play in the World Cup in Switzerland but that trip was not to pay off until much later and not until the captain, Jock Stein, came back to the club as manager. He had learned much.

That good Aberdeen team had to stay, formidable but unacclaimed in their North-East corner of Scotland where they found good players to keep content the captive audience they had there. In addition spectators elsewhere, with Saturday a free day and transport speeding up, attached themselves to Celtic and Rangers and travelled with them.

In the 'twenties almost every little town around Scotland had its football team and such as Armadale, Bathgate, and Boness had their League teams. They existed for they had a captive audience. Men then worked on a Saturday until lunch time and public transport was slow and scarce and motor cars were not yet for the football followers. Working men had time only to go home from work, wash, change, and eat and go to the local football match. There was great community involvement in the clubs.

After the war Saturday ceased to be a working day, buses were easy to hire, and there was time on a Saturday to travel even from the Central Belt to Aberdeen. There was a deplorable urge to become identified with the big ones and many passed their local grounds to travel to Ibrox Stadium or Celtic Park so that local football languished while the rich grew richer. Social change had brought an unfortunate trend.

20

The Cup Moves Around

During the early 'fifties the game was throbbing beneath the surface but bound by a heavy crust of tradition. Sir George Graham and the president Harry Swan toured the north spurred by criticism of the organisation of the Scottish Cup. The big clubs complained of the prevalence of 'rabbits' threatening their reaching the later stages.

A scheme was canvassed for exempting the First Division clubs from the early rounds but Sir George said, 'Everywhere we were asked what was in it for the clubs. We promised that none would lose money from a change and that any deficit would be made up from a pool but they did not want money, just a chance of having their wee bit of glory.' It was much later before the change was made.

And then the Scottish League was testing its strength with the Scottish Football Association and getting bigger representation on the council and a vice president and the president of the League, it was agreed, would be chairman of any S.F.A. committee of his choosing. He invariably chose the International Selection Committee.

In the East of Scotland the traditional question, 'Is this Hearts' Year?' was at last answered in the affirmative and there were to be many Hearts' years as Tommy Walker, after eighteen years as a player at the top level, served his apprenticeship under Davie McLean and proved that he was not too soft to be a manager. He won for his Hearts players what he had never won himself, a medal in a national competition.

From the days of the first captain, Tom Purdie, through the times of the great Bobby Walker, and in the 'thirties Hearts were a team to follow as long as one did not expect to have the ultimate satisfaction of seeing their captain hold a national trophy aloft.

Tommy Walker had gone as assistant manager in 1948 and took full charge in 1951. Then the players of Davie McLean, Alfie Conn, and Willie Bauld began to blend with some of Walker's players such as Dave Mackay and Jimmy Wardhaugh, who was born in Berwick but insisted forcibly, 'There is nothing English about me'. Alfie Conn joined Bauld and Wardhaugh to make as spectacular a scoring combination as were Hibs Famous Five.

They were smoothly blended for scoring goals through the middle of a defence. Conn, the sturdy worker with the subtle touch, Bauld almost languid in his movements but decisive in shooting and powerfully accurate in the air, Wardhaugh the runner with the sure shot.

Hearts' Terrible Trio: Alfie Conn, Willie Bauld (*with ball*), and Jimmy Wardhaugh, the highest-scoring inside forwards in Scottish football.

These three as one reached their peak in season 1957–58 when, after being runners up in the League the previous season, Hearts at last won the Championship finishing 13 points clear of Rangers who were in second place. Hearts, that season, scored the record number of 132 goals. Bauld had 28 of them, Wardhaugh 28, but there was scoring ability deep into the team, scoring in all their minds and it is in minds that goalscoring starts.

Tommy Walker contrary to what had been assumed from his own playing style made a conscious effort to stiffen the Hearts team. He brought to full-back, Bobby Parker, a big enthusiastic player who put physical realism to the silky tradition of the play. Then the powerful Dave Mackay, masterly in technique, and a fiery red-head, John Cumming, brought vigour and perception to the midfield behind the scorers. Tommy Walker admitted after the Scottish Cup had been won, 'They're more determined to win than in my days as a player'.

There was an illusion that Walker had been a soft player. Gentlemanliness had been mistaken for softness and none of the Hearts players who played against him in practice matches, when he was manager, thought he was soft after they had taken the weight of his tackles.

There were great expectations in Edinburgh after Hearts beat the good Motherwell team of Bobby Ancell in the League Cup-Final of 1954–55. Motherwell had such delicate graceful players as Hearts used to have in Pat Quinn, Ian St John, Willie Hunter, and Bert McCann. Willie Bauld scored three goals and Wardhaugh one against their two and Edinburgh was thinking that at last it might be Hearts' year.

There had been an old joke that Hearts would win the Scottish Cup when the trams stopped running along Gorgie Road and this was remembered when Edinburgh Corporation started tearing up the tram tracks in Gorgie Road and a formidable Hearts team moved ever near the Final.

Hearts did reach the Final. Celtic were there to meet them and 132,000 spectators gathered; all Edinburgh seemed to be there. If at last it was going to be Hearts' year then they were going to be in at the moment of glory and then hurry back to the capital to welcome Hearts in the triumphant drive which had been planned.

Celtic were not too well-prepared for the Final. Jock Stein had broken down and Bobby Evans moved back to take his place. Bobby Collins was injured and a novice, Craig, took his place on the right-wing while there was the extraordinary selection of Haughney being moved from right-back to partner him at inside-right.

Hearts sent their supporters into ecstasies by triumphing over themselves and once they had done that Celtic were easy. The spirit of the new Hearts was seen in John Cumming with blood trickling down his face tackling and chasing like a fury.

The Hearts team was: Duff; Kirk, McKenzie; Mackay, Glidden, Cumming; Young, Conn, Bauld, Wardhaugh, Crawford. The left-winger scored two goals. Haughney raised Celtic hopes with a goal but Conn near the end smashed all fear of a wrong result with a third goal.

Hearts took the cup through Edinburgh in an open topped bus and the citizens acclaimed them and then were again in ecstasies of delight the following season when Hearts went cantering gaily through the League programme and lost only one match, to Clyde. The League Cup was won again in 1959 and in 1960 they held off Kilmarnock in 1959–60 to win the League Championship again.

And then financial pressures forced Hearts to sell and the Cup-winning team was broken up. Dave Mackay went to Spurs and began an impressive progression through various grades of English football. Alex Young, a sophisticated forward, went to Everton, age caught up on others, and Hearts slipped back.

Yet in some ways success had spoiled them and especially their supporters. At one time Hearts football was the attraction and in the days of Barney Battles and John White, and later Andy Anderson, Alex Massie, and Andy Black it was pure and exciting football. It was enough and there was the hope each year of a success but such was not important. But when they had tasted success they liked the flavour and cried for more and the football became secondary.

The exhilaration of Hearts cup night was to be reproduced in other quarters and even those who thought that success was their right had to stand back and enjoy the fun as the Cup was brought to unexpected places.

In 1959 St Mirren had crept up on an unsuspecting public. They were as plain and straightforward as their manager Willie Reid. Yet he was a little ahead of his time when he said, 'I want my defenders to be football players. Nothing more disconcerts a forward than to find a back is a better football player than he is'. He had another happy philosophy, 'A pass rising a yard above the ground should be a foul. A player receiving a pass has two feet and only one head.'

St Mirren with delicate inside-forwards, Gemmill and Bryceland, later to be their manager, and Gerry Baker, a fast-chasing and hard-shooting centre-forward and brother of Joe, worked calmly to the Final. There they found yet another good Aberdeen team but one without luck and it is strange how often luck deserted Aberdeen at Hampden.

The Aberdeen full-back, Hogg, strained a leg muscle and went off the field to have it strapped and then had to move to the right-wing. Hather, the winger, took his place. Bryceland headed one goal and Gemmill scored another. Wishart and Davidson strove to turn the game for the handicapped Aberdeen but then Clunie, the centre-half, slipped and Baker was past him and scoring a third goal. Aberdeen were left to wonder about what might have happened had Hogg not been injured.

David Lapsley, an exemplary player, received the Cup on his last day as a football player and then the Saints went marching in to Paisley. The town turned out, the Provost spoke from the City Chambers balcony, and a convivial night was had by all.

And there was such another night in Dunfermline two years later in 1961. Jock Stein had taken over the club in his first managerial appointment in 1960. They were a miserable team who had not won a game for months. They seemed certain to be relegated but then under Stein they won the next five matches and were saved. Stein said, 'The difficulty was in making a provincial team think they were as good as a big city one'.

The following season Stein had them marching ten feet tall and striding to Hampden for the Scottish Cup-Final and it was their first time there in the seventy-six years of their existence. It was a happy coincidence that Stein's former club Celtic were the opposition.

That day Pat Crerand played one of his best-ever games for Celtic but the Dunfermline goalkeeper Connachan was letting nothing past and there was a no-scoring draw. Again in the replay Connachan was unbeatable. Dunfermline won by 2–0 and Jock Stein was out on the Hampden track with coat-tails flying and arms flung wide to welcome them to the presentation.

They say it was Dunfermline's biggest night since Malcolm Canmore brought his good Queen Margaret to the town 900 years before. At any rate Stein had Dunfermline thinking they were as big as anybody and for the next few years they were strong in European competition and they spent a quarter-of-a-million pounds on ground improvements. They played ten Fairs' Cup-ties and went to the semi-final of the Cup Winners' Cup after they won the Scottish Cup again in 1968 against a fading Hearts in the first Final for nine years without Celtic or Rangers.

They had previously beaten Everton in a Fairs' Cup-tie but in the Cup Winners' Cup of 1968–69 they beat the F.A. Cup holders, West Bromwich Albion, but lost in the semi-final to Slovan Bratislava, a side with many Czech internationalists.

21

Bonnie Dundee

The development of the game from the 'fifties was progressing steadily when a happening in England drained much of the quality out of it. The regulation imposing a maximum wage in English League football was cancelled. Until then the most an English club could pay a player legitimately per week was £20. With such terms it was difficult to tempt Scottish players to England for they could do better with the more successful clubs at home.

But soon Johnny Haynes was being proclaimed as the first £100-a-week player and Scots were streaming south to claim some of the unlimited wealth. Scottish football continued to be creamed by rich English clubs and this had an effect not just on the game at home but also on the national team. Clubs in England demanded that a player's first allegiance should be to the club who paid his wages and were reluctant to release their men for international football.

Bob Shankly just escaped this development when he built a Dundee team to win the Scottish League championship in season 1961–62. Bob Shankly, the brother of the Liverpool manager, Bill, often had his name used by journalists merely as an excuse for naming his Junior Club, Glenbuck Cherrypickers.

Dundee had never previously had a sound backing for fame. They never could organise full return for the quality they often had. The club had been formed in 1893 by the amalgamation of two clubs in the town, East End and Our Boys. They might at that time when uniting have taken the name of the other town team, Dundee United. The United only changed their name to that from Dundee Hibernian in 1923, the year they were elected to the Second Division of the Scottish League.

Over the years Dundee had had many players of fame: the Englishman Herbert Dainty, David Halliday, later to be manager of Aberdeen, wee Alec Troup, who was only kept out of the international team by Alan Morton, Bert Juliussan who scored thirteen goals in two matches in the year they won promotion after the war.

George Anderson, a flamboyant showman took that team to a decisive match in 1949. Dundee, playing at Falkirk, had to win to make certain of the Championship. In that match the Falkirk crowd seemed to want Dundee to win but they missed a penalty-kick at a vital stage and were strangled by nerves and eventually beaten by 4–1 with every goal greeted by a moan from the crowd.

A measure of George Anderson's enterprise was that he paid Derby County £23,500 for Billy Steel. It was a record Scottish fee then and as startling as the £5,000 paid by Falkirk to West Ham for Syd Puddefoot in 1922.

The Dundee team of 1961–62, with the Scottish League Championship Trophy. *Standing:* Liney, Smith, Gilzean, Wishart, Ure, Sammy Kean (Trainer), Seith. *Seated:* Penman, Cox, Hamilton, Cousins, Robertson.

There had been other such great players as Scot Symon, Jimmy Guthrie, and Alec Forbes who went to Arsenal before Bob Shankly brought forth his team. He had bought a brave little goalkeeper, Bert Slater, from his brother at Liverpool to work behind a consistent pair of full-backs, the extrovert Alex Hamilton and the more sober Bobby Cox. At centre-half there was the blond man of muscle, Ian Ure, with two composed wing-halves, Bobby Seith and Bobby Wishart, whose football was sound and safe.

The forward line was smooth and functional. Gordon Smith had been brought from Hearts specifically to take the ball from the defence. He was always available for the pass from the harassed defender and could be depended upon to hold the ball until good order had been restored.

As targets for his passes he had two tall strikers with good shots and both marvellously accurate headers of the ball. Alan Gilzean and Alan Cousin were always racing through the middle inviting the Smith cross. The young Andy Penman with his running linked defence and attack and there was a straight running orthodox left-winger in the bouncy Hugh Robertson.

The team had been under-rated as they won the League Championship and not until they went charging through Europe startling more famous clubs in the European Cup for Champions were they really noticed. Indeed they had not been expected to go beyond the first round when they were drawn against Cologne F.C., who were one of the favourites for the trophy.

And then in one of the most sensational European ties played in Scotland, Dundee won by 8–1 and there were startled looks throughout football. There was some sinister talk from the West German club officials afterwards and the gist was that Cologne's goalkeeper had been hurt in Dundee and maybe Dundee's goal-keeper would be hurt in Cologne.

Billy Steel (Scotland, Morton, Derby County, Dundee) one of the post-war greats.

The Cologne players were told that they had a great shame hanging over them and in the second leg of the match they furiously tried to lift it. Seven goals was indeed a heavy shame to shift yet they nearly did the job and had they not lost their heads they could well have won the tie.

There was some incredible happenings and Bert Slater was indeed kicked on the head after diving to save. He was put quickly on a stretcher and was being carried from the stadium when he realised what was happening and fought back into the ground. He played on the wing for a few minutes with his head swathed in bandage but he could not stand watching the goalkeeping of his deputy, Andy Penman, and went back into goal. He held the scoring of the emotional Cologne to four goals.

The game finished with the crowd thick round the touchlines and police holding them back with dogs on long leads. So nasty was the atmosphere of the match that Dundee refused to join Cologne at the after-match banquet.

In the next round Dundee lost a controversial goal to Sporting Club, Lisbon in Portugal when the referee ruled that the ball had crossed the line in the last minute as Wishart breasted it away. Dundee won the second leg by an impressive 4–1 and then had to go to Brussels to play Anderlecht.

Dundee soon won that one. They scored in 90 seconds, led by 2 goals in 17 minutes, and eventually had 4 to the Belgian champions' 1. Gilzean scored twice to bring his record in the tournament to 8. Dundee won 2–1 in the second leg and then there was A.C. Milan and a sad tale to tell of mistaken ambition.

Against the formidable Italian champions, in Milan, Dundee were drawing 1–1 at half-time. During the interval talk they allowed their previous success to go to their heads and they talked rashly of going out to beat the Italians and scorned holding the draw as they seemed well able to do.

There was the usual tight Italian defence and Milan had the accomplished Rivera in midfield, but more important was the big-scoring centre, Altafini, and a big left-winger, Barison. With Dundee ambitious in the second half and the defence thin the Italians started throwing the ball high across to Slater's right-hand post where Barison and Altafini were jumping better than Alex Hamilton or Ian Ure.

They hammered away monotonously at that left post and scored four second-half goals there. It was frustrating for Dundee to beat them 1–0 at Dens Park. Benfica won the Final that year but Dundee on their day would probably have beaten them and so, but for that rash half-time talk, they might have been the first British team to win the European Championship.

They were to get no further chance for soon the team was disintegrating. Ian Ure was transferred to Arsenal for £62,000, Alan Gilzean to Spurs for £72,000, and Alan Cousins to Hibs. Gordon Smith went into honourable retirement.

22

The Artistry of the 'Sixties

While Hearts and Dundee moved in and took their bows and retired reluctantly Rangers were re-organising. John Lawrence a builder, had been taken on to the board of directors, in March 1954, and his keen business mind had been jarred by the haphazard finances of football. He set about fitting Rangers' financial structure to the prestige of the club and when he was satisfied it was the largest financial organisation in football in Britain. There were, through re-organisation, 340,000 nominal £1 shares in circulation and they were dealt in shares of about £5.

Scot Symon returned to Ibrox from Preston North End to be manager three months after John Lawrence and he found, there, sumptuous offices with a marble stairway leading to them. There was, however, a team which was past its best and which had been neglected for too long.

In the next twelve years Scot Symon worked to such purpose that the League Championship was won six times, the Scottish Cup five times, and the Scottish League Cup four times. If there was a disappointment it was that Rangers had not won a European trophy although they had been in the Final of the European Cup Winners' Cup in 1961 and the semi-final of the European Champion Clubs' Cup in 1959–60.

When the history of the Rangers football club was written in 1966 a whole page was needed to list Scot Symon's achievement but that did not prevent him being sacked later. He moved to manage Partick Thistle and then to become their general manager.

In Scot Symon's first season Willie Woodburn and Sammy Cox retired while George Young went the following season. They were difficult to replace. A sound little goalkeeper, George Niven, became established. A sturdy full-back, Bobby Shearer, teamed with a more sophisticated one, Eric Caldow. There were two good progressive wingers, Alex Scott on the right and David Wilson, who was to have a long, consistent and exemplary career. Jimmy Millar, a strong and intelligent centre, struggled against injury to remain an important team man.

And still Scot Symon needed a player of class, a Gillick. He found one in Airdrie in Ian McMillan a clever and gentlemanly player who brought out the best in the others and made a team of them. McMillan signed for Rangers in October 1958 and they had him for six successful seasons before he returned to Airdrie and eventually was their manager.

Rangers' success had come to be expected in League and Cup and Symon was given no credit even when Rangers took the Scottish Cup in three successive seasons and then again after missing one but he did carry out the principal task of a Rangers manager and that was to beat Celtic. In the 12 seasons of Symon Rangers played Celtic in 24 League matches and lost only 4 of them.

There was a good run in the European Champions Clubs' Cup in 1959–60 and Anderlecht, Red Star, Belgrade, and Sparta, Rotterdam were beaten before losing to Eintracht, Frankfurt, who then played the memorable Final with Real Madrid at Hampden Park.

There was an acceptance that things were going right when Rangers beat Hibs 3–2 in the Scottish Cup in 1960, and then beat Celtic in the semi-final in a replay qualifying to meet Kilmarnock in the Final. Rangers had been without the Scottish Cup since 1953 and although they had not lost a Cup-Final since 1929, when they ended the cupless twenty-five years which had become a joke. They worried lest another unsuccessful stretch was ahead.

A controversial post-war Rangers player, the powerful Don Kitchenbrand, against Partick Thistle in 1956.

Ian McColl made a comeback for that match and when the Kilmarnock centre-half, Willie Toner, injured an ankle and limped on a touchline afterwards it was McColl who rallied and inspired Rangers. Scot Symon's reputation was established.

Even with a team that could win the Scottish Cup Symon was not satisfied. He knew he needed one player in the middle of the field who could bring flair to the team and then he saw him when Raith Rovers came to Ibrox. He was a slim young man made to look frail by a mop of hair above a slender frame and legs made to look even more spindly by not wearing shin guards. He was Jim Baxter.

The slim one had been born in Hill o' Beath in Fife and worked in the pits when he was fifteen years old. He had signed for Raith Rovers in 1957 and had come under the influence of a fine player and gentleman, Willie McNaught, a man who, in the obscurity of Raith Rovers, was never given full credit for his worth.

Baxter had learned from McNaught, had appreciated his excellence and resolved, 'I'll make something out of this football and not finish up like Willie McNaught with nothing but admiration'. In that mood he went to Ibrox resenting Rangers for their success as is the way of the underprivileged.

He played magnificently, scored as good a goal as anybody could remember at Ibrox and, to the astonishment of one and all, Rangers were beaten 2–1. Baxter had previously been under Rangers' scrutiny and Hearts and East Fife also looked at him but in June 1960 Rangers signed him.

Scot Symon knew that he had signed a great player but he was not to know the torment that player would cause him later as he strode arrogantly across football overawed by nobody, laughing when others were tense, listening but ignoring, knowing that his way was the right way. Within three years there was some dispute as to whether he or the club was the greater. He insisted cheekily that he was worth £100 a week to Rangers and delayed signing until the matter was argued.

He was quickly a folk hero but in the pattern of Benny Lynch, with that inherent urge to self-destruction which the Scottish sporting heroes seem to have. His alleged exploits off the field fed those who would gossip but there was no denying his skill as a football player.

Some saw him as standing in a spotlight of changing colours but when he had the ball at his feet in midfield he was as a man standing in a field with the dawn behind him. Then he would draw that golf club left foot of his and the instep would strike the leather and the leg would twist in a distortion of art. The ball would travel with that strange velocity, not fast, not slow, weightless and with a kind of gentleness.

That was a Jim Baxter pass, something that did to the emotions of those who appreciated football as an art form what music and poetry would normally do. Like Benny Lynch the imperfections of slim Jim Baxter off the field were tolerated when he displayed his unique skills.

Baxter had the right blend in Rangers to cover his deficiency in tackling. He had good tacklers all round him in Shearer and Caldow, and Harold Davis, besides tackling, was prepared to run for him. The wingers, Scott and Wilson, and the twin centres, Millar and Brand, flourished from the Baxter service. Rangers won the League Championship that season, the Scottish Cup the following season, and the League and Cup double in the next two seasons.

New players came into the team and flourished under the Baxter influence. There were new goalscorers in the erratic George McLean, signed from St Mirren, and the speedy Jim Forrest who was custom-made for the Baxter through-passes. There was a new right-winger, Willie Henderson, an impish player, an entertaining dribbler of the ball. There was a new worker alongside Baxter in John Greig whose great worth was first discovered in a tour of the U.S.S.R.

Jim Baxter was to have an exciting influence on international football. He represented the essential Scottishness of the Scottish game, the arrogance which would be expressed in torturing the opposition not with goals but with contempt, in teasing them, humiliating them, and enjoying it.

It is irrational and it stems from a great conceit or, perhaps, a myth, that in Scottish football there is an inspired, spontaneous geometry of purest origin which, when it comes right, will benefit even the defeated. For they could learn from the vision of perfection, a perfection that is of people, made by people, by wee, bitter, narrow, ill-educated men yet full of light and luminous grace.

Jim Baxter was prepared to establish this philosophy as an undeniable law and he had many around him to support the cause impulsively. Denis Law had the Scottish thing developed from his flashing feet to the top of his blond head. Pat Crerand was an aggressive supporter of the cause. John White, who was later tragically killed during a thunderstorm on a golf course, backed the more physical campaigners with his sophisticated skills and was maybe more truly Scottish than any of them.

He had been taken from Alloa Athletic by Falkirk after Rangers had had him watched 13 times and like others had decided he was too light and frail. He developed later with Spurs into a gentle player who floated unobtrusively and made chances with grace and precision, what used to be called a typical Scottish inside forward.

Jim Baxter played 33 times for Scotland and only 10 of those games were lost. He played 5 times against England and 4 of those games were won. In December 1964 there was an interruption to his career which might have finished it and did instead diminish it. He had a leg broken in the closing minute of a European Cup-tie in Vienna. He had almost completed what was maybe his best game.

Rangers went to play Vienna Rapid in the first round of the European Champion Clubs' Cup holding a single goal lead from the first leg in Glasgow. The Prater Stadium had a frightening reputation for Scottish clubs and Baxter's plan was to keep the game calm and maybe hush the 70,000 to sleep. Indeed he nearly did as he took all the excitement out of the game.

He seemed never to be off the ball. He was greedy for it and he dragged it around, slowing the play, and entertaining the crowd with his tricks until they forgot about the serious business of cutting back Rangers' lead. Then Baxter made a goal for Forrest and another one for Wilson and went on with his performance.

In the last minute, with the game won, he took the ball from the Rapid penalty-area back towards his own goal, as the Viennese gaped, and when still untackled went back down the left-wing with it. Then Walter Skocik went in from behind and Baxter went down. A leg was broken. Typically he said, 'I overdid it'.

He lost much with the enforced idleness. While he played regularly he was hard and lean. When the playing pattern was broken he softened and the old hardness was never regained. He was transferred to Sunderland but was never completely successful there. He was a Scottish player. Eventually he returned to Rangers but when he was well past his best and out of condition. He did little other than revive great memories.

In the Baxter era mis-directed Scottish chauvinism ran high on the international field. Games which should have been show matches became little wars and at times it seemed that the hostilities would spread to the press boxes. Those players with

Arms aloft, Ian St John acclaims a great goal by Jim Baxter, hidden behind number 3, England's Gerry Byrne, Wembley, 1963.

English clubs played with a frenzy directed at stopping the dressing room taunts they had to endure about the quality of Scottish football.

Just before Baxter came on the scene there had been the humiliation of a tiny tots Scotland team being outmatched physically and beaten 9–3 at Wembley. That game was to provide a coaching film for many years for Scotland teams as, with the camera running back over the play which cost each goal, every imaginable mistake could be shown. Yet poor Frank Haffey, the happy, extrovert goalkeeper, had to carry most of the blame.

The 1963 Wembley started with high drama. In the fifth minute Eric Caldow was carried from the field with his left leg broken. Scotland overcame the misfortune because they had adaptable players. David Wilson went to left-back and was as good a back as he was upfield. He was the forerunner of the development which was soon to follow when full-backs extended their influence to playing up the wings.

Baxter and Dave Mackay switched from defence to attack naturally and were more effective than Flowers and Moore who were committed to stodgy destruction. John White had the England defence worried with the cunning balls he flighted across goal and, in the two minutes from the twenty-ninth, Scotland scored twice. Baxter dispossessed Armfield and strode on to shoot past Banks. Then Willie Henderson was jinking in on goal when he was tripped. Baxter scored with the penalty-kick and clearly he had no thought of missing.

At Hampden in 1964 Scotland had a third successive win over England for the first time this century. Baxter and Law had been languid in the first half and then began to breathe fire. In the seventy-second minute Alan Gilzean headed a spectacular goal to win the match. Gordon Banks kept the score down to that goal.

The next match against England also should have been won. Baxter was not at Wembley to take advantage of an England team reduced to nine men when Wilson and Byrne were injured, and one of the few blunders in Gordon Banks' career gave Scotland a draw.

In 1966 Scotland's arrogance survived for only half an hour in the cool April sun. There had been boasts about what Scotland's attacking flair would do to the academic methods of the football Alf Ramsey was devising for the World Cup. Two bad passes gave England two goals and Scotland were down to earth. Baxter's lack of pace put heavy work on Bremner and Crerand and Scotland went down by 4–3.

And then England won the World Cup and that was sufficient challenge for that flock of cocky Scots. They could not get to Wembley quickly enough to substantiate the irrational claim that a team which did not qualify for the final stages of the World Cup were better than the winners.

And, as has happened so often, memorable circumstances arose to perpetuate the conceit and Sir Alf Ramsey's World Cup champions were subdued, tormented, and outclassed. The energy of Billy Bremner, the elegance of Baxter, and the run-

Jimmy Johnstone scores Scotland's second goal against England at Hampden Park in 1966 from Denis Law's pass despite the efforts of Newton and Jackie Charlton.

ning of a new boy, Jim McCalliog, had dominated the midfield in which England's play was centred. John Greig played mightily and Tommy Gemmell with dash while Denis Law waged furious war among the defenders.

The task was made easier by an injury to Jackie Charlton but Scotland gloated over the goals by Law, Billy Lennox, and Jim McCalliog. They resisted the temptation to make the match hectic and played relaxed, controlled, and almost arrogant football. England's two goals in the last five minutes distorted the picture. Who could argue then that Scotland's heaven-sent supremacy had not been established.

There was predictable Scottish ecstasy over the win but little regard paid to the fact that, in the match, the free, instinctive play of which Scotland had been so proud had been discarded and that a formation of four backs, three midfield players and three forwards, for which Sir Alf Ramsey had been so heavily criticised for using, had been adopted by Scotland's manager, Bobby Brown.

Tommy Gemmell and Eddie McCreadie had played as full-backs, John Greig and Ronnie McKinnon as centre-backs. Jim Baxter, Billy Bremner, and Jim McCalliog were in the midfield and forward, Denis Law had two wingers, Willie Wallace and Bobby Lennox, on his flanks.

In that match was set the pattern of play for the end of the century. The numbers given to formations were new but the formations were not. Even the Wembley

Bobby Lennox (Celtic), looks for a chink in the Dunfermline defence.

Wizards of 1928 had midfield men and never more than four forwards for Alex James although named as a forward really played in the midfield.

All that was new was that the centre-half had developed a cover and that the full-backs were released from their duties as destroyers and allowed to take part in the constructive aspect of the game. Gemmell and McCreadie were as liable to be found far up their wings in attack as deep in defence and the wingers could be found back covering. Fuller all-round use was made of the players and defenders had to be as skilful with the ball as forwards.

And away from the international field the way was being cleared for the final and most prestigious phase in Scottish football, a phase which did indeed inspire admiration throughout the world. But first Kilmarnock, who had been snapping at the heels of Rangers, had to win the League Championship which they had so richly deserved.

They had been for five years idle during the war when their ground was taken over by the Army. Their manager Jimmy McGrory had returned to Celtic. They had been placed in the Second Division of the Scottish League after being for forty-eight years in the First Division. Malcolm MacDonald rebuilt the team but it took them seven years to get back to the First Division. Then the former Rangers player, Willie Waddell, took over the team and made it functional.

In five seasons they had been four times runners-up in the Scottish League and then came a momentous day, the last one in the 1964–65 season. Kilmarnock went to Edinburgh to play Hearts who led them by two points and had a slightly better goal average. Willie Waddell had all along insisted that his team would catch Hearts and to do so they needed to win that day at Tynecastle Park by two goals to nil. That they did, provided maybe the most exciting finish ever to a Scottish League Championship.

The aftermath was less exciting. It had been expected that playing as champions would again entice the citizens of Kilmarnock to flock to the matches and the board of directors encouraged them by massive improvements in the amenities at Rugby Park but in that disappointing season the champions could not average crowds of 10,000 and mostly they were much below that figure. They were ill-rewarded for their enterprise.

23

The Last and Greatest Phase

The final phase in a century of Scottish football started on a March morning in 1965 with a few simple words spoken by the chairman of the Celtic Football Club, Mr Robert Kelly. Solemnly he told Jock Stein, 'It's all yours now'. And so was installed Celtic's fourth manager to follow Willie Maley, Jimmy McStay, and Jimmy McGrory, all, like himself, former Celtic players. Another former player, Sean Fallon, was appointed assistant manager and the likeable Jimmy McGrory became public relations officer.

It was a momentous occasion yet calmly enacted in the Celtic board room for nobody could have guessed at the full significance of the event. Stein, as a manager, had been extraordinarily successful with Dunfermline and with Hibs and there was never any doubt that he would make a memorable mark with Celtic. But nobody had considered that he who had played non-League football in Wales would produce the greatest club team of the whole century.

In the next seven seasons Stein's Celtic won seven successive Scottish League Championships and became the first British team to win the European Champion Clubs' Cup. They were admired throughout the world for the attractiveness and excellence of their football.

In that team was crystallised all the fine aims which had inspired those who had started the Scottish Football Association, the craft, the distinctive Scottish skill on the ball, the sporting challenge, the concentration on scoring goals.

These ideals had been obsessing the mind of the traditionalist, Robert Kelly, but there was nobody who could bring them to effectiveness before that morning when Jock Stein took charge. Celtic before then had been naive in football matters. It was typical that in the European Cup Winners' Cup in 1963–64 they should have gone to Budapest in the second leg of the semi-final, acknowledged the best team in the competition, and with a four goals lead over M.T.K. attack indiscriminately and lose four goals and the tie.

Mr Kelly was committed to the idealism of attacking football and even in such circumstances would not use discretion in even slightly compromising with defence. Jock Stein was as enthusiastic about attractive, attacking football but he was more of a realist.

Celtic won the Scottish Cup a month after Stein took charge but he would take no credit for that. He said, 'I only took them in the run in over the final furlong'. He inherited a young team on the brink of success and when the style of management had changed to suit his talents.

Earlier managers worked from an office chair, he went out on the practice field with his players. Before there had been a concentration on running for stamina and the main training was monotonous lapping of the track. His players worked with a ball and under his eye and his direction. He encouraged them to talk football, cunningly planted ideas in their minds so they thought that they were their own and then congratulated them when they produced them as original.

Skills were developed, football thinking was stimulated but, above all, sustained speed was added to craft and this was the development which eventually defeated the best in Europe. There, since the Hungarians of 1953, they had produced marvellous skill but they played their matches in spasms and, particularly the Italians, with frequent rests.

It was Celtic's ability to sustain the pace of their attacking football without break which made them champions of Europe and almost champions of the world. Stein was successful beyond any other Scottish manager and reasons for this were sought. It was said he handled players well, he could teach, he had great humanity, he was a disciplinarian, players worked for him. The simple explanation was that he knew more about football than anybody else.

He could look at opponents and see almost immediately the pattern of their play and draw their game on the back of an envelope. He had a tremendous memory for football, for players, and for play. He surprised some a few years after the European Cup-Final when he was shown a picture postcard of the National Stadium in Lisbon. Although the players were but mere dots, he recognised the game as the Final and the play as that leading up to the second goal, and he detailed the players and the moves up to the scoring. This was startling recall.

In the previous ten years Celtic had lost four Scottish Cup-Finals and Stein's appointment before the Final of 1965 against Dunfermline was a calculated risk that he would alter immediately that dismal record. Stein had his first trial of strength with the dominating chairman when he told him the team for the Final. He had named Murdoch as a half-back. Kelly reminded him that he was a forward and insisted he was not a half-back. Stein answered, 'You'll see on Saturday that he is'. Kelly never again questioned a Stein selection and they lived thereafter in mutual respect.

Bertie Auld twice equalised Dunfermline goals in the Final and then in the closing minutes Billy McNeil, the young captain, headed a spectacular winning goal, something he was to repeat on various important occasions. The team had served its appenticeship and in the next season, saturated with the mood of change, impressively won the League Championship and opened the door to Europe.

The Championship was won after a long struggle with Rangers and during the season significant changes were made. Into goal went Ronnie Simpson, son of a former Rangers captain, and an astonishing thirty-five years of age. Simpson played his first League match for Queen's Park when he was fourteen years old and he had played for Third Lanark, Newcastle United, and Hibs before going to Celtic for a small fee to bring experience to their young second eleven. He won his first Scottish cap when he was thirty-six years old and seemed to get better with age until he damaged a shoulder and had to retire. He was a model in character and temperament and skill for all goalkeepers.

The other significant change in the team was the bringing back of Bertie Auld who had gone from Celtic to Blackburn Rovers in 1961 after a troublesome period with Scottish referees. Stein brought him back for the simple reason that he could pass the ball and it is strange how few can do that well.

Bertie Auld, with maturity bringing a greater sense of responsibility was to bring his cunning and subtlety, a delight to the perceptive spectator, to form a midfield partnership with Bobby Murdoch. This was the basis of the team's success. Murdoch, strong and marvellously aggressive with the long forward pass, was watched by an agent of Racing, Buenos Aires, before the World Club Championship match, and he said tersely afterwards, 'Celtic – One Man – Murdoch'. That was a ridiculous over-simplification but most high-level observers rated Bobby Murdoch the key man in the team.

Yet it was a team of all the talents from the dashing full-backs, Jim Craig and Tommy Gemmell, to the nippy goal-scoring forwards. There was fun in the team too with Tommy Gemmell, the heaviest shot in Britain and the scorer of spectacular goals, playing the clown as relief to the persisting strain of competition.

And these full-backs Jim Craig, a dentist in private life, and Tommy Gemmell might have been forwards as they developed the new thinking on backs overlapping their forwards which grew from the greater fitness of players and their ability to sustain flat-out running.

There were such exciting forwards in that championship team. The long and the short on the wings, the massive but unpredictable John Hughes and maybe the trickiest ball-player of the century in Jimmy Johnstone. Had he had the composure of Alan Morton or Sir Stanley Matthews then he could have been one of the greatest players of all time but, had he been composed and rational, then perhaps he would not have been jinking Jimmy Johnstone.

To work in the middle of the attack were the speedy Bobby Lennox and the courageous Steve Chalmers but they took such punishment against determined defences that Stein reinforced them with Joe McBride, whom he bought from Motherwell, and Willie Wallace, a buy from Hearts.

Both were spectacularly successful in the Celtic team. Joe McBride was able to indulge the goal-scoring urge he could not express with Wolves, Partick Thistle, and Motherwell. Wallace was a marvellously comprehensive player, safe with the scoring chance, perceptive in the build up. Stein paid just over £50,000 for the two of them to show there was more to his skill as a manager than winning championships.

The captain Billy McNeill, was officer material, impressive in bearing, authoritative in his territory in front of the goal. He had been one of Stein's young players when he was coach at Celtic Park and Stein himself had taught him the basic defensive skills and made him so formidable in the air. What set McNeill apart from all the others was that he was the only one with authority to alter, on the field, a Stein order. No matter what had been decided before, McNeill could nominate a penalty-kick taker if he thought Stein's choice was not playing well.

In Stein's philosophy it was accepted that all eleven players would not be at their best on the same day. He was prepared for one or two being off form and the others were indoctrinated in this so that they could cover for the unfortunate one without annoyance knowing that it could be their turn next to need help.

And in the middle of the defence Celtic had John Clark a cold, knowledgeable player, safe and unhurried when the action boiled in the penalty-box and inspiring when, with short steps and pouting chest, he took the ball calmly out of the goal-mouth rumpus.

And thus equipped and proudly bearing the title, 'Champions of Scotland', Celtic for the first time challenged in the European Cup of 1966–67 and Stein pitted his wits against the highly paid and temperamental managers of Europe.

Celtic went with an adventurous, attacking style in contrast to the deplorable, defensive methods of the Italians which were inhibiting the skills and strangling the joys of football spectating. They had been drilled to the *catenaccio* formation with a sweeper playing behind four backs so with one more defender there had to be one less attacker. Unfortunately, before Stein nobody had devised a counter.

Confident from a run of forty-two games without defeat there was a smooth start for Celtic. Zurich were beaten home and away and so too were Nantes. There was little concern shown when Vojvodina took a one-goal lead in their home leg but soon consternation showed when, with but a minute remaining of the second leg, Celtic had done no more than pull back that lead. And then Billy McNeill rose majestically to head a spectacular winning goal and Celtic were through to the semi-final against Dukla, Prague, the formidable Czechoslovakian Army team.

And as Celtic continued to win at home and the League Cup was theirs, Europe began to notice their obsession with goals. Dukla were beaten 3–1 in Glasgow and with the prospect of competing in the Final just a game away and Celtic, with a two-goal start in that game, a bubbling mixture of emotions confused Stein. There was apprehension, an urge to do the right thing for the players, his realisation that they depended upon him for so much, his responsibility to Celtic and to Scotland. In the confusion he made a decision which he swore later he would never repeat.

He went to Prague to defend and defended so courageously as would have shamed an Italian tactics master. Only Steve Chalmers was left in attack and he took a terrible buffeting as he held the ball and ran with it buying the defenders precious seconds of relief. The justification was a no-scoring draw and a place in the Final in Lisbon.

The Final could not have been better scripted. The setting was the National Stadium in Lisbon, a glorious field in a wooded park. The opponents were Celtic, the new adventurous cavaliers of international club football, against the hard defenders of Internazionale Milan. The directors were Helenio Herrera, the high priest of defence which inhibited spectacle, and Jock Stein, the messiah of the spectators, preaching his doctrine of goals.

Before Celtic went into training for the event they drew with Rangers at the beginning of May at Ibrox Stadium and that was enough to win them the League Championship and complete a grand slam of Scottish football. They had won every tournament in which they had competed: the Scottish Cup, the League Cup, the Glasgow Cup, and the Scottish League. Herrera watched the match against Rangers and rated Celtic the fittest team he had ever seen. He was soon to have confirmation.

There was the usual gamesmanship from the managers before the teams met on Thursday, May 25. Suarez was unable to play and so Inter had an all-Italian team and Celtic an all-Scots one. That was a change from the cosmopolitan Real Madrid which had won the first five European Cups and Benfica who followed them. Stein kept amazingly composed, declaring, 'We have come to play a game of football not to fight a war'.

The European Cup is won by Celtic and it's too much for the veteran goalkeeper, Ronnie Simpson, as he breaks down in the arms of Jock Stein.

Steve Chalmers and Tommy Gemmell, Celtic's goalscorers in the European Champions' Cup-Final, 1967.

He tried on a hat in a shop in Estoril where the team were staying and when the shop girl told him, 'It's too small', he answered, 'It would have fitted me last year'. His good humour and wit kept the team relaxed.

He won over the locals when he declared his creed for the Final, 'Inter will play defensively. That's their way and it's their business. We have a duty to play the game our way and that is to attack. We can be as hard and professional as anyone but I mean it when I say, that we don't just want to win this Cup. We want to win it playing good football to make neutrals glad we've won it, glad to remember how we did it.' It was one of the great speeches on the eve of a memorable event.

Of course Celtic did win it and with all Europe watching on television and being glad they were watching and glad that Celtic had won playing the kind of football which is universally approved by the spectators.

Scotland basked in reflected glory puzzled as some talked of Celtic as they used to talk of Real Madrid, as they talked of the unshakable assurance of Clark, the creative cunning of Auld, the astonishing virtuosity of Johnstone, the ceaseless running of Chalmers. Nothing symbolised the spirit of the team more than the incredible display of Gemmell. Inter had led from a penalty-kick. Gemmell kept charging up the left side until he was drooping with exhaustion. Then he would gasp and go again and he was almost on his knees when he shot that thunderous equalising goal in the sixty-third minute. It was a goal to make heroic poetry in any language. And then there was Steve Chalmers' winner and the final whistle and Stein by that time in the dressing room unable to wait and watch any more.

Then there were the jollifications and the team at last in the dressing room with the Cup and Stein being urged to drink champagne from it and even in such a moment of self-fulfilment refusing to break his abstinence from alcoholic drink. The final scene could not have been scripted. On cue Bill Shankly burst in with hands spread to the heavens shouting, 'John, You're immortal'. He was only exaggerating slightly.

Congratulations for Celtic from the House of Commons.

No. 187 **10145**

NOTICES OF QUESTIONS AND MOTIONS

given on

Wednesday 26th April 1967

QUESTIONS

NOTE: Questions marked thus * *are for oral answer*

FRIDAY 28th APRIL

520 *CONGRATULATIONS TO GLASGOW CELTIC FOOTBALL CLUB*

Mr Richard Buchanan
Mr James Bennett
Dr Miller
Mrs Alice Cullen
Mr William Small

That this House congratulates the Glasgow Celtic Football Club on reaching the final of the European Champions' Cup and wishes them success in the next stage, and would deplore any attempt by the air charter companies or travel agencies to exploit the occasion by charging excessive fares in conveying the supporters to the final in Lisbon.

Within a day or two the Portuguese had won back their city from the 7,000 city supporters who had travelled and the goings-on went into the folklore of football. The story was told a thousand times of the consulate official who matched Stein's immortality when he said, 'Every time I open a cupboard a Celtic supporter falls out'. Another favourite was of those who were bundled on planes at Lisbon airport and then in Glasgow remembered they had gone by car. The best was of the lone hiker with green and white favours on the road outside Lisbon who when offered a lift asked, 'Where are you going?' and when told Edinburgh, said, 'That's no use – I'm going to Glasgow'.

Celtic's record for the season was: played 65 games, won 53, drawn 8, lost 4: goals for 201, against 49. There was just time to wonder at it and then to switch to Rangers who, the following week, were bound for Nuremburg to play Bayern Munich in the Final of the European Cup Winners' Cup. The exciting prospect was that the two principal trophies in European club football would go to Scotland.

Rangers' expedition got off to a bad start. Team changes were made necessary and then the chairman, Mr John Lawrence, in an unfortunate press conference, described, with misplaced realism, Rangers team as makeshift for they had three half-backs as inside-forwards. Then he described Celtic as the yardstick in Scottish football. It was hard for Rangers people to take such official talk.

He was soon shown to be right. In the Final Rangers had many chances to win and at times all that was needed was for a foot to push out smartly. But their forwards were indeed heavier footed than goal-scorers should be and Bayern scored in extra-time to ruin what could have been the most exciting Scottish week of the century.

Unfortunately for Rangers they did make Stein's Celtic the yardstick and then tried to match it too quickly. There were arguments about the training methods after their heavy footedness was compared with the nimble skills of Celtic. Almost half a million pounds were spent on new players to try and bring an end to Celtic's dominance. But Rangers had created a crisis for themselves and panic was the wrong mood for buying.

They sought to alter the management control. Eddie Turnbull, then making his way promisingly with Aberdeen, was offered the post as assistant to Scot Symon but the homework had not been done and an arrangement worked out with Symon. In the consequent discussion Eddie Turnbull refused the post and that was a blow to Rangers' prestige.

The play at Ibrox continued to deteriorate and David White was taken from Clyde as assistant to the manager. He had impressed the chairman, John Lawrence, by taking Clyde, a part-time club, to third position in the Scottish League. Things went from bad to worse and Celtic's triumphant run continued to disturb. Scot Symon was sacked with undue haste and David White took over but, as it turned out, before he was ready for the job. Then when he did show signs of learning he, too, was sent away and the former exciting right-winger, Willie Waddell, moved into the manager's office.

Celtic continued winning but with a defeat here and there to prove they were indeed human. They had been praised for their discipline and then went to the Argentine with a one goal lead over Racing in the World Club Championship. But even before the start, in Buenos Aires, Ronnie Simpson was struck on the back of the head with a missile and had to be substituted. They lost a goal, had to replay in Montevideo, and disgraced themselves when they could not resist provocation, losing the Cup and their good name. The Celtic management fined them £250 per head for their indiscretions.

The following season they were quickly out of the European Cup to Kiev Dynamo. They became irritated with their own failings and lost their rhythm. They took some time to recover from their grand-slam season.

A blunder by Billy McNeill, who had won so many ties, gifted A.C. Milan a goal in the quarter-finals of the next European Cup and they could not match it. In the following season they played, in the semi-final, the final before the Final against Leeds United the English champions. There has maybe been no better game of football played between clubs from the two countries from which football first came.

Celtic won both legs and went to meet the Dutch champions, Feyenoord, in the Final in Milan, but not even the blaring horns of the many thousands of Dutch supporters could wake them from their complacency or rouse them from their languor and they lost by a goal in extra-time. The Dutch in the form of Ajax eliminated them the following year but by then Celtic were clearly in a transition period and the new men George Connelly, Lou Macari, and Kenny Dalglish were mere European apprentices. Stein's dream of a second European Cup was not working out.

The 1970 Scottish Cup-Final. Aberdeen 3, Celtic 1. Joe Harper scores the first goal from the penalty-spot.

Ian St John scores at Hampden.

An Aberdeen team brilliantly conceived by Eddie Turnbull became the principal challengers at home and against all the odds, but in keeping with Eddie Turnbull's faith, beat Celtic 3–1 in the 1970 Scottish Cup-Final. Celtic had won five successive League Cups but the sixteen-year-old Derek Johnstone headed a goal against them in 1970–71 to give Rangers the trophy to bolster the hopes of their depressed supporters. The following season the new, bright Partick Thistle of David McParland beat them in another League Cup-Final by 4–1 to delight many who wish well to the underdogs. But with the Scottish Cup and the League Championship both won again, Celtic pushed into the final season of the century still masters but masters with the young ones such as Hibs and Aberdeen and Dundee snapping at their heels and Rangers under yet another manager, Jock Wallace, striving mightily to recover their glories of other days.

Rangers finished the century in deep depression. Despite playing miserably at home they surged past such formidable opposition as Torino and Bayern Munich in the European Cup Winners' Cup, then beat Moscow Dynamo in a dramatic Final in Barcelona. Then joy overcame discretion and Rangers were punished for the excesses of their supporters. They were suspended by U.E.F.A. from European Competition for two years, a sentence which was later halved. They would hope a new century would see them assume their old position of authority.

Another Scottish Cup, another celebration. After the 1967 Final: Jimmy Johnstone, Tommy Gemmell, Bob Rooney, and Neil Mochan.

The excitement of the Scottish Cup. The winning team of 1970 arrives back in Aberdeen.

24

The Century Ends

A few sports-minded men met in Glasgow on March 13, 1873 to talk about forming an association to bring good order and controlled manliness to a new game in which they saw a way of achieving the then popular aim of a sound mind in a sound body. They had watched the centuries-old pastime of kicking a ball about but had disliked the coarseness of the mob game and the handling adaptation of it in the rugby rules.

They did their work well and a game emerged which has surpassed in popular appeal any game which was devised before or since. When one writes of it the attention is naturally drawn to the spectacular top level, to the heroes of the spectators. It dare not be forgotten, however, that the game starts in the school playground and is developed in the various grades where men, as they did years ago, work unselfishly to produce a sound mind in a sound body.

There, among the juveniles, the amateurs, and the juniors the game is played for glory. There is regret that in the higher flights of world competition they think the game is about winning and have forgotten that it is about glory. When Scots forget about glory then they are no longer playing Scottish football.

The Scottish Football Association have been handed down the charge from those pioneers and it is to promote the game, the whole game, from the schools to the psychosomatic crust at the top. It is to the benefit of the flowering branch up above that they pay attention to what is happening at the roots.

And so the first century has gone and left its memories, happy and sad. There is regret, deep and bitter, that a grand old club such as Third Lanark was allowed through mismanagement to flounder and sink but there is the brighter memory of Tam Fergusson, a coal merchant in Stirling, going to look at a field as potential grazing for his horses and seeing in it a football stadium and forming Stirling Albion.

When he shocked the S.F.A. council by telling someone that he did not know 'a bee from a bull's foot' there were tolerant nods, 'He's a terrible man', but of such were the game built.

And there were more happy memories than the other kind. There was Hal Stewart flamboyantly selling Greenock Morton to an unwilling public and stimulating interest in bringing to Cappielow the Scandinavians. There was Bobby Ancell, angry at Celtic and Rangers supporters passing his fine team in Motherwell to jump on the bandwagon at Celtic Park or Ibrox, and saying of them that they were the only ones who wore woollen scarves in summer time.

Officials of the Scottish Football Association 1972–73, *Seated:* E. Walker (Assistant Secretary), G. F. Fox (Hon. Treasurer), W. P. Allan, J.P. (Secretary), H. S. Nelson, J.P. (President), R. G. Grimshaw (Vice-President), J. R. Aitkin (Vice-President). *Standing:* P. Scott, M.B.E. (Past President), A. Wilson Strachan (Past Hon. Treasurer).

There was Haige Gordon bringing to solemn, international occasions good Border conviviality, and the president, Tom Reid, urbane and jovial, charming the foreigners and maybe throwing in a song and soft shoe act.

The fierceness of some of the partisanship was funny and a friend, a Hearts supporter, was lamenting that the sun was shining in Edinburgh one Saturday and Hibs would have a good gate.

There were worries ninety years ago about rough play and about hooliganism. There are still worries about these deplorable practices but a reasonable look will show that conduct has not deteriorated in football as much as it has away from the game in the streets and in the dark corners off them.

There is still one matter to settle. On Monday, December 15, 1890 the Rutherglen Club with the sanction of the North Eastern Association asked the S.F.A. if it was absolutely necessary for the ground club to supply balls to the end of a game and if a tie could be awarded to a club who still have five minutes of a game to play when the last ball burst. It is time they had an answer.

Scotland in International Football

Summary of Results

ENGLAND *v.* SCOTLAND

PLAYED: 89; England won 32, Scotland won 35, Drawn 22. GOALS: England 160, Scotland 156.

Year	*Venue*	*Goals* E.	S.	*Year*	*Venue*	*Goals* E.	S.	*Year*	*Venue*	*Goals* E.	S.
1872	Glasgow	0	0	1902	Birmingham	2	2	1937	Glasgow	1	3
1873	Kennington Oval	4	2	1903	Sheffield	1	2	1938	Wembley	0	1
1874	Glasgow	1	2	1904	Glasgow	1	0	1939	Glasgow	2	1
1875	Kennington Oval	2	2	1905	Crystal Palace	1	0	1947	Wembley	1	1
1876	Glasgow	0	3	1906	Glasgow	1	2	1948	Glasgow	2	0
1877	Kennington Oval	1	3	1907	Newcastle	1	1	1949	Wembley	1	3
1878	Glasgow	2	7	1908	Glasgow	1	1	WC1950	Glasgow	1	0
1879	Kennington Oval	5	4	1909	Crystal Palace	2	0	1951	Wembley	2	3
1880	Glasgow	4	5	1910	Glasgow	0	2	1952	Glasgow	2	1
1881	Kennington Oval	1	6	1911	Everton	1	1	1953	Wembley	2	2
1882	Glasgow	1	5	1912	Glasgow	1	1	WC1954	Glasgow	4	2
1883	Sheffield	2	3	1913	Chelsea	1	0	1955	Wembley	7	2
1884	Glasgow	0	1	1914	Glasgow	1	3	1956	Glasgow	1	1
1885	Kennington Oval	1	1	1920	Sheffield	5	4	1957	Wembley	2	1
1886	Glasgow	1	1	1921	Glasgow	0	3	1958	Glasgow	4	0
1887	Blackburn	2	3	1922	Aston Villa	0	1	1959	Wembley	1	0
1888	Glasgow	5	0	1923	Glasgow	2	2	1960	Glasgow	1	1
1889	Kennington Oval	2	3	1924	Wembley	1	1	1961	Wembley	9	3
1890	Glasgow	1	1	1925	Glasgow	0	2	1962	Glasgow	0	2
1891	Blackburn	2	1	1926	Manchester	0	1	1963	Wembley	1	2
1892	Glasgow	4	1	1927	Glasgow	2	1	1964	Glasgow	0	1
1893	Richmond	5	2	1928	Wembley	1	5	1965	Wembley	2	2
1894	Glasgow	2	2	1929	Glasgow	0	1	1966	Glasgow	4	3
1895	Everton	3	0	1930	Wembley	5	2	EC1967	Wembley	2	3
1896	Glasgow	1	2	1931	Glasgow	0	2	EC1968	Glasgow	1	1
1897	Crystal Palace	1	2	1932	Wembley	3	0	1969	Wembley	4	1
1898	Glasgow	3	1	1933	Glasgow	1	2	1970	Glasgow	0	0
1899	Birmingham	2	1	1934	Wembley	3	0	1971	Wembley	3	1
1900	Glasgow	1	4	1935	Glasgow	0	2	1972	Glasgow	1	0
1901	Crystal Palace	2	2	1936	Wembley	1	1				

WC = World Cup EC = European Nations' Cup

SCOTLAND *v.* IRELAND

PLAYED 77; Scotland won 56, Ireland won 10, Drawn 11. GOALS: Scotland 237, Ireland 72.

Year	*Venue*	*Goals* S.	I.	*Year*	*Venue*	*Goals* S.	I.	*Year*	*Venue*	*Goals* S.	I.
1884	Belfast	5	0	1892	Belfast	3	2	1900	Belfast	3	0
1885	Glasgow	8	2	1893	Glasgow	6	1	1901	Glasgow	11	0
1886	Belfast	7	2	1894	Belfast	2	1	1902	Belfast	5	1
1887	Glasgow	4	1	1895	Glasgow	3	1	1903	Glasgow	0	2
1888	Belfast	10	2	1896	Belfast	3	3	1904	Dublin	1	1
1889	Glasgow	7	0	1897	Glasgow	5	1	1905	Glasgow	4	0
1890	Belfast	4	1	1898	Belfast	3	0	1906	Dublin	1	0
1891	Glasgow	2	1	1899	Glasgow	9	1	1907	Glasgow	3	0

Year	Venue	Goals S.	Goals I.
1908	Dublin	5	0
1909	Glasgow	5	0
1910	Belfast	0	1
1911	Glasgow	2	0
1912	Belfast	4	1
1913	Dublin	2	1
1914	Belfast	1	1
1920	Glasgow	3	0
1921	Belfast	2	0
1922	Glasgow	2	1
1923	Belfast	1	0
1924	Glasgow	2	0
1925	Belfast	3	0
1926	Glasgow	4	0
1927	Belfast	2	0
1928	Glasgow	0	1
1929	Belfast	7	3
1930	Glasgow	3	1
1931	Belfast	0	0
1932	Glasgow	3	1
1933	Belfast	4	0
1934	Glasgow	1	2
1935	Belfast	1	2
1936	Edinburgh	2	1
1937	Belfast	3	1
1938	Aberdeen	1	1
1939	Belfast	2	0
1947	Glasgow	0	0
1948	Belfast	0	2
1949	Glasgow	3	2
1950	Belfast	8	2
1951	Glasgow	6	1
1952	Belfast	3	0
1953	Glasgow	1	1
1954	Belfast	3	1
1955	Glasgow	2	2
1956	Belfast	1	2
1957	Glasgow	1	0
1958	Belfast	1	1
1959	Glasgow	2	2
1960	Belfast	4	0
1961	Glasgow	5	2
1962	Belfast	6	1
1963	Glasgow	5	1
1964	Belfast	1	2
1965	Glasgow	3	2
1966	Belfast	2	3
1967	Glasgow	2	1
1968	Belfast	0	1
1969	Glasgow	1	1
1970	Belfast	1	0
1971	Glasgow	1	0
1972	Glasgow	2	0

SCOTLAND *v*. WALES

PLAYED: 85; Scotland won 51, Wales won 15, Drawn 19. GOALS: Scotland 219, Wales 39.

Year	Venue	Goals S.	Goals W.
1876	Glasgow	4	0
1877	Wrexham	2	0
1878	Glasgow	9	0
1879	Wrexham	3	0
1880	Glasgow	5	1
1881	Wrexham	5	1
1882	Glasgow	5	0
1883	Wrexham	4	1
1884	Glasgow	4	1
1885	Wrexham	8	1
1886	Glasgow	4	1
1887	Wrexham	2	0
1888	Edinburgh	5	1
1889	Wrexham	0	0
1890	Paisley	5	0
1891	Wrexham	4	3
1892	Edinburgh	6	1
1893	Wrexham	8	0
1894	Kilmarnock	5	2
1895	Wrexham	2	2
1896	Dundee	4	0
1897	Wrexham	2	2
1898	Motherwell	5	2
1899	Wrexham	6	0
1900	Aberdeen	5	2
1901	Wrexham	1	1
1902	Greenock	5	1
1903	Cardiff	1	0
1904	Dundee	1	1
1905	Wrexham	1	3
1906	Edinburgh	0	2
1907	Wrexham	0	1
1908	Dundee	2	1
1909	Wrexham	2	3
1910	Kilmarnock	1	0
1911	Cardiff	2	2
1912	Tynecastle	1	0
1913	Wrexham	0	0
1914	Glasgow	0	0
1920	Cardiff	1	1
1921	Aberdeen	2	1
1922	Wrexham	1	2
1923	Paisley	2	0
1924	Cardiff	0	2
1925	Tynecastle	3	1
1926	Cardiff	3	0
1927	Glasgow	3	0
1928	Wrexham	2	2
1929	Ibrox	4	2
1930	Cardiff	4	2
1931	Glasgow	1	1
1932	Wrexham	3	2
1933	Edinburgh	2	5
1934	Cardiff	2	3
1935	Aberdeen	3	2
1936	Cardiff	1	1
1937	Dundee	1	2
1938	Cardiff	1	2
1939	Edinburgh	3	2
1947	Wrexham	1	3
1948	Glasgow	1	2
1949	Cardiff	3	1
1950	Glasgow	2	0
1951	Cardiff	3	1
1952	Glasgow	0	1
1953	Cardiff	2	1
1954	Glasgow	3	3
1955	Cardiff	1	0
1956	Glasgow	3	0
1957	Cardiff	2	2
1958	Glasgow	1	1
1959	Cardiff	3	0
1960	Glasgow	1	1
1961	Cardiff	0	2
1962	Glasgow	2	0
1963	Cardiff	3	2
1964	Glasgow	2	1
1965	Cardiff	2	3
1966	Glasgow	4	1
1967	Cardiff	1	1
1968	Glasgow	3	2
1969	Wrexham	5	3
1970	Glasgow	0	0
1971	Cardiff	0	0
1972	Glasgow	1	0

v. AUSTRIA

Year	Date	Venue	Goals S.	Goals A.
1931	May 16	Vienna	0	5
1933	Nov. 29	Glasgow	2	2
1937	May 9	Vienna	1	1
1950	Dec. 13	Glasgow	0	1
1951	May 27	Vienna	0	4
WC1954	June 16	Zurich	0	1
1955	May 19	Vienna	4	1
1956	May 2	Glasgow	1	1
1960	May 29	Vienna	1	4
1963	May 8	Glasgow	4	1
		(abandoned after 79 mins.)		
WC1968	Nov. 6	Glasgow	2	1
WC1969	Nov. 5	Vienna	0	2

v. BELGIUM

			S.	B.
1947	May 18	Brussels	1	2
1948	April 28	Glasgow	2	0
1951	May 20	Brussels	5	0
EC1971	Feb. 3	Liege	0	3
EC1971	Nov. 10	Glasgow	1	0

v. BRAZIL

			S.	B.
1966	June 25	Glasgow	1	1

v. CYPRUS

			S.	C.
WC1968	Dec. 11	Nicosia	5	0
WC1969	May 17	Glasgow	8	0

v. CZECHOSLOVAKIA

			S.	C.
1937	May 22	Prague	3	1
1937	Dec. 8	Glasgow	5	0
WC1961	May 14	Bratislava	0	4
WC1961	Sept. 26	Glasgow	3	2
WC1961	Nov. 29	Brussels	2	4

v. DENMARK

			S.	D.
1951	May 12	Glasgow	3	1
1952	May 25	Copenhagen	2	1
1968	Oct. 16	Copenhagen	1	0
EC1970	Nov. 11	Glasgow	1	0
EC1971	June 9	Copenhagen	0	1

v. FINLAND

			S.	F.
1954	May 25	Helsinki	2	1
WC1964	Oct. 21	Glasgow	3	1
WC1965	May 27	Helsinki	2	1

v. FRANCE

Year	Date	Venue	Goals S.	Goals F.
1930	May 18	Paris	2	0
1932	May 8	Paris	3	1
1948	May 23	Paris	0	3
1949	April 27	Glasgow	2	0
1950	May 27	Paris	1	0
1951	May 16	Glasgow	1	0
WC1958	June 15	Orebro	1	2

v. WEST GERMANY

			S.	W.G.
1929	June 1	Berlin	1	1
1936	Oct. 14	Glasgow	2	2
1957	May 22	Stuttgart	3	1
1959	May 6	Glasgow	3	2
1964	May 12	Hanover	2	2
WC1969	April 16	Glasgow	1	1
WC1969	Oct. 22	Hamburg	2	3

v. HUNGARY

			S.	H.
1938	Dec. 7	Glasgow	3	1
1954	Dec. 8	Glasgow	2	4
1955	May 29	Budapest	1	3
1958	May 7	Glasgow	1	1
1960	June 5	Budapest	3	3

v. ITALY

			S.	I.
1931	May 20	Rome	0	3
WC1965	Nov. 9	Glasgow	1	0
WC1965	Dec. 7	Naples	0	3

v. LUXEMBOURG

			S.	L.
1947	May 24	Luxembourg	6	0

v. NETHERLANDS

			S.	N.
1929	June 4	Amsterdam	2	0
1938	May 21	Amsterdam	3	1
1959	May 27	Amsterdam	2	1
1966	May 11	Glasgow	0	3
1968	May 30	Amsterdam	0	0
1971	Dec. 1	Rotterdam	1	2

v. NORWAY

			S.	N.
1929	May 28	Oslo	7	3
1954	May 5	Glasgow	1	0
1954	May 19	Oslo	1	1
1963	June 4	Bergen	3	4
1963	Nov. 7	Glasgow	6	1

v. PARAGUAY

			S.	P.
WC1958	June 11	Norrkoping	2	3

v. PERU

Year	*Date*	*Venue*	*Goals* S.	P.
1972	April 26	Glasgow	2	0

v. POLAND

			S.	P.
1958	June 1	Warsaw	2	1
1960	May 4	Glasgow	2	3
WC1965	May 23	Chorzow	1	1
WC1965	Oct. 13	Glasgow	1	2

v. PORTUGAL

			S.	P.
1950	May 21	Lisbon	2	2
1955	May 4	Glasgow	3	0
1959	June 3	Lisbon	0	1
1966	June 18	Glasgow	0	1
EC1971	April 21	Lisbon	0	2
EC1971	Oct. 13	Glasgow	2	1

v. SPAIN

			S.	Sp.
WC1957	May 8	Glasgow	4	2
WC1957	May 26	Madrid	1	4
1963	June 13	Madrid	6	2
1965	May 8	Glasgow	0	0

v. SWEDEN

			S.	Swe.
1952	May 30	Stockholm	1	3
1953	May 6	Glasgow	1	2

v. SWITZERLAND

Year	*Date*	*Venue*	*Goals* S.	Switz.
1931	May 24	Geneva	3	2
1948	May 17	Berne	1	2
1950	April 26	Glasgow	3	1
WC1957	May 19	Basle	2	1
WC1957	Nov. 6	Glasgow	3	2

v. TURKEY

			S.	T.
1960	June 8	Ankara	2	4

v. URUGUAY

			S.	U.
WC1954	June 19	Basle	0	7
1962	May 2	Glasgow	2	3

v. U.S.A.

			S.	U.S.A.
1952	April 30	Glasgow	6	0

v. U.S.S.R.

			S.	R.
1967	May 10	Glasgow	0	2
1971	June 14	Moscow	0	1

v. YUGOSLAVIA

			S.	Y.
1955	May 15	Belgrade	2	2
1956	Nov. 21	Glasgow	2	0
WC1958	June 8	Vasteras	1	1

The Scottish team which played Wales in Aberdeen in 1934. *Back row:* Alex Massie, Peter McGonagle, Andy Anderson, Alan McClory, Dally Duncan, George Brown. *Front row:* Willie Cook, Tommy Walker, Jimmy Simpsson, Charlie Napier, Dave McCulloch.

Full Scotland International Matches

Versus England 1872–1972

Date. November 30, 1872
Venue. Partick, Glasgow
Result. Scotland 0 England 0
Referee. W. Keay (Queen's Park)
Linesmen. H. N. Smith (Pres. Queen's Park)
C. W. Alcock (Hon. Sec. F.A.)

R. Gardner (Captain)	Queen's Park
J. Taylor	Queen's Park
W. Ker	Queen's Park
J. Thomson	Queen's Park
J. Smith	Queen's Park
W. McKinnon	Queen's Park
J. Weir	Queen's Park
R. Leckie	Queen's Park
D. Wotherspoon	Queen's Park
R. Smith	Queen's Park
A. Rhind	Queen's Park

Date. March 8, 1873
Venue. Oval, London
Result. England 4 Scotland 2
Linesmen. A. Rae
C. W. Alcock (Hon. Sec. F.A.)

R. Gardner (Captain)	Queen's Park
J. Taylor	Queen's Park
W. Ker	Queen's Park
J. Thomson	Queen's Park
J. Smith	Queen's Park
W. McKinnon	Queen's Park
R. Tailyour	Royal Engineers
A. Kinnaird	Wanderers
G. Blackburn	Royal Engineers
W. Gibb	Clydesdale
J. Weir	Queen's Park

Date. March 7, 1874
Venue. Partick, Glasgow
Result. Scotland 2 England 1
Referee. A. Rae (Queen's Park)
Linesman. W. Keay (Queen's Park)

R. Gardner	Clydesdale
J. Hunter	Third Lanark
J. Taylor	Queen's Park
C. Campbell	Queen's Park
J. Thomson (Captain)	Queen's Park
J. Weir	Queen's Park
J. Ferguson	Vale of Leven
H. McNeil	Queen's Park
W. McKinnon	Queen's Park
A. McKinnon	Queen's Park
F. Anderson	Clydesdale

Date. March 6, 1875
Venue. Oval, London
Result. England 2 Scotland 2
Referee. A. Stair (Hon. Sec. F.A.)
Linesmen. J. C. Mackay (Granville)
Major Marindin (Royal Engineers)

R. Gardner	Clydesdale
J. Hunter	Third Lanark
J. Taylor (Captain)	Queen's Park
A. Kennedy	Eastern
A. McLintock	Vale of Leven
J. Weir	Queen's Park
W. McKinnon	Queen's Park
H. McNeil	Queen's Park
T. Highet	Queen's Park
P. Andrews	Eastern
J. McPherson	Clydesdale

Date. March 14, 1876
Venue. Partick, Glasgow
Result. Scotland 3 England 0

A. McGeoch	Dumbreck
J. Taylor (Captain)	Queen's Park
J. Hunter	Third Lanark
A. McLintock	Vale of Leven
A. Kennedy	Eastern
H. McNeil	Queen's Park
W. McKinnon	Queen's Park
T. Highet	Queen's Park
W. Miller	Third Lanark
J. Ferguson	Vale of Leven
J. Baird	Vale of Leven

Date.March 3, 1877
Venue. Oval, London
Result. England 1 Scotland 3
Referee. R. A. Ogilvie (Clapham Rovers)
Linesmen. W. Dick (Hon. Sec. S.F.A.)
H. Heron (Wanderers)

A. McGeoch	Dumbreck
R. Neil	Queen's Park
T. Vallance	Rangers
C. Campbell (Captain)	Queen's Park
J. Phillips	Queen's Park
J. Richmond	Clydesdale
J. McDougal	Vale of Leven
W. McKinnon	Queen's Park
J. McGregor	Vale of Leven
J. Ferguson	Vale of Leven
J. Smith	Mauchline

Date. March 2, 1878
Venue. Hampden Park, Glasgow
Result. Scotland 7 England 2
Goalscorers. Scotland: McKinnon (2), McDougal (3), McNeil (2)
England: Wylie, Cursham
Referee. W. Dick (Hon. Sec. S.F.A.)
Linesmen. R. B. Colquhoun (Lennox)
G. Turner (Edinburgh University)

R. Gardner	Clydesdale
A. McIntyre	Vale of Leven
T. Vallance	Rangers
C. Campbell (Captain)	Queen's Park
A. Kennedy	Third Lanark
J. Richmond	Queen's Park
J. McGregor	Vale of Leven
J. McDougal	Vale of Leven
T. Highet	Queen's Park
W. McKinnon	Queen's Park
H. McNeil	Queen's Park

Date. April 5, 1879
Venue. Oval, London
Result. England 5 Scotland 4
Linesman. R. B. Colquhoun (Lennox)

R. Parlane	Vale of Leven
W. Somers	Third Lanark
T. Vallance	Rangers
C. Campbell (Captain)	Queen's Park
J. McPherson	Vale of Leven
R. Paton	Vale of Leven
W. Beveridge	Ayr Academy
W. McKinnon	Queen's Park
J. Smith	Mauchline
H. McNeil	Queen's Park
J. McDougal	Vale of Leven

Date. March 13, 1880
Venue. Hampden Park, Glasgow
Result. Scotland 5 England 4
Goalscorers. Scotland: Ker (3), Baird, Kay
England: Mosforth, Bambridge (2), Sparks
Referee. D. Hamilton (Parkgrove)
Linesmen. J. Nicholson (Vale of Leven)
W. Pierce Dix (Sheffield Assoc.)

A. Rowan	Caledonian
A. McLintock	Vale of Leven
R. Neill (Captain)	Queen's Park
C. Campbell	Queen's Park
J. McPherson	Vale of Leven
J. Smith	Edinburgh University
M. McNeil	Rangers
G. Ker	Queen's Park
J. McGregor	Vale of Leven
J. Baird	Vale of Leven
J. Kaye	Queen's Park

Date. March 12, 1881
Venue. Oval, London
Result. England 1 Scotland 6

G. Gillespie	Rangers
A. Watson	Queen's Park
A. McIntyre	Vale of Leven
C. Campbell (Captain)	Queen's Park
P. Miller	Dumbarton
E. Fraser	Queen's Park
W. Anderson	Queen's Park
G. Ker	Queen's Park
W. Harrower	Queen's Park
J. Kaye	Queen's Park
J. McPherson	Arthurlie

Date. March 11, 1882
Venue. Hampden Park, Glasgow
Result. Scotland 5 England 1
Goalscorers. Scotland: Harrower, Ker (2), McPherson, Kaye
England: Vaughton
Referee. J. Wallace (Beith)
Linesmen. T. Anderson (Renfrew)
Mr Bastard (F.A.)

G. Gillespie	Rangers
A. Watson	Queen's Park
A. McIntyre	Vale of Leven
C. Campbell (Captain)	Queen's Park
P. Miller	Dumbarton
E. Fraser	Queen's Park
W. Anderson	Queen's Park
G. Ker	Queen's Park
W. Harrower	Queen's Park
J. Kaye	Queen's Park
J. McPherson	Arthurlie

Date. March 10, 1883
Venue. Sheffield
Result. England 2 Scotland 3
Goalscorers. England: Mitchell, Cobbald
Scotland: Smith (3)
Referee. S. Sinclair (Ireland)
Linesmen. T. Lawrie (Vice-Pres. S.F.A.)
J. C. Clegg (Sheffield Assoc.)

J. McAulay	Dumbarton
A. Holm (Captain)	Queen's Park
M. Paton	Dumbarton
P. Miller	Dumbarton
J. McPherson	Vale of Leven
E. Fraser	Queen's Park
W. Anderson	Queen's Park
Dr J. Smith	Edinburgh University
J. Inglis	Rangers
J. Kaye	Queen's Park
W. McKinnon	Dumbarton

Date. March 15, 1884
Venue. Hampden Park, Glasgow
Result. Scotland 1 England 0
Goalscorer. Smith
Referee. J. Sinclair (Ireland)
Linesmen. T. Lawrie (Pres. S.F.A.)
Major Marindin (F.A.)

J. McAulay	Dumbarton
W. Arnott	Queen's Park
J. Forbes	Vale of Leven
C. Campbell (Captain)	Queen's Park
J. McPherson	Vale of Leven
W. Anderson	Queen's Park
F. Shaw	Pollockshields Athletic
Dr J. Smith	Queen's Park
J. Lindsay	Dumbarton
R. Christie	Queen's Park
W. McKinnon	Dumbarton

Date. March 21, 1885
Venue. Oval, London
Result. England 1 Scotland 1
Goalscorers. England: Bambridge
Scotland: Lindsay

J. McAulay	Dumbarton
W. Arnott	Queen's Park
M. Paton	Dumbarton
C. Campbell	Queen's Park
J. Gow	Queen's Park
W. Anderson	Queen's Park
A. Hamilton	Queen's Park
W. Sellar	Battlefield
J. Lindsay	Dumbarton
D. Allan	Queen's Park
R. Calderwood	Cartvale

Date. March 27, 1886
Venue. Hampden Park, Glasgow
Result. Scotland 1 England 1
Goalscorers. Scotland: Somerville
England: Lindley
Referee. Mr Hunter (Welsh F.A.)
Linesmen. N. L. Jackson (Hon. Sec. London Assoc.)
A. Stuart (Vice-Pres. S.F.A.)

J. McAulay	Dumbarton
W. Arnott (Captain)	Queen's Park
M. Paton	Dumbarton
C. Campbell	Queen's Park
J. McDonald	Edinburgh University
A. Hamilton	Queen's Park
W. Sellar	Battlefield
G. Somerville	Queen's Park
J. Lindsay	Dumbarton
W. Gray	Pollockshields Athletic
R. Aitken	Dumbarton

Date. March 19, 1887
Venue. Blackburn
Result. England 2 Scotland 3
Goalscorers. England: Lindley, Dewhurst
Scotland: Keir, McColl (2)
Referee. Mr Sinclair (Irish Assoc.)
Linesmen. Mr Gregson (England)
Mr Browne (Scotland)

J. McAulay (Captain)	Dumbarton
W. Arnott	Queen's Park
J. Forbes	Vale of Leven
J. Kelso	Renton
J. Auld	3rd L.R.V.
L. Keir	Dumbarton
J. Marshall	3rd L.R.V.
W. Robertson	Dumbarton
W. Sellar	Battlefield
J. McColl	Renton
J. Allan	Queen's Park

Date. March 17, 1888
Venue. Hampden Park, Glasgow
Result. Scotland 0 England 5
Referee. J. Sinclair (Irish Assoc.)
Linesmen. A. Kennedy (Pres. S.F.A.)
M. P. Betts (England)

J. Lindsay	Renton
W. Arnott	Queen's Park
D. Gow (Captain)	Rangers
J. Kelly	Renton
L. Keir	Dumbarton
R. Kelso	Renton
A. Hamilton	Queen's Park
W. Berry	Queen's Park
W. Sellars	Battlefield
J. McColl	Renton
J. Lambie	Queen's Park

Date. April 13, 1889
Venue. Oval, London
Result. England 2 Scotland 3

W. Arnott	Queen's Park
W. Berry	Queen's Park
G. Dewar	Dumbarton
J. Kelly	Celtic
A. Latta	Dumbarton
J. McLaren	Celtic
J. McPherson	Cowlairs
N. Munro	Abercon
J. Oswald	Third Lanark
R. Smellie	Queen's Park
J. Wilson	Vale of Leven

Date. April 5, 1890
Venue. Hampden Park, Glasgow
Result. Scotland 1 England 1
Goalscorers. Scotland: Johnstone
England: Wood
Referee. J. Reid (Irish Assoc.)
Linesmen. C. Campbell (Pres. S.F.A.)
R. P. Gregson (Lancashire Assoc.)

J. Wilson	Vale of Leven
W. Arnott	Queen's Park
M. McKeown	Celtic
T. Robertson	Queen's Park
J. Kelly	Celtic
J. McLaren (Captain)	Celtic
W. Groves	Celtic
W. Berry	Queen's Park
W. Johnstone	Third Lanark
J. McPherson	Cowlairs
J. McCall	Renton

Date. April 6, 1891 *Venue*. Blackburn *Result*. England 2 Scotland 1	W. Arnott	Queen's Park
	D. Baird	Heart of Midlothian
	I. Begbie	Heart of Midlothian
	W. Berry	Queen's Park
	J. Hill	Heart of Midlothian
	J. McPherson	Heart of Midlothian
	G. Rankin	Vale of Leven
	W. Sellar	Queen's Park
	R. Smellie	Queen's Park
	F. Watt	Kilbirnie
	J. Wilson	Vale of Leven
Date. April 2, 1892 *Venue*. Glasgow *Result*. Scotland 0 England 4	W. Arnott	Queen's Park
	J. Bell	Dumbarton
	D. Doyle	Celtic
	J. Kelly	Celtic
	J. McLeod	Dumbarton
	A. McMahon	Celtic
	D. Mitchell	Rangers
	W. Sellar	Queen's Park
	D. C. Sillars	Queen's Park
	W. Taylor	Heart of Midlothian
	T. Waddell	Queen's Park
Date. April 1, 1893 *Venue*. Richmond *Result*. England 5 Scotland 2	W. Arnott	Queen's Park
	J. Campbell	Celtic
	J. Hamilton	Queen's Park
	J. Kelly	Celtic
	J. Lindsay	Renton
	A. McMahon	Celtic
	W. Maley	Celtic
	D. Mitchell	Rangers
	W. Sellar	Queen's Park
	R. Smellie	Queen's Park
	T. Waddell	Queen's Park
Date. April 7, 1894 *Venue*. Glasgow *Result*. Scotland 2 England 2	I. Begbie	Heart of Midlothian
	J. Blessington	Celtic
	D. Doyle	Celtic
	W. Gulliland	Queen's Park
	D. Haddow	Rangers
	W. Lambie	Queen's Park
	A. McCreadie	Rangers
	A. McMahon	Celtic
	J. McPherson	Rangers
	D. Mitchell	Rangers
	D. C. Sillars	Queen's Park
Date. April 6, 1895 *Venue*. Goodison Park, Liverpool *Result*. England 3 Scotland 0 *Goalscorers*. Bloomer, Smith, Gibson (o.g.)	D. McArthur	Celtic
	J. Drummond	Rangers
	D. Doyle	Celtic
	J. Simpson	Third Lanark
	J. Russell	Heart of Midlothian
	N. Gibson	Rangers
	W. Gulliland	Queen's Park
	T. Waddell	Queen's Park
	J. Oswald (Captain)	St Bernard
	J. McPherson	Rangers
	W. Lambie	Queen's Park

Date. April 4, 1896
Venue. Celtic Park, Glasgow
Result. Scotland 2 England 1
Goalscorers. Scotland: Lambie, Bell
England: Bassett
Referee. H. Jones (Wales)
Linesmen. Mr Harrison (Scotland)
Mr Jackson (England)

J. Doig	Sunderland
J. Drummond (Captain)	Rangers
T. Brandon	Blackburn Rovers
J. Cowan	Aston Villa
N. Gibson	Rangers
E. Hogg	Heart of Midlothian
W. Lambie	Queen's Park
A. King	Heart of Midlothian
T. Hyslop	Stoke City
J. Bell	Everton
J. Blessington	Celtic

Date. April 3, 1897
Venue. Crystal Palace, London
Result. England 1 Scotland 2
Goalscorers. England: Bloomer
Scotland: Hyslop, Millar
Referee. R. T. Gough (Wales)
Linesmen. Mr Crichton (Scotland)
Mr Sherrington (England)

J. Patrick	St Mirren
N. Smith	Rangers
D. Doyle	Celtic
N. Gibson	Rangers
J. Cowan	Aston Villa
H. Wilson	Sunderland
J. Bell	Everton
J. Millar	Rangers
J. Allan	Liverpool
T. Hyslop	Rangers
W. Lambie (Captain)	Queen's Park

Date. April 2, 1898
Venue. Celtic Park, Glasgow
Result. Scotland 1 England 3
Goalscorers. Scotland: Millar
England: Wheldon, Bloomer (2)
Referee. T. Robertson

K. Anderson	Queen's Park
J. Drummond	Rangers
D. Doyle	Celtic
N. Gibson	Rangers
J. Cowan	Aston Villa
J. Robertson	Everton
J. Bell	Everton
J. Campbell	Celtic
W. Maxwell	Stoke City
J. Millar	Rangers
A. Smith	Rangers

Date. April 8, 1899
Venue. Birmingham
Result. England 2 Scotland 1

J. Bell	Everton
J. Campbell	Rangers
A. J. Christie	Queen's Park
J. E. Doig	Arbroath
N. Gibson	Rangers
R. C. Hamilton	Rangers
R. S. McColl	Queen's Park
H. Morgan	St Mirren
J. T. Robertson	Southampton
N. Smith	Rangers
D. Storrier	Celtic

Date. April 7, 1900
Venue. Celtic Park, Glasgow
Result. Scotland 4 England 1

H. Rennie	Heart of Midlothian
N. Smith	Rangers
J. Drummond	Rangers
N. Gibson	Rangers
A. Raisbeck	Liverpool
J. Robertson (Captain)	Rangers
J. Bell	Celtic
R. Walker	Heart of Midlothian
R. McColl	Queen's Park
J. Campbell	Celtic
A. Smith	Rangers

Date. March 30, 1901
Venue. Crystal Palace, London
Result. England 2 Scotland 2

H. Rennie	Hibernian
B. Battles	Celtic
J. Drummond	Rangers
A. Aitken	Newcastle United
A. Raisbeck	Liverpool
J. Robertson (Captain)	Rangers
R. Walker	Heart of Midlothian
J. Campbell	Celtic
R. McColl	Queen's Park
R. Hamilton	Rangers
A. Smith	Rangers

Date. April 5, 1902
Venue. Ibrox Park, Glasgow
Result. Scotland 1 England 1
Remarks. Ibrox Disaster – match declared unofficial

J. Doig	Sunderland
N. Smith	Rangers
J. Drummond	Rangers
A. Aitken	Newcastle United
A. Raisbeck	Liverpool
J. Robertson	Rangers
R. Templeton	Aston Villa
R. Walker	Heart of Midlothian
A. Brown	Tottenham Hotspur
G. Livingstone	Celtic
A. Smith	Rangers

Date. May 3, 1902
Venue. Birmingham
Result. England 2 Scotland 2

H. Rennie	Hibernian
N. Smith	Rangers
J. Drummond	Rangers
A. Aitken (Captain)	Newcastle United
A. Raisbeck	Liverpool
J. Robertson	Rangers
R. Templeton	Aston Villa
R. Walker	Heart of Midlothian
R. McColl	Newcastle United
R. Orr	Newcastle United
A. Smith	Rangers

Date. April 4, 1903
Venue. Sheffield
Result. England 1 Scotland 2

J. Doig	Sunderland
A. McCombie	Sunderland
J. Watson	Sunderland
A. Aitken	Newcastle United
A. Raisbeck	Liverpool
J. Robertson	Rangers
R. Templeton	Newcastle United
R. Walker	Heart of Midlothian
R. Hamilton	Rangers
F. Speedie	Rangers
A. Smith	Rangers

Date. April 9, 1904
Venue. Celtic Park, Glasgow
Result. Scotland 0 England 1
Goalscorer. Bloomer
Referee. Mr Nunnerley (Wales)

P. McBride	Preston North End
T. Jackson	St Mirren
J. Watson	Sunderland
A. Aitken	Newcastle United
A. Raisbeck	Liverpool
J. Robertson (Captain)	Rangers
R. Templeton	Newcastle United
R. Orr	Newcastle United
A. Brown	Middlesbrough
R. Walker	Heart of Midlothian
T. Niblo	Aston Villa

Date. April 1, 1905
Venue. Crystal Palace, London
Result. England 1 Scotland 0

J. Lyall	Sheffield Wednesday
A. McCombie	Newcastle United
J. Watson	Sunderland
A. Aitken	Newcastle United
C. Thomson	Heart of Midlothian
P. McWilliam	Newcastle United
R. Walker	Heart of Midlothian
J. Howie	Newcastle United
A. Young	Everton
P. Somers	Celtic
G. Wilson	Heart of Midlothian

Date. April 7, 1906
Venue. Hampden Park, Glasgow
Result. Scotland 2 England 1

P. McBride	Preston North End
D. McLeod	Celtic
W. Dunlop	Liverpool
A. Aitken	Newcastle United
A. Raisbeck	Liverpool
P. McWilliam	Newcastle United
G. Stewart	Hibernian
J. Howie	Newcastle United
A. Menzies	Heart of Midlothian
G. Livingstone	Manchester City
A. Smith	Rangers

Date. April 6, 1907
Venue. St James Park, Newcastle
Result. England 1 Scotland 1
Goalscorers. England: Bloomer
Scotland: Crompton (o.g.)
Referee. T. Robertson (Glasgow)
Linesmen. A. G. Hines (England)
J. Liddell (Scotland)

P. McBride	Preston North End
J. Sharp	Arsenal
G. Thomson	Heart of Midlothian
A. Aitken	Middlesbrough
A. Raisbeck (Captain)	Liverpool
P. McWilliam	Newcastle United
G. Stewart	Manchester City
R. Walker	Heart of Midlothian
A. Wilson	Sheffield Wednesday
W. White	Bolton Wanderers
G. Wilson	Everton

Date. April 4, 1908
Venue. Hampden Park, Glasgow
Result. Scotland 1 England 1
Goalscorers. Scotland: Wilson
England: Windridge
Referee. J. Mason (Burslem)
Linesmen. J. Liddell (Scotland)
J. Lewis (England)

P. McBride	Preston North End
A. McNair	Celtic
J. Sharp	Arsenal
A. Aitken	Middlesbrough
C. Thomson (Captain)	Heart of Midlothian
J. May	Rangers
J. Howie	Newcastle United
R. Walker	Heart of Midlothian
A. Wilson	Sheffield Wednesday
W. White	Bolton Wanderers
J. Quinn	Celtic

Date. April 3, 1909
Venue. Crystal Palace, London
Result. England 2 Scotland 0
Goalscorer. Wall (2)

J. Brownlie	Third Lanark
J. Cameron	Chelsea
J. Watson	Middlesbrough
A. McNair	Celtic
J. Stark	Rangers
P. McWilliam	Newcastle United
A. Bennett	Rangers
R. Walker	Heart of Midlothian
J. Quinn	Celtic
G. Wilson	Newcastle United
H. Paul	Queen's Park

Date. April 2, 1910
Venue. Hampden Park, Glasgow
Result. Scotland 2 England 0
Goalscorers. McMenemy, Quinn
Referee. J. Mason (Burslem)
Linesmen. W. Lorimer (Scotland)
J. Lewis (England)

J. Brownlie	Third Lanark
G. Law	Rangers
J. Hay	Celtic
A. Aitken	Leicester Fosse
C. Thomson (Captain)	Sunderland
P. McWilliam	Newcastle United
A. Bennett	Rangers
J. McMenemy	Celtic
J. Quinn	Celtic
A. Higgins	Newcastle United
R. Templeton	Kilmarnock

Date. April 1, 1911
Venue. Goodison Park, Liverpool
Result. England 1 Scotland 1
Goalscorers. England: Stewart
Scotland: Higgins
Referee. W. Nunnerly (Wales)
Linesmen. S. D. Peers (England)
A. M. Robertson (Scotland)

J. Lawrence	Newcastle United
D. Colman	Aberdeen
J. Walker	Swindon Town
A. Aitken	Leicester Fosse
W. Low	Newcastle United
J. Hay (Captain)	Celtic
A. Bennett	Rangers
J. McMenemy	Celtic
W. Reid	Rangers
A. Higgins	Newcastle United
A. Smith	Rangers

Date. March 23, 1912
Venue. Hampden Park, Glasgow
Result. Scotland 1 England 1
Goalscorers. Scotland: Wilson
England: Holley
Referee. J. Mason (Burslem)
Linesmen. J. Black (Scotland)
G. Wagstaff Simmons (England)

J. Brownlie	Third Lanark
A. McNair (Captain)	Celtic
J. Walker	Swindon Town
J. Gordon	Rangers
C. Thomson	Sunderland
J. Hay	Newcastle United
R. Templeton	Kilmarnock
R. Walker	Heart of Midlothian
D. McLean	Sheffield Wednesday
A. Wilson	Sheffield Wednesday
J. Quinn	Celtic

Date. April 5, 1913
Venue. Stamford Bridge, London
Result. England 1 Scotland 0
Goalscorer. Hampton
Referee. A. A. Jackson (Glasgow)
Linesmen. A. Kingscott (England)
H. S. McLauchlan (Scotland)

J. Brownlie	Third Lanark
A. McNair	Celtic
J. Walker	Swindon Town
J. Gordon	Rangers
C. Thomson (Captain)	Sunderland
D. Wilson	Oldham Athletic
J. Donnachie	Oldham Athletic
R. Walker	Heart of Midlothian
W. Reid	Rangers
A. Wilson	Sheffield Wednesday
G. Robertson	Sheffield Wednesday

Date. April 4, 1914
Venue. Hampden Park, Glasgow
Result. Scotland 3 England 1
Goalscorers. Scotland: Thomson, McMenemy, Reid
England: Fleming
Referee. H. S. Bamlett (Gateshead)
Linesmen. D. Campbell (Scotland)
M. Bilston (England)

J. Brownlie	Third Lanark
A. McNair	Celtic
J. Dodds	Celtic
J. Gordon (Captain)	Rangers
C. Thomson	Sunderland
J. Hay	Newcastle United
A. Donaldson	Bolton Wanderers
J. McMenemy	Celtic
W. Reid	Rangers
J. A. Croal	Falkirk
J. Donnachie	Oldham Athletic

Date. April 26, 1919
Venue. Goodison Park, Liverpool
Result. England 2 Scotland 2
Goalscorers. England: Turnbull, Puddefoot
Scotland: Wright, McMenemy
Referee. A. Warner (Nottingham)
Remarks. Unofficial 'Victory' match

J. Brownlie	Morton
A. McNair	Celtic
J. Blair	Rangers
J. Gordon	Rangers
J. Wright	Morton
J. McMullan	Partick Thistle
A. Donaldson	Bolton Wanderers
J. Bowie	Rangers
J. Richardson	Ayr United
J. McMenemy	Celtic
A. Morton	Queen's Park

Date. May 3, 1919
Venue. Hampden Park, Glasgow
Result. Scotland 3 England 4
Goalscorers. Scotland: Wilson (2), Morton
England: Grimsdell (2), Puddefoot (2)
Referee. A. A. Jackson (Glasgow)
Remarks. Unofficial 'Victory' match

J. Brownlie	Morton
A. McNair	Celtic
J. Blair	Rangers
J. Gordon	Rangers
J. Wright	Morton
J. McMullan	Partick Thistle
J. Reid	Airdrieonians
J. Bowie	Rangers
A. Wilson	Heart of Midlothian
J. McMenemy	Celtic
A. Morton	Queen's Park

Date. April 10, 1920
Venue. Hillsborough, Sheffield
Result. England 4 Scotland 4
Goalscorers. England: Kelly (2), Morris, Cock, Quantrill
Scotland: Miller (2), Wilson, Donaldson
Referee. T. Dougray (Scotland)

K. Campbell	Liverpool
A. McNair (Captain)	Celtic
J. Blair	Sheffield Wednesday
J. Bowie	Rangers
W. Low	Newcastle United
J. Gordon	Rangers
A. Donaldson	Bolton Wanderers
T. Miller	Liverpool
A. Wilson	Dunfermline
J. Paterson	Leicester City
A. Troup	Dundee

Date. April 9, 1921
Venue. Hampden Park, Glasgow
Result. Scotland 3 England 0
Goalscorers. Wilson, Morton, Cunningham
Referee. A. Ward (Kirkham)

J. Ewart	Bradford City
J. Marshall (Captain)	Middlesbrough
J. Blair	Cardiff City
S. Davidson	Middlesbrough
G. Brewster	Everton
J. McMullan	Partick Thistle
A. McNab	Morton
T. Miller	Manchester United
A. Wilson	Dunfermline Athletic
A. Cunningham	Rangers
A. Morton	Rangers

Date. April 8, 1922
Venue. Villa Park, Birmingham
Result. England 0 Scotland 1
Goalscorer. Wilson
Referee. T. Dougray (Bellshill)

K. Campbell	Partick Thistle
J. Marshall	Middlesbrough
J. Blair (Captain)	Cardiff City
J. Gilchrist	Celtic
W. Cringan	Celtic
N. McBain	Manchester United
A. Archibald	Rangers
J. Crosbie	Birmingham City
A. Wilson	Middlesbrough
T. Cairns	Rangers
A. Morton	Rangers

Date. April 14, 1923
Venue. Hampden Park, Glasgow
Result. Scotland 2 England 2
Goalscorers. Scotland: Cunningham, Wilson
England: Kelly, Watson
Referee. A. Ward (Kirkham)

W. Harper	Hibernian
J. Hutton	Aberdeen
J. Blair	Cardiff City
D. Steele	Huddersfield Town
W. Cringan (Captain)	Celtic
T. Muirhead	Rangers
D. Lawson	St Mirren
A. Cunningham	Rangers
A. Wilson	Middlesbrough
T. Cairns	Rangers
A. Morton	Rangers

Date. April 12, 1924
Venue. Wembley, London
Result. England 1 Scotland 1
Goalscorers. England: Walker
Scotland: Cowan
Referee. T. Dougray (Bellshill)

W. Harper	Hibernian
J. Smith	Ayr United
P. McCloy	Ayr United
W. Clunas	Sunderland
D. Morris	Raith Rovers
J. McMullan (Captain)	Partick Thistle
A. Archibald	Rangers
W. Cowan	Newcastle United
N. Harris	Newcastle United
A. Cunningham	Rangers
A. Morton	Rangers

Date. April 4, 1925
Venue. Hampden Park, Glasgow
Result. Scotland 2 England 0
Goalscorer. Gallacher (2)
Referee. A. Ward (Kirkham)

W. Harper	Hibernian
W. McStay	Celtic
P. McCloy	Ayr United
D. Meiklejohn	Rangers
D. Morris (Captain)	Raith Rovers
J. McMullan	Partick Thistle
A. Jackson	Aberdeen
W. Russell	Airdrieonians
H. Gallacher	Airdrieonians
T. Cairns	Rangers
A. Morton	Rangers

Date. April 17, 1926
Venue. Old Trafford, Manchester
Result. England 0 Scotland 1
Goalscorer. Jackson
Referee. T. Dougray (Bellshill)

W. Harper	Arsenal
J. Hutton	Aberdeen
W. McStay (Captain)	Celtic
J. Gibson	Partick Thistle
W. Summers	St Mirren
J. McMullan	Manchester City
A. Jackson	Huddersfield Town
A. Thomson	Celtic
H. Gallacher	Newcastle United
A. Cunningham	Rangers
A. Troup	Everton

Date. April 2, 1927
Venue. Hampden Park, Glasgow
Result. Scotland 1 England 2
Goalscorers. Scotland: Morton
England: Dean (2)
Referee. A. Ward (Kirkham)

J. Harkness	Queen's Park
W. McStay	Celtic
R. Thomson	Falkirk
T. Morrison	St Mirren
J. Gibson	Partick Thistle
J. McMullan	Manchester City
A. McLean	Celtic
A. Cunningham	Rangers
H. Gallacher	Newcastle United
R. McPhail	Airdrieonians
A. Morton	Rangers

Date. March 31, 1928
Venue. Wembley, London
Result. England 1 Scotland 5
Goalscorers. England: Kelly
Scotland: Jackson (3), James (2)
Referee. W. Bell (Motherwell)

J. Harkness	Queen's Park
J. Nelson	Cardiff City
T. Law	Chelsea
J. Gibson	Aston Villa
T. Bradshaw	Bury
J. McMullan	Manchester City
A. Jackson	Huddersfield Town
J. Dunn	Hibernian
H. Gallacher	Newcastle United
A. James	Preston North End
A. Morton	Rangers

Date. April 13, 1929
Venue. Hampden Park, Glasgow
Result. Scotland 1 England 0
Goalscorer. Cheyne
Referee. A. Josephs (South Shields)

J. Harkness	Heart of Midlothian
J. Crapnell	Airdrieonians
J. Nibloe	Kilmarnock
J. Buchanan	Rangers
D. Meiklejohn	Rangers
J. McMullan (Captain)	Manchester City
A. Jackson	Huddersfield Town
A. Cheyne	Aberdeen
H. Gallacher	Newcastle United
A. James	Preston North End
A. Morton	Rangers

Date. April 5, 1930
Venue. Wembley, London
Result. England 5 Scotland 2
Goalscorers. England: Watson (2), Rimmer (2), Jack
Scotland: Fleming (2)
Referee. W. McLean (Ireland)

J. Harkness	Heart of Midlothian
D. Gray	Rangers
T. Law	Chelsea
J. Buchanan	Rangers
D. Meiklejohn	Rangers
T. Craig	Rangers
A. Jackson	Huddersfield Town
A. James	Arsenal
J. Fleming	Rangers
G. Stevenson	Motherwell
A. Morton	Rangers

Date. March 28, 1931
Venue. Hampden Park, Glasgow
Result. Scotland 2 England 0
Goalscorers. Stevenson, McGrory
Referee. A. J. Atwood (Wales)

J. Thomson	Celtic
D. Blair	Clyde
J. Nibloe	Kilmarnock
C. McNab	Dundee
D. Meiklejohn (Captain)	Rangers
J. Miller	St Mirren
A. Archibald	Rangers
G. Stevenson	Motherwell
J. McGrory	Celtic
R. McPhail	Rangers
A. Morton	Rangers

Date. April 9, 1932
Venue. Wembley, London
Result. England 3 Scotland 0
Goalscorers. Waring, Barclay, Crook
Referee. S. Thompson (Belfast)
Linesmen. S. F. Rous (Herts)
T. Dougary (Rutherglen)

T. Hamilton	Rangers
J. Crapnell (Captain)	Airdrieonians
J. Nibloe	Kilmarnock
C. McNab	Dundee
A. Craig	Motherwell
G. C. P. Brown	Rangers
A. Archibald	Rangers
J. Marshall	Rangers
N. Dewar	Third Lanark
C. Napier	Celtic
A. Morton	Rangers

Date. April 1, 1933 *Venue*. Hampden Park, Glasgow *Result*. Scotland 2 England 1 *Goalscorers*. Scotland: McGrory (2) England: Hunt *Referee*. S. Thompson (Belfast)	J. Jackson A. Anderson W. McGonagle P. Wilson R. Gillespie G. Brown J. Crawford J. Marshall J. McGrory R. McPhail D. Duncan	Partick Thistle Heart of Midlothian Celtic Celtic Queen's Park Rangers Queen's Park Rangers Celtic Rangers Derby County
Date. April 14, 1934 *Venue*. Wembley, London *Result*. England 3 Scotland 0 *Goalscorers*. Bastin, Brooke, Bowers *Referee*. S. Thompson (Belfast)	J. Jackson A. Anderson W. McGonagle A. Massie (Captain) J. Smith J. Miller W. Cook J. Marshall H. Gallacher G. Stevenson J. Connor	Chelsea Heart of Midlothian Celtic Heart of Midlothian Kilmarnock St Mirren Bolton Wanderers Rangers Chelsea Motherwell Sunderland
Date. April 6, 1935 *Venue*. Hampden Park, Glasgow *Result*. Scotland 2 England 0 *Goalscorer*. Duncan (2) *Referee*. S. Thompson (Belfast)	J. Jackson A. Anderson G. Cummings A. Massie J. Simpson G. Brown C. Napier T. Walker H. Gallacher R. McPhail D. Duncan	Chelsea Heart of Midlothian Partick Thistle Heart of Midlothian Rangers Rangers Celtic Heart of Midlothian Derby County Rangers Derby County
Date. April 4, 1936 *Venue*. Wembley, London *Result*. England 1 Scotland 1 *Goalscorers*. England: Camsell Scotland: Walker *Referee*. W. R. Hamilton (Ireland)	J. Dawson A. Anderson G. Cummings A. Massie J. Simpson G. Brown J. Crum T. Walker D. McCulloch A. Venters D. Duncan	Rangers Heart of Midlothian Aston Villa Aston Villa Rangers Rangers Celtic Heart of Midlothian Brentford Rangers Derby County
Date. April 17, 1937 *Venue*. Hampden Park, Glasgow *Result*. Scotland 3 England 1 *Goalscorers*. Scotland: O'Donnell, McPhail (2) England: Steele *Referee*. W. McClean (Ireland)	J. Dawson A. Anderson A. Beattie A. Massie J. Simpson G. Brown J. Delaney T. Walker F. O'Donnell R. McPhail D. Duncan	Rangers Heart of Midlothian Preston North End Aston Villa Rangers Rangers Celtic Heart of Midlothian Preston North End Rangers Derby County

Date. April 9, 1938
Venue. Wembley, London
Result. England 0 Scotland 1
Goalscorer. Walker
Referee. W. R. Hamilton (Belfast)

D. Cumming	Middlesbrough
A. Anderson	Heart of Midlothian
A. Beattie	Preston North End
W. Shankley	Preston North End
T. Smith	Preston North End
G. Brown	Rangers
J. Milne	Middlesbrough
T. Walker	Heart of Midlothian
F. O'Donnell	Blackpool
G. Mutch	Preston North End
R. Reid	Brentford

Date. April 15, 1939
Venue. Hampden Park, Glasgow
Result. Scotland 1 England 2
Goalscorers. Scotland: Dougal
England: Beasley, Lawton
Referee. W. R. Hamilton (Belfast)

J. Dawson	Rangers
J. Carabine	Third Lanark
G. Cummings	Aston Villa
W. Shankley	Preston North End
R. Baxter	Middlesbrough
A. McNab	West Bromwich Albion
A. McSpadyen	Partick Thistle
T. Walker	Heart of Midlothian
J. Dougal	Preston North End
A. Venters	Rangers
J. Milne	Middlesbrough

Date. October 14, 1944
Venue. Wembley, London
Result. England 6 Scotland 2
Goalscorers. Scotland: Walker, Milne

D. Cumming	Middlesbrough
J. F. Stephen	Bradford
G. Cumming	Aston Villa
R. B. Thyne	Darlington
R. Baxter	Middlesbrough
A. Macaulay	West Ham United
G. Smith	Hibernian
T. Walker	Heart of Midlothian
A. Milne	Hibernian
A. Black	Heart of Midlothian
J. Caskie	Everton

Date. February 3, 1945
Venue. Villa Park, Birmingham
Result. England 2 Scotland 3
Goalscorers. Scotland: Delaney, Dodds

R. Brown	Queen's Park
J. Harley	Liverpool
J. F. Stephen	Bradford
M. Busby	Liverpool
R. B. Thyne	Darlington
A. Macaulay	West Ham United
J. Delaney	Celtic
W. Fagan	Liverpool
E. Dodds	Blackpool
A. Black	Heart of Midlothian
W. Liddell	Liverpool

Date. April 14, 1945
Venue. Hampden Park, Glasgow
Result. Scotland 1 England 6
Goalscorer. Scotland: Johnstone
Referee. J. S. Cox (Rutherglen)
Linesmen. M. A. Mann (Perth)
A. Watt (Edinburgh)
Remarks. Bogan sustained a broken leg in the first minute and was replaced by L. Johnstone (Clyde) after 15-minutes' play

R. Brown	Queen's Park
J. Harley	Liverpool
J. F. Stephen	Bradford
M. Busby	Liverpool
J. Harris	Wolverhampton Wanderers
A. Macaulay	West Ham United
W. Waddell	Rangers
T. Bogan	Hibernian
A. Harris	Queen's Park
A. Black	Heart of Midlothian
R. Kelly	Greenock Morton

Date. April 13, 1946 *Venue.* Hampden Park, Glasgow *Result.* Scotland 1 England 0 *Goalscorer.* Delaney *Referee.* P. Craigmyle (Aberdeen)	R. Brown D. Shaw J. Shaw W. Campbell F. Brennan J. Husband W. Waddell N. Dougal J. Delaney G. Hamilton W. Liddell	Queen's Park Hibernian Rangers Greenock Morton Airdrieonians Partick Thistle Rangers Birmingham City Manchester United Aberdeen Liverpool
Date. April 12, 1947 *Venue.* Wembley, London *Result.* England 1 Scotland 1 *Goalscorer.* Scotland: McLaren *Referee.* C. H. Delasalle (France) *Linesman.* A. Watt (Edinburgh)	W. Miller G. Young J. Shaw A. Macaulay W. Woodburn A. Forbes G. Smith A. McLaren J. Delaney W. Steel T. Pearson	Celtic Rangers Rangers Brentford Rangers Sheffield United Hibernian Preston North End Manchester United Greenock Morton Newcastle United
Date. April 10, 1948 *Venue.* Hampden Park, Glasgow *Result.* Scotland 0 England 2 *Linesman.* L. J. Oates (Kirkcaldy)	I. Black J. Govan D. Shaw W. Campbell G. Young A. Macaulay J. Delaney R. Coombe W. Thornton W. Steel W. Liddell	Southampton Hibernian Hibernian Morton Rangers Arsenal Manchester United Hibernian Rangers Derby County Liverpool
Date. April 9, 1949 *Venue.* Wembley, London *Result.* England 1 Scotland 3 *Goalscorers.* England: Milburn Scotland: Mason, Steel, Reilly *Referee.* B. M. Griffiths (Newport) *Linesmen.* F. Owen (Llay) F. Roberts (Bangor)	J. Cowan G. Young (Captain) S. R. Cox R. Evans W. A. Woodburn G. Aitken W. Waddell J. Mason W. Houliston W. Steel L. Reilly	Morton Rangers Rangers Celtic Rangers East Fife Rangers Third Lanark Queen of the South Derby County Hibernian
Date. April 15, 1950 *Venue.* Hampden Park, Glasgow *Result.* Scotland 0 England 1	J. Cowan G. Young S. Cox I. McColl W. Woodburn A. Forbes W. Waddell W. Moir W. Bauld W. Steel W. Liddell	Greenock Morton Rangers Rangers Rangers Rangers Arsenal Rangers Bolton Wanderers Heart of Midlothian Derby County Liverpool

Date. April 14, 1951 *Venue*. Wembley, London *Result*. England 2 Scotland 3 *Goalscorers*. Scotland: Johnstone, Reilly, Liddell	J. Cowan G. Young S. Cox R. Evans W. Woodburn W. Redpath W. Waddell R. Johnstone L. Reilly W. Steel W. Liddell	Greenock Morton Rangers Rangers Celtic Rangers Motherwell Rangers Hibernian Hibernian Dundee Liverpool
Date. April 5, 1952 *Venue*. Hampden Park, Glasgow *Result*. Scotland 1 England 2 *Goalscorers*. Scotland: Reilly England: Pearson (2) *Referee*. P. Morris (Belfast) *Linesmen*. T. J. Mitchell (Lurgan) J. Davidson (Newtonards)	R. Brown G. Young (Captain) W. McNaught J. Scoular W. Woodburn W. Redpath G. Smith R. Johnstone L. Reilly J. L. McMillan W. Liddell	Rangers Rangers Raith Rovers Portsmouth Rangers Motherwell Hibernian Hibernian Hibernian Airdrieonians Liverpool
Date. April 18, 1953 *Venue*. Wembley, London *Result*. England 2 Scotland 2 *Goalscorers*. Scotland: Reilly (2) *Referee*. T. J. Mitchell *Linesmen*. R. J. Quail J. Davidson	G. Farm G. Young S. Cox T. Docherty F. Brennan D. Cowie T. Wright R. Johnstone L. Reilly W. Steel W. Liddell	Blackpool Rangers Rangers Preston North End Newcastle United Dundee Sunderland Hibernian Hibernian Dundee Liverpool
Date. April 3, 1954 *Venue*. Hampden Park, Glasgow *Result*. Scotland 2 England 4 *Goalscorers*. Scotland: Brown, Byrne (o.g.)	G. Farm M. Haughney S. Cox R. Evans F. Brennan G. Aitken J. McKenzie R. Johnstone J. Henderson A. Brown W. Ormond	Blackpool Celtic Rangers Celtic Newcastle United Sunderland Partick Thistle Hibernian Portsmouth Blackpool Hibernian
Date. April 2, 1955 *Venue*. Wembley, London *Result*. England 7 Scotland 2 *Goalscorers*. England: Wilshaw (4), Lofthouse (2), Revie Scotland: Reilly, Docherty *Referee*. B. M. Griffiths (Newport) *Linesmen*. T. L. Davies (Glamorgan) H. Williams (Glamorgan)	F. Martin W. Cunningham (Captain) H. Haddock T. Docherty J. Davidson J. Cumming J. McKenzie R. Johnstone L. Reilly J. L. McMillan T. Ring	Aberdeen Preston North End Clyde Preston North End Partick Thistle Heart of Midlothian Partick Thistle Manchester City Hibernian Airdrieonians Clyde

Date. April 14, 1956
Venue. Hampden Park, Glasgow
Result. Scotland 1 England 1
Goalscorers. Scotland: Leggat
England: Haynes
Referee. L. Callaghan (Merthyr Tydfil)
Linesmen. N. H. Jones (Wrexham)
G. H. Lewis (Aberdare)

T. Younger	Hibernian
A. H. Parker	Falkirk
J. Hewie	Charlton Athletic
R. Evans	Celtic
G. Young (Captain)	Rangers
A. Glen	Aberdeen
G. Leggat	Aberdeen
R. Johnstone	Manchester City
L. Reilly	Hibernian
J. L. McMillan	Airdrieonians
G. Smith	Hibernian

Date. April 6, 1957
Venue. Wembley, London
Result. England 2 Scotland 1
Goalscorers. England: Grainger, Edwards
Scotland: Ring
Referee. P. P. Roomer (Holland)
Linesmen. W. Beltman (Holland)
K. Schipper (Holland)

T. Younger	Liverpool
E. Caldow	Rangers
J. Hewie	Charlton Athletic
I. McColl	Rangers
G. Young (Captain)	Rangers
T. Docherty	Preston North End
R. Collins	Celtic
W. Fernie	Celtic
L. Reilly	Hibernian
J. K. Mudie	Blackpool
T. Ring	Clyde

Date. April 19, 1958
Venue. Hampden Park, Glasgow
Result. Scotland 0 England 4
Goalscorers. Charlton, Kevan (2), Douglas
Referee. A. Dusch (Germany)
Linesmen. K. Karle (Germany)
K. Tschenscher (Germany)

T. Younger	Liverpool
A. H. Parker	Falkirk
H. Haddock	Clyde
I. McColl	Rangers
R. Evans	Celtic
T. Docherty (Captain)	Preston North End
G. Herd	Clyde
J. Murray	Heart of Midlothian
J. K. Mudie	Blackpool
T. Forrest	Motherwell
T. Ewing	Partick Thistle

Date. April 11, 1959
Venue. Wembley, London
Result. England 1 Scotland 0
Goalscorer. Charlton
Referee. J. Campos (Portugal)
Linesmen. H. Soaves (Portugal)
E. Gouvlia (Portugal)

W. D. F. Brown	Dundee
D. MacKay	Celtic
E. Caldow	Rangers
T. Docherty	Arsenal
R. Evans (Captain)	Celtic
D. C. Mackay	Tottenham Hotspur
G. Leggat	Fulham
R. Collins	Everton
D. Herd	Arsenal
J. Dick	West Ham United
W. Ormond	Hibernian

Date. April 9, 1960
Venue. Hampden Park, Glasgow
Result. Scotland 1 England 1
Goalscorers. Scotland: Leggat
England: Charlton (pen.)
Referee. E. Sramko (Hungary)
Linesmen. I. Zsolt (Hungary)
V. Kostner (Hungary)

F. Haffey	Celtic
D. MacKay	Celtic
E. Caldow	Rangers
J. Cumming	Heart of Midlothian
R. Evans (Captain)	Celtic
R. J. McCann	Motherwell
G. Leggat	Fulham
A. Young	Heart of Midlothian
I. St John	Motherwell
D. Law	Manchester City
A. Weir	Motherwell

Date. April 15, 1961
Venue. Wembley, London
Result. England 9 Scotland 3
Goalscorers. England: Greaves (3), Haynes (2), Smith (2), Robson, Douglas
Scotland: Wilson (2), Mackay
Referee. M. Lequesne (France)
Linesmen. A. Carette (France)
R. Poncin (France)

F. Haffey	Celtic
R. Shearer	Rangers
E. Caldow (Captain)	Rangers
D. C. Mackay	Tottenham Hotspur
W. McNeill	Celtic
R. J. McCann	Motherwell
J. M. Macleod	Hibernian
D. Law	Manchester City
I. St John	Motherwell
P. Quinn	Motherwell
D. Wilson	Rangers

Date. April 14, 1962
Venue. Hampden Park, Glasgow
Result. Scotland 2 England 0
Goalscorers. Wilson, Caldow (pen.)
Referee. L. Horn (Holland)
Linesmen. D. van Male (Holland)
A. van Leeuwen (Holland)

W. D. F. Brown	Tottenham Hotspur
A. W. Hamilton	Dundee
E. Caldow (Captain)	Rangers
P. T. Crerand	Celtic
W. McNeill	Celtic
J. Baxter	Rangers
A. Scott	Rangers
J. A. White	Tottenham Hotspur
I. St John	Liverpool
D. Law	Turin
D. Wilson	Rangers

Date. April 6, 1963
Venue. Wembley, London
Result. England 1 Scotland 2
Goalscorers. England: Douglas
Scotland: Baxter (2, 1 pen.)
Referee. L. Horn (Holland)
Linesmen. L. van Ravens (Holland)
Van der Veer (Holland)
Remarks. Caldow suffered a fracture of both bones of the left leg six minutes after kick-off and took no further part in the game

W. D. F. Brown	Tottenham Hotspur
A. W. Hamilton	Dundee
E. Caldow (Captain)	Rangers
D. C. Mackay	Tottenham Hotspur
J. F. Ure	Dundee
J. Baxter	Rangers
W. Henderson	Rangers
J. A. White	Tottenham Hotspur
I. St John	Liverpool
D. Law	Manchester United
D. Wilson	Rangers

Date. April 11, 1964
Venue. Hampden Park, Glasgow
Result. Scotland 1 England 0
Goalscorer. Gilzean
Referee. L. Horn (Holland)
Linesmen. A. Aalbrecht (Holland)
C. Arkenbout (Holland)

R. C. Forsyth	Kilmarnock
A. W. Hamilton	Dundee
J. Kennedy	Celtic
J. Greig	Rangers
W. McNeill (Captain)	Celtic
J. Baxter	Rangers
W. Henderson	Rangers
J. A. White	Tottenham Hotspur
A. J. Gilzean	Dundee
D. Law	Manchester United
D. Wilson	Rangers

Date. April 10, 1965
Venue. Wembley, London
Result. England 2 Scotland 2
Goalscorers. England: Charlton, Greaves
Scotland: Law, St John
Referee. I. Zsolt (Hungary)
Linesmen. J. Fohervari (Hungary)
G. Emsberger (Hungary)
Remarks. England played all of the second half without their left-back, Wilson

W. D. F. Brown	Tottenham Hotspur
A. W. Hamilton	Dundee
E. G. McCreadie	Chelsea
P. T. Crerand	Manchester United
W. McNeill (Captain)	Celtic
J. Greig	Rangers
W. Henderson	Rangers
R. Collins	Leeds United
I. St John	Liverpool
D. Law	Manchester United
D. Wilson	Rangers

Date. April 2, 1966
Venue. Hampden Park, Glasgow
Result. Scotland 3 England 4
Goalscorers. Scotland: Law, Johnstone (2)
England: Hurst, Hunt (2), Charlton
Referee. H. Faucheux (France)
Linesmen. J. Lamour (France)
J. Malleville (France)

R. Ferguson	Kilmarnock
J. Greig (Captain)	Rangers
T. Gemmell	Celtic
R. Murdoch	Celtic
R. McKinnon	Rangers
J. Baxter	Sunderland
J. Johnstone	Celtic
D. Law	Manchester United
W. S. B. Wallace	Heart of Midlothian
W. J. Bremner	Leeds United
W. Johnston	Rangers

Date. April 15, 1967
Venue. Wembley, London
Result. England 2 Scotland 3
Goalscorers. England: J. Charlton, Hurst
Scotland: Law, Lennox, McCalliog
Referee. G. Schulenburg (West Germany)
Linesmen. E. Schafer (West Germany)
U. Wolf (West Germany)

R. Simpson	Celtic
T. Gemmell	Celtic
E. McCreadie	Chelsea
J. Greig (Captain)	Rangers
R. McKinnon	Rangers
J. Baxter	Sunderland
W. Wallace	Celtic
W. Bremner	Leeds United
J. McCalliog	Sheffield Wednesday
D. Law	Manchester United
R. Lennox	Celtic

Date. February 24, 1968
Venue. Hampden Park, Glasgow
Result. Scotland 1 England 1
Goalscorers. Scotland: Hughes
England: Peters
Referee. L. van Ravens (Holland)
Linesmen. W. J. M. Schalks (Holland)
J. Byleveld (Holland)

R. Simpson	Celtic
T. Gemmell	Celtic
E. McCreadie	Chelsea
W. McNeil	Celtic
R. McKinnon	Rangers
J. Greig (Captain)	Rangers
C. Cooke	Chelsea
W. Bremner	Leeds United
J. Hughes	Celtic
W. Johnston	Rangers
R. Lennox	Celtic

Date. May 10, 1969
Venue. Wembley, London
Result. England 4 Scotland 1
Goalscorers. England: Peters (2), Hurst (2)
Scotland: Stein
Referee. R. Helies (France)
Linesmen. A. Carette (France)
L. Dhumberelle (France)
Remarks. W. Wallace (Celtic) substituted for Gilzean towards the end of the match

J. Herriot	Birmingham City
E. McCreadie	Chelsea
T. Gemmell	Celtic
R. Murdoch	Celtic
W. McNeil	Celtic
J. Greig	Rangers
W. Henderson	Rangers
W. Bremner (Captain)	Leeds United
C. Stein	Rangers
A. Gilzean	Tottenham Hotspur
E. Gray	Leeds United

Date. April 25, 1970
Venue. Hampden Park, Glasgow
Result. Scotland 0 England 0
Referee. G. Schulenburg (West Germany)
Linesmen. W. Horstmann (West Germany)
E. Schafer (West Germany)
Remarks. A. Gilzean (Tottenham Hotspur) substituted for Moncur a few minutes from the end of the match

J. Cruickshank	Heart of Midlothian
T. Gemmell	Celtic
W. Dickson	Kilmarnock
J. Greig (Captain)	Rangers
R. MacKinnon	Rangers
R. Moncur	Newcastle United
J. Johnstone	Celtic
D. Hay	Celtic
C. Stein	Rangers
J. O'Hare	Derby County
W. Carr	Coventry City

Date. May 22, 1971
Venue. Wembley, London
Result. England 3 Scotland 1
Goalscorers. England: Peters, Chivers (2)
Scotland: Curran
Referee. D. F. Dorpmans (Holland)
Linesmen. K. Brouwer (Holland)
L. W. v.d. Kroft (Holland)
Remarks. F. Munro (Wolverhampton Wanderers) and A. Jarvie (Airdrieonians) were substituted for H. Curran and A. Green respectively in the second half

R. Clark	Aberdeen
J. Greig	Rangers
J. Brogan	Celtic
W. Bremner	Leeds United
F. McLintock	Arsenal
R. Moncur (Captain)	Newcastle United
J. Johnstone	Celtic
D. Robb	Aberdeen
H. Curran	Wolverhampton Wanderers
A. Green	Blackpool
P. Cormack	Nottingham Forest

Date. May 27, 1972
Venue. Hampden Park, Glasgow
Result. Scotland 0 England 1
Goalscorer. Ball
Referee. S. Gonella (Italy)
Linesmen. A. Picasso (Italy)
A. Trono (Italy)
Remarks. A. Gemmill was substituted by J. Johnstone (Celtic), and W. Donachie by A. Green (Newcastle United) during the second half

R. Clark	Aberdeen
J. Brownlie	Hibernian
W. Donachie	Manchester City
W. Bremner (Captain)	Leeds United
W. McNeill	Celtic
R. Moncur	Newcastle United
P. Lorimer	Leeds United
R. A. Hartford	West Bromwich Albion
L. Macari	Celtic
D. Law	Manchester United
A. Gemmill	Derby County

Versus Ireland 1885–1920

Date. March 14, 1885
Venue. Hampden Park, Glasgow
Result. Scotland 8 Ireland 2
Referee. Mr Pierce Dix

W. Chalmers	Rangers
N. McHardy	Rangers
J. Niven	Moffat
R. Kelso	Renton
J. McPherson	Vale of Leven
A. Barbour	Renton
J. Marshall	Third Lanark
W. Turner	Pollokshields Athletic
A. Higgins	Kilmarnock
R. Calderwood	Cartvale
W. Lamont	Pilgrims

Date. March 20, 1886
Venue. Belfast
Result. Ireland 2 Scotland 7
Goalscorers. Ireland: Condy, Johnston
Scotland: Lambie, Heggie (4),
Gourlay, Dunbar
Referee. Mr Woolstewholme
Linesmen. Mr McKillop
Mr Sinclair

J. Connor	Lorettonians
A. Thompson	Arthurlie
W. McLeod	Queens' Park
A. Cameron	Rangers
L. Keir	Dumbarton
R. Fleming	Morton
J. Lambie	Queen's Park
C. Heggie	Rangers
W. Turner	Pollockshields Athletic
J. Gourlay	Cambuslang
J. Dunbar	Cartvale

Date. February 19, 1887
Venue. Hampden Park, Glasgow
Result. Scotland 4 Ireland 1
Goalscorers. Scotland: Jenkinson, Watt, Lowe, Johnstone
Ireland: Browne

E. Doig	Arbroath
A. Whitelaw	Vale of Leven
R. Smellie	Queen's Park
J. Weir	3rd L.R.V.
T. McMillan	Dumbarton
J. Hutton	St Bernards
W. Jenkinson	Heart of Midlothian
J. Lambie (Captain)	Queen's Park
W. Watt	Queen's Park
J. Lowe	St Bernards
W. Johnstone	3rd L.R.V.

Date. March 24, 1888.
Venue: Cliftonville, Belfast
Result. Ireland 2 Scotland 10
Referee. Mr Parlane

J. McLeod	Dumbarton
D. Stewart	Dumbarton
J. McCall	Renton
A. Stewart	Queen's Park
G. Dewar	Dumbarton
A. Jackson	Cambuslang
N. McCallum	Renton
J. Gow	Rangers
W. Dickson	Strathmore
T. Brackrenridge	Heart of Midlothian
R. Aitken	Dumbarton

Date. March 9, 1889
Venue. Ibrox Park, Glasgow
Result. Scotland 7 Ireland 0

E. Doig	Arbroath
J. Adams	Hearts
M. McKeown	Celtic
T. Robertson	Queen's Park
D. Calderhead	Queen of South Wanderers
J. Buchanan	Cambuslang
F. Watt	Kilbirnie
T. McInnes	Cowlairs
W. Groves	Celtic
R. Boyd	Mossend Swifts
D. Black	Hurlford

Date. March 28th, 1891
Venue. Celtic Park, Glasgow
Result. Scotland 2 Ireland 1
Referee. W. H. Staley

G. Gillespie	Queen's Park
D. Sillars	Queen's Park
W. Paul	Dykebar
T. Hamilton	Hurlford
J. Cleland	Royal Albert
J. Campbell	Kilmarnock
J. Low	Cambuslang
R. Clements	Leith Athletic
W. Bowie	Linthouse
T. Waddell	Queen's Park
J. Fraser	Moffat

Date. March 19, 1892
Venue. Cliftonville, Belfast
Result. Ireland 2 Scotland 3
Referee. Mr Taylor

W. Baird	St Bernard
G. Bowman	Montrose
J. Drummond	Rangers
R. Marshall	Rangers
T. Robertson	Queen's Park
P. Dowds	Celtic
W. Gulliland	Queen's Park
D. McPherson	Kilmarnock
J. Ellis	Mossend Swifts
W. Lambie	Queen's Park
A. Keillor	Dundee

Date. March 25, 1893
Venue. Celtic Park, Glasgow
Result. Scotland 6 Ireland 1
Referee. Mr Taylor

J. Lindsay	Renton
J. Adams	Heart of Midlothian
R. Smellie	Queen's Park
W. Maley	Celtic
J. Kelly	Celtic
D. Mitchell	Rangers
W. Sellar	Queen's Park
T. Waddell	Queen's Park
J. Hamilton	Queen's Park
A. McMahon	Celtic
J. Campbell	Celtic

Date. March 31, 1894
Venue. Cliftonville, Belfast
Result. Ireland 1 Scotland 2
Referee. Mr Phennah

F. Barret	Dundee
D. Crawford	St Mirren
J. Drummond	Rangers
R. Marshall	Rangers
W. Logair	Dundee
D. Stewart	Queen's Park
J. Taylor	St Mirren
J. Blessington	Celtic
D. Alexander	East Stirlingshire
R. Scott	Airdrie
A. Keillor	Dundee

Date. March 1895
Venue. Glasgow
Result. Scotland 3 Ireland 1

D. McArthur	Celtic
J. Drummond (Captain)	Rangers
D. Doyle	Celtic
I. Begbie	Heart of Midlothian
J. Russell	Heart of Midlothian
N. Gibson	Rangers
J. Taylor	St Mirren
T. Waddell	Queen's Park
J. McPherson	Rangers
R. Walker	Heart of Midlothian
W. Lambie	Queen's Park

Date. March 28, 1896
Venue. Belfast
Result. Ireland 3 Scotland 3
Goalscorers. Ireland: Barron (2), Milne
Scotland: McColl (2), Murray
Referee. Mr Cooper (Blackburn)

K. Anderson	Queen's Park
P. Meechan	Celtic
J. Drummond	Rangers
N. Gibson	Rangers
J. Kelly	Celtic
G. Hogg	Heart of Midlothian
P. Murray	Hibernian
J. Blessington	Celtic
R. McColl	Queen's Park
J. Cameron	Queen's Park
W. Lambie	Queen's Park

Date. March 27, 1897
Venue: Ibrox Park, Glasgow
Result. Scotland 5 Ireland 1
Goalscorers. Scotland: Gibson, McPherson, McColl, King
Referee. Mr Cooper (Blackburn)

M. Dickie	Rangers
D. McLean	St Bernard
J. Drummond	Rangers
N. Gibson	Rangers
W. Baird	St Bernard
D. Stewart	Queen's Park
T. Low	Rangers
J. McPherson	Rangers
R. McColl	Queen's Park
A. King	Celtic
W. Lambic	Queen's Park

Date. March 26, 1898
Venue. Cliftonville, Belfast
Result. Ireland 0 Scotland 3
Goalscorers. Stewart, McColl, Robertson

K. Anderson	Queen's Park
R. Kelso	Dundee
D. Doyle	Celtic
W. Thomson	Dumbarton
D. Russell	Celtic
A. King	Celtic
W. Stewart	Queen's Park
J. Campbell	Celtic
R. McColl	Queen's Park
J. Walker	Heart of Midlothian
T. Robertson	Heart of Midlothian

Date. March 25, 1899
Venue. Celtic Park, Glasgow
Result. Scotland 9 Ireland 1
Referee. Mr Sutcliffe

M. Dickie	Rangers
N. Smith	Rangers
D. Storrier	Celtic
N. Gibson	Rangers
A. Christie	Queen's Park
A. King	Celtic
J. Campbell	Celtic
R. Hamilton	Rangers
R. McColl	Queen's Park
D. Berry	Queen's Park
J. Bell	Everton

Date. March 3, 1900
Venue. Cliftonville, Belfast
Result. Ireland 0 Scotland 3
Referee. Mr Sutcliffe

H. Rennie	Heart of Midlothian
N. Smith	Rangers
R. Glen	Hibernian
N. Gibson	Rangers
H. Marshall	Celtic
W. Orr	Celtic
W. Stewart	Queen's Park
R. Walker	Heart of Midlothian
J. Campbell	Celtic
P. Callaghan	Hibernian
A. Smith	Rangers

Date. February 23, 1901
Venue. Celtic Park, Glasgow
Result. Scotland 11 Ireland 0
Referee. Mr Gough

G. MacWattie	Queen's Park
N. Smith	Rangers
B. Battles	Celtic
D. Russell	Celtic
G. Anderson	Kilmarnock
J. Robertson	Rangers
R. Campbell	Rangers
J. Campbell	Celtic
R. Hamilton	Rangers
A. McMahon	Celtic
A. Smith	Rangers

Date. March 21, 1903
Venue. Celtic Park, Glasgow
Result. Scotland 0 Ireland 2
Referee. Mr Kirkham

H. Rennie	Hibernian
A. Gray	Hibernian
J. Drummond	Rangers
J. Cross	Third Lanark
J. Robertson	Rangers
W. Orr	Celtic
J. Lindsay	Renton
R. Walker	Heart of Midlothian
W. Porteous	Heart of Midlothian
F. Speedie	Rangers
A. Smith	Rangers

Date. February 26, 1904
Venue. Dalymount Park, Dublin
Result. Ireland 1 Scotland 1
Goalscorers. Ireland: Sheridan
Scotland: Hamilton
Referee. Mr Kirkham (Preston)

H. Rennie	Hibernian
T. Jackson	St Mirren
J. Cameron	St Mirren
G. Henderson	Rangers
C. Thomson	Heart of Midlothian
J. Robertson	Rangers
J. Walker	Rangers
R. Walker	Heart of Midlothian
R. Hamilton	Rangers
H. Wilson	Third Lanark
A. Smith	Rangers

Date. March 18, 1905
Venue. Celtic Park, Glasgow
Result. Scotland 4 Ireland 0

W. Howden	Partick Thistle
D. McLeod	Celtic
W. McIntosh	Partick Thistle
N. Gibson	Partick Thistle
C. Thomson	Heart of Midlothian
J. Hay	Celtic
R. Walker	Heart of Midlothian
J. McMenemy	Celtic
J. Quinn	Celtic
P. Somers	Celtic
G. Wilson	Heart of Midlothian

Date. March 11, 1906
Venue. Dublin
Result. Ireland 0 Scotland 1

H. Rennie	Hibernian
D. McLeod	Celtic
D. Hill	Third Lanark
J. Young	Celtic
C. Thomson	Heart of Midlothian
J. May	Rangers
G. Hamilton	Port Glasgow Athletic
R. Walker	Heart of Midlothian
J. Quinn	Celtic
T. Fitchie	Woolwich Arsenal
A. Smith	Rangers

Date. March 16, 1907
Venue. Celtic Park, Glasgow
Result. Scotland 3 Ireland 0
Referee. J. Lewis

W. Muir	Dundee
T. Jackson	St Mirren
W. Agnew	Kilmarnock
W. Key	Queen's Park
C. Thomson	Heart of Midlothian
A. McNair	Celtic
A. Bennett	Celtic
R. Walker	Heart of Midlothian
F. O'Rourke	Airdrieonians
P. Somers	Celtic
J. Fraser	Dundee

Date. March 14, 1908
Venue. Dalymount Park, Dublin
Result. Ireland 0 Scotland 5
Goalscorers. Quinn (4), Galt

H. Rennie	Hibernian
J. Mitchell	Kilmarnock
W. Agnew	Kilmarnock
J. May	Rangers
C. Thomson	Heart of Midlothian
J. Galt	Rangers
R. Templeton	Kilmarnock
R. Walker	Heart of Midlothian
J. Quinn	Celtic
R. McColl	Newcastle United
W. Lennie	Aberdeen

Date. March 15, 1909
Venue. Ibrox Park, Glasgow
Result. Scotland 5 Ireland 0
Goalscorers. McMenemy (2), McFarlane, Thomson, Paul

J. Brownlie	Third Lanark
J. Main	Hibernian
J. Watson	Middlesbrough
W. Walker	Clyde
J. Stark	Rangers
J. Hay	Celtic
A. Bennett	Rangers
J. McMenemy	Celtic
W. Thomson	Dundee
A. McFarlane	Dundee
H. Paul	Queen's Park

Date. March 19, 1910
Venue. Linfield's Ground, Belfast
Result. Ireland 1 Scotland 0
Goalscorer. Thompson

J. Brownlie	Third Lanark
G. Law	Rangers
J. Mitchell	Kilmarnock
W. Walker	Clyde
W. Loney	Celtic
J. Hay (Captain)	Celtic
G. Sinclair	Heart of Midlothian
J. McTavish	Falkirk
J. Quinn	Celtic
A. Higgins	Newcastle United
R. Templeton	Kilmarnock

Date. March 18, 1911
Venue. Celtic Park, Glasgow
Result. Scotland 2 Ireland 0
Goalscorers. Reid, McMenemy
Referee. H. S. Bamlett (Gateshead)
Linesmen. O. Branigan (Scotland)
J. Stewart (Ireland)

J. Brownlie	Third Lanark
D. Colman	Aberdeen
J. Walker	Swindon Town
A. Aitken (Captain)	Leicester Fosse
C. Thomson	Sunderland
J. Hay	Celtic
A. Douglas	Chelsea
J. McMenemy	Celtic
W. Reid	Rangers
A. Higgins	Newcastle United
A. Smith	Rangers

Date. March 16, 1912
Venue. Windsor Park, Belfast
Result. Ireland 1 Scotland 4
Goalscorers. Ireland: McKnight
Scotland: Aitkenhead (2), Reid, Walker

J. Brownlie	Third Lanark
A. McNair	Celtic
J. Walker	Swindon Town
J. Gordon	Rangers
W. Low	Newcastle United
A. Bell	Manchester United
G. Sinclair	Heart of Midlothian
R. Walker	Heart of Midlothian
W. Reid	Rangers
W. Aitkenhead	Blackburn Rovers
R. Templeton	Kilmarnock

Date. March 15, 1913
Venue. Dalymount Park, Dublin
Result. Ireland 1 Scotland 2
Goalscorers. Ireland: McKnight
Scotland: Reid, Bennett

J. Brownlie	Third Lanark
D. Colman	Aberdeen
J. Walker	Swindon Town
R. Mercer	Heart of Midlothian
T. Logan	Falkirk
P. Nellies	Heart of Midlothian
A. Bennett	Rangers
J. Gordon	Rangers
W. Reid	Rangers
J. Croal	Falkirk
G. Robertson	Sheffield Wednesday

Date. March 14, 1914
Venue. Windsor Park, Belfast
Result. Ireland 1 Scotland 1
Goalscorers. Ireland: Young
Scotland: Donnachie

J. Brownlie	Third Lanark
A. McNair	Celtic
J. Dodds	Celtic
J. Gordon	Rangers
C. Thomson	Sunderland
J. Hay	Newcastle United
A. Donaldson	Bolton Wanderers
J. McMenemy	Celtic
W. Reid	Rangers
A. Wilson	Sheffield Wednesday
J. Donnachie	Oldham Athletic

Date. March 22, 1919
Venue. Ibrox Park, Glasgow
Result. Scotland 2 Ireland 1
Goalscorers. Scotland: Wilson (2)
Ireland: Halligan
Referee. A. A. Jackson (Glasgow)
Remarks. Unofficial 'Victory' match

J. Brownlie	Morton
A. McNair	Celtic
R. Orr	Third Lanark
J. Gordon	Rangers
W. Cringan	Celtic
J. McMullan	Partick Thistle
A. Donaldson	Bolton Wanderers
J. Bowie	Rangers
A. Wilson	Middlesbrough
G. Miller	Heart of Midlothian
A. Morton	Queen's Park

Date. April 19, 1919
Venue. Windsor Park, Belfast
Result. Ireland 0 Scotland 0
Referee. A. Cowan (Belfast)
Remarks. Unofficial 'Victory' match

J. Brownlie	Morton
J. Marshall	St Mirren
J. Blair	Rangers
J. Gordon	Rangers
W. McNamee	Hamilton Academicals
J. McMullan	Partick Thistle
A. Donaldson	Bolton Wanderers
J. Crosbie	Ayr United
J. Richardson	Ayr United
T. Cairns	Rangers
M. McPhail	Kilmarnock

Versus Northern Ireland 1920–1972

Date. March 13, 1920
Venue. Parkhead, Glasgow
Result. Scotland 3 Northern Ireland 0
Goalscorers. Wilson, Morton, Cunningham
Referee. J. Mason (Burslem)

K. Campbell	Liverpool
A. McNair	Celtic
J. Blair	Sheffield Wednesday
J. Bowie	Rangers
W. Low	Newcastle United
J. Gordon	Rangers
A. Donaldson	Bolton Wanderers
J. McMenemy	Celtic
A. Wilson	Dunfermline Athletic
A. Cunningham	Rangers
A. Morton	Queen's Park

Date. February 26, 1921
Venue. Windsor Park, Belfast
Result. Northern Ireland 0 Scotland 2
Goalscorers. Wilson, Cassidy
Referee. A. Ward (Kirkham)

K. Campbell	Partick Thistle
J. Marshall	Middlesbrough
W. McStay	Celtic
J. Harris	Partick Thistle
A. Graham	Arsenal
J. McMullan	Partick Thistle
T. Miller	Manchester United
A. McNab	Morton
A. Wilson (Captain)	Dunfermline Athletic
J. Cassidy	Celtic
A. Troup	Dundee

Date. March 4, 1922
Venue. Parkhead, Glasgow
Result. Scotland 2 Northern Ireland 1
Goalscorers. Scotland: Wilson (2)
Northern Ireland: Gillespie
Referee. A. Ward (Kirkham)

K. Campbell	Partick Thistle
J. Marshall	Middlesbrough
D. McKinlay	Liverpool
J. Hogg	Ayr United
W. Cringan	Celtic
T. Muirhead	Rangers
A. Donaldson	Bolton Wanderers
J. Kinloch	Partick Thistle
A. Wilson	Middlesbrough
A. Cunningham (Captain)	Rangers
A. Troup	Dundee

Date. March 3, 1923
Venue. Windsor Park, Belfast
Result. Northern Ireland 0 Scotland 1
Goalscorer. Wilson
Referee. A. Ward (Kirkham)

W. Harper	Hibernian
J. Hutton	Aberdeen
J. Blair (Captain)	Cardiff City
D. Steele	Huddcrsfield Town
D. Morris	Raith Rovers
N. McBain	Everton
A. Archibald	Rangers
J. White	Heart of Midlothian
A. Wilson	Middlesbrough
J. Cassidy	Celtic
A. Morton	Rangers

Date. March 1, 1924
Venue. Celtic Park, Glasgow
Result. Scotland 2 Northern Ireland 0
Goalscorers. Cunningham, Morris
Referee. G. N. Watson (Nottingham)

W. Harper	Hibernian
J. Hutton	Aberdeen
J. Hamilton	St Mirren
P. Kerr	Hibernian
D. Morris	Raith Rovers
J. McMullan	Partick Thistle
J. Reid	Airdrieonians
A. Cunningham	Rangers
H. Gallacher	Airdrieonians
T. Cairns	Rangers
A. Morton	Rangers

Date. February 28, 1925
Venue. Windsor Park, Belfast
Result. Northern Ireland 0 Scotland 3
Goalscorers. Meiklejohn, Gallacher, Dunn
Referee. G. N. Watson (Nottingham)

W. Harper	Hibernian
W. Nelson	Cardiff City
W. McStay	Celtic
D. Meiklejohn	Rangers
D. Morris	Raith Rovers
R. Bennie	Airdrieonians
R. Jackson	Aberdeen
J. Dunn	Hibernian
H. Gallacher	Airdrieonians
T. Cairns	Rangers
A. Morton	Rangers

Date. February 27, 1926
Venue. Ibrox Park, Glasgow
Result. Scotland 4 Northern Ireland 0
Goalscorers. Gallacher (3), Cunningham
Referee. G. N. Watson (Nottingham)

W. Harper	Arsenal
J. Hutton	Aberdeen
W. McStay	Celtic
P. Wilson	Celtic
J. McDougall	Airdrieonians
R. Bennie	Airdrieonians
A. Jackson	Huddersfield Town
A. Cunningham	Rangers
H. Gallacher	Newcastle United
T. McInally	Celtic
A. McLean	Celtic

Date. February 26, 1927
Venue. Belfast
Result. Northern Ireland 0 Scotland 2
Goalscorer. Morton (2)
Referee. G. N. Watson (Nottingham)

J. Harkness	Queen's Park
J. Hutton	Blackburn Rovers
W. McStay	Celtic
T. Muirhead	Rangers
J. Gibson	Partick Thistle
T. Craig	Rangers
A. Jackson	Huddersfield Town
J. Dunn	Hibernian
H. Gallacher	Newcastle United
J. Howieson	St Mirren
A. Morton	Rangers

Date. February 25, 1928
Venue. Firhill Park, Glasgow
Result. Scotland 0 Northern Ireland 1
Goalscorer. Chambers
Referee. A. Ward (Kirkham)

A. McClory	Motherwell
J. Hutton	Blackburn Rovers
W. McStay	Celtic
T. Muirhead	Rangers
D. Meiklejohn	Rangers
T. Craig	Rangers
H. Ritchie	Hibernian
J. Dunn	Hibernian
J. McGrory	Celtic
G. Stevenson	Motherwell
A. Morton	Rangers

Date. February 23, 1929
Venue. Windsor Park, Belfast
Result. Northern Ireland 3 Scotland 7
Goalscorers. N. Ireland: Bambrick (2), Rowley
Scotland: Gallacher (4), Jackson (2), James
Referee. A. E. Fogg (Bolton)

J. Harkness	Heart of Midlothian
D. Gray	Rangers
D. Blair	Clyde
T. Muirhead	Rangers
D. Meiklejohn	Rangers
J. McMullan	Manchester City
A. Jackson	Huddersfield Town
W. Chalmers	Queen's Park
H. Gallacher	Newcastle United
A. James	Preston North End
A. Morton	Rangers

Date. February 22, 1930
Venue. Celtic Park, Glasgow
Result. Scotland 3 Northern Ireland 1
Goalscorers. Scotland: Gallacher (2), Stevenson
N. Ireland: McCaw
Referee. A. Josephs (England)

R. Middleton	Cowdenbeath
D. Gray	Rangers
W. Wiseman	Queen's Park
J. Gibson	Aston Villa
D. Meiklejohn	Rangers
T. Craig	Rangers
A. Jackson	Huddersfield Town
G. Stevenson	Motherwell
H. Gallacher	Newcastle United
A. James	Arsenal
A. Morton	Rangers

Date. February 21, 1931
Venue. Windsor Park, Belfast
Result. Northern Ireland 0 Scotland 0
Referee. H. E. Hull (Burnley)

J. Thomson	Celtic
J. Crapnell	Airdrieonians
J. Nibloe	Kilmarnock
P. Wilson	Celtic
G. Walker	St Mirren
F. Hill	Aberdeen
J. Murdoch	Motherwell
P. Scarff	Celtic
B. Yorston	Aberdeen
R. McPhail	Rangers
A. Morton	Rangers

Date. May 19, 1932
Venue. Ibrox Park, Glasgow
Result. Scotland 3 Northern Ireland 1
Goalscorers. Scotland: Stevenson, McGrory, McPhail
N. Ireland: Dunne
Referee. I. Caswell (Blackburn)

R. Hepburn	Ayr United
D. Blair	Clyde
R. McAulay	Rangers
A. Massie	Heart of Midlothian
D. Meiklejohn	Rangers
G. Brown	Rangers
J. Crawford	Queen's Park
G. Stevenson	Motherwell
J. McGrory	Celtic
R. McPhail	Rangers
J. Connor	Sunderland

Date. September 19, 1933
Venue. Windsor Park, Belfast
Result. Northern Ireland 0 Scotland 4
Goalscorers. McPhail (2), King, McGrory
Referee. W. P. Harper (Stourbridge)

A. McLaren	St Johnstone
D. Gray	Rangers
J. Crapnell	Airdrieonians
A. Massie	Heart of Midlothian
J. Johnstone	Heart of Midlothian
W. Telfer	Motherwell
J. Crawford	Queen's Park
G. Stevenson	Motherwell
J. McGrory	Celtic
R. McPhail	Rangers
J. King	Hamilton Academicals

Date. September 16, 1934
Venue. Celtic Park, Glasgow
Result. Scotland 1 Northern Ireland 2
Goalscorers. Scotland: McPhail
N. Ireland: Martin (2)
Referee. E. Wood (Sheffield)

J. Harkness	Heart of Midlothian
A. Anderson	Heart of Midlothian
W. McGonagle	Celtic
A. Massie	Heart of Midlothian
A. Low	Falkirk
W. Telfer	Motherwell
J. Boyd	Newcastle United
A. Venters	Cowdenbeath
J. McGrory	Celtic
R. McPhail	Rangers
J. King	Hamilton Academicals

Date. October 20, 1935
Venue. Belfast
Result. Northern Ireland 2 Scotland 1
Goalscorers. N. Ireland: Martin, Coulter
Scotland: Gallacher
Referee. H. N. Mee (England)

J. Dawson	Rangers
A. Anderson	Heart of Midlothian
W. McGonagle	Celtic
A. Massie	Heart of Midlothian
J. Simpson	Rangers
A. Herd	Heart of Midlothian
W. Cook	Bolton Wanderers
G. Stevenson	Motherwell
J. Smith	Rangers
P. Gallacher	Sunderland
J. Connor	Sunderland

Date. November 13, 1936
Venue. Tynecastle Park, Edinburgh
Result. Scotland 2 Northern Ireland 1
Goalscorers. Scotland: Walker, Duncan
N. Ireland: Kelly
Referee. H. Natrass (New Seaham)

J. Jackson	Chelsea
A. Anderson	Heart of Midlothian
G. Cummings	Partick Thistle
A. Massie	Heart of Midlothian
J. Simpson	Rangers
A. Hastings	Sunderland
J. Delaney	Celtic
T. Walker	Heart of Midlothian
M. Armstrong	Aberdeen
W. Mills	Aberdeen
D. Duncan	Derby County

Date. October 31, 1937
Venue. Belfast
Result. Northern Ireland 1 Scotland 3
Goalscorers. N. Ireland: Kernoghan
Scotland: Napier, Munro, McCulloch
Referee. T. Thomson (England)

J. Dawson	Rangers
A. Anderson	Heart of Midlothian
R. Ancell	Newcastle United
A. Massie	Aston Villa
J. Simpson	Rangers
G. Brown	Rangers
A. Munro	Heart of Midlothian
T. Walker	Heart of Midlothian
D. McCulloch	Brentford
C. Napier	Derby County
D. Duncan	Derby County

Date. November 10, 1938
Venue Pittodrie Park, Aberdeen
Result. Scotland 1 Northern Ireland 1
Goalscorers. Scotland: Smith
N. Ireland: P. Doherty

J. Dawson	Rangers
A. Anderson	Heart of Midlothian
G. Cummings	Aston Villa
D. McKenzie	Brentford
J. Simpson	Rangers
A. Hastings	Sunderland
J. Delaney	Celtic
T. Walker	Heart of Midlothian
J. Smith	Rangers
R. McPhail	Rangers
R. Reid	Brentford

Date. October 8, 1939
Venue. Belfast
Result. Northern Ireland 0 Scotland 2
Goalscorers. Delaney, Walker
Referee. R. A. Mortimer (Huddersfield)

J. Dawson	Rangers
J. Carabine	Third Lanark
A. Beattie	Preston North End
W. Shankly	Preston North End
J. Dykes	Heart of Midlothian
G. Paterson	Celtic
J. Delaney	Celtic
T. Walker	Heart of Midlothian
J. Crum	Celtic
J. Divers	Celtic
T. Gillick	Everton

Date. February 2, 1946
Venue. Windsor Park, Belfast
Result. Northern Ireland 2 Scotland 3
Goalscorers. N. Ireland: Walsh (2)
Scotland: Liddell (2), Hamilton
Referee. D. Maxwell (Belfast)

R. Brown	Queen's Park
J. McGowan	Partick Thistle
J. Shaw	Rangers
W. Campbell	Greenock Morton
A. Paton	Motherwell
G. Paterson	Celtic
W. Waddell	Rangers
G. Hamilton	Aberdeen
E. Dodds	Blackpool
K. Chisholm	Queen's Park
W. Liddell	Liverpool

Date. November 27, 1947
Venue. Hampden Park, Glasgow
Result. Scotland 0 Northern Ireland 0
Referee. G. Reader (Southampton)
Linesmen. A. Watt (Edinburgh)
T. McNiven (Inverness)

R. Brown	Rangers
G. Young	Rangers
D. Shaw (Captain)	Hibernian
W. Campbell	Morton
F. Brennan	Newcastle United
H. Long	Clyde
G. Smith	Hibernian
G. Hamilton	Aberdeen
W. Thornton	Rangers
J. Duncanson	Rangers
W. B. Liddell	Liverpool

Date. October 4, 1948
Venue. Windsor Park, Belfast
Result. Northern Ireland 2 Scotland 0
Referee. T. Smith (Atherstone)
Linesman. J. B. Smillie (Law)

W. Miller	Celtic
G. Young	Rangers
J. Shaw	Rangers
A. Macaulay	Arsenal
W. Woodburn	Rangers
A. Forbes	Sheffield United
J. Delaney	Manchester United
J. Watson	Motherwell
W. Thornton	Rangers
W. Steel	Derby County
W. Liddell	Liverpool

Date. November 12, 1949
Venue. Hampden Park, Glasgow
Result. Scotland 3 Northern Ireland 2
Goalscorers. Scotland: Houliston (2), Mason
Referee. H. E. Evans (Liverpool)
Linesman. H. J. Gallacher (Glasgow)

R. Brown	Rangers
J. Govan	Hibernian
D. Shaw	Hibernian
R. Evans	Celtic
G. Young	Rangers
W. Redpath	Motherwell
W. Waddell	Rangers
J. Mason	Third Lanark
W. Houliston	Queen of the South
W. Steel	Derby County
J. Kelly	Barnsley

Date. October 7, 1950
Venue. Windsor Park, Belfast
Result. Northern Ireland 2 Scotland 8
Goalscorers. Scotland: Morris (3), Waddell (2),
Steel, Reilly, Mason
Referee. R. Mortimer (Huddersfield)
Linesman. W. G. Livingstone (Glasgow)

J. Cowan	Greenock Morton
G. Young	Rangers
S. Cox	Rangers
R. Evans	Celtic
W. Woodburn	Rangers
G. Aitken	East Fife
W. Waddell	Rangers
J. Mason	Third Lanark
H. Morris	East Fife
W. Steel	Derby County
L. Reilly	Hibernian

Date. November 1, 1951
Venue. Hampden Park, Glasgow
Result. Scotland 6 Northern Ireland 1
Goalscorers. Scotland: Steel (4), McPhail (2)
N. Ireland: McGarry
Referee. B. M. Griffiths (Newport)
Linesmen. G. O. Hancock (Bargoed)
J. S. Edwards (Llandudno)

J. Cowan	Morton
G. Young (Captain)	Rangers
W. McNaught	Raith Rovers
I. McColl	Rangers
W. A. Woodburn	Rangers
A. Forbes	Arsenal
R. Collins	Celtic
J. Mason	Third Lanark
J. McPhail	Celtic
W. Steel	Dundee
W. B. Liddell	Liverpool

Date. October 6, 1952
Venue. Windsor Park, Belfast
Result. Northern Ireland 0 Scotland 3
Goalscorers. Johnstone (2), Orr

J. Cowan	Greenock Morton
G. Young	Rangers
S. Cox	Rangers
R. Evans	Celtic
W. Woodburn	Rangers
W. Redpath	Motherwell
W. Waddell	Rangers
R. Johnstone	Hibernian
L. Reilly	Hibernian
T. Orr	Greenock Morton
W. Liddell	Liverpool

Date. November 5, 1953
Venue. Hampden Park, Glasgow
Result. Scotland 1 Northern Ireland 1
Goalscorers. Scotland: Reilly
N. Ireland: D'Arcy
Referee. R. E. Smith (Newport)
Linesmen. J. S. Edwards (Llandudno)
F. Roberts (Bangor)

G. Farm	Blackpool
G. Young (Captain)	Rangers
S. R. Cox	Rangers
J. Scoular	Portsmouth
F. Brennan	Newcastle United
G. Aitken	Sunderland
T. Wright	Sunderland
J. Logie	Arsenal
L. Reilly	Hibernian
W. Steel	Dundee
W. B. Liddell	Liverpool

Date. November 3, 1954
Venue. Hampden Park, Glasgow
Result. Scotland 2 Ireland 2
Goalscorers. Scotland: Davidson, Johnstone
Ireland: Bingham, McAdams
Referee. A. Bond (London)
Linesmen. F. H. Gerrard (Preston)
H. Hawthorne (Willington)

W. Fraser	Sunderland
G. Young (Captain)	Rangers
W. McNaught	Raith Rovers
R. Evans	Celtic
J. Davidson	Partick Thistle
D. Cowie	Dundee
W. Waddell	Rangers
R. Johnstone	Hibernian
P. Buckley	Aberdeen
W. Fernie	Celtic
T. Ring	Clyde

Date. November 3, 1955.
Venue. Hampden Park, Glasgow
Result. Scotland 2 Northern Ireland 2
Goalscorers. Scotland: Davidson, Johnstone
N. Ireland: Bingham, McAdams
Referee. A. Bond (London)
Linesmen. F. H. Gerrard (Preston)
H. Hawthorne (Willington)

W. Fraser	Sunderland
G. Young (Captain)	Rangers
W. McNaught	Raith Rovers
R. Evans	Celtic
J. Davidson	Partick Thistle
D. Cowie	Dundee
W. Waddell	Rangers
R. Johnstone	Hibernian
P. Buckley	Aberdeen
W. Fernie	Celtic
T. Ring	Clyde

Date. October 8, 1956
Venue. Windsor Park, Belfast
Result. Northern Ireland 2 Scotland 1
Goalscorer. Scotland: Reilly
Referee. J. Kelly (Chorley)

T. Younger	Hibernian
A. H. Parker	Falkirk
J. McDonald	Sunderland
R. Evans	Celtic
G. Young	Rangers
A. Glen	Aberdeen
G. Smith	Hibernian
R. Collins	Celtic
L. Reilly	Hibernian
R. Johnstone	Manchester City
W. Liddell	Liverpool

Date. November 7, 1957
Venue. Hampden Park, Glasgow
Result. Scotland 1 Northern Ireland 0
Goalscorer. Scott
Referee. R. J. Leafe (Nottingham)
Linesmen. J. E. Meade (London)
G. W. Ward (Selby)

T. Younger	Liverpool
A. H. Parker	Falkirk
J. Hewie	Charlton Athletic
I. McColl	Rangers
G. Young (Captain)	Rangers
D. Cowie	Dundee
A. Scott	Rangers
J. K. Mudie	Blackpool
L. Reilly	Hibernian
J. Wardhaugh	Heart of Midlothian
W. Fernie	Celtic

Date. October 5, 1958
Venue. Windsor Park, Belfast
Result. Northern Ireland 1 Scotland 1
Goalscorers. N. Ireland: Simpson
Scotland: Leggat
Referee. L. Callaghan (Merthyr Tydfil)
Linesmen. J. J. Bailey (Llantrisant)
N. A. Jones (Wrexham)

T. Younger	Liverpool
A. H. Parker	Falkirk
E. Caldow	Rangers
I. McColl	Rangers
R. Evans	Celtic
T. Docherty (Captain)	Preston North End
G. Leggat	Aberdeen
R. Collins	Celtic
J. K. Mudie	Blackpool
S. Baird	Rangers
T. Ring	Clyde

Date. November 5, 1959
Venue. Hampden Park, Glasgow
Result. Scotland 2 Northern Ireland 2
Goalscorers. Scotland: Herd, Collins
N. Ireland: Caldow (o.g.), McIlroy
Referee. J. H. Clough (Bolton)
Linesmen. H. Burns (Leyland)
L. Dalkin (Ashington)

W. D. F. Brown	Dundee
J. Grant	Hibernian
E. Caldow	Rangers
D. C. Mackay (Captain)	Heart of Midlothian
W. Toner	Kilmarnock
T. Docherty	Arsenal
G. Leggat	Fulham
R. Collins	Everton
D. Herd	Arsenal
D. Law	Huddersfield Town
J. Henderson	Arsenal

Date. November 9, 1960
Venue. Hampden Park, Glasgow
Result. Scotland 5 Ireland 2
Goalscorers. Scotland: Law, Caldow (pen.), Young, Brand (2)
Ireland: Blanchflower (pen.), McParland
Referee. K. Howley (Middlesbrough)
Linesmen. R. Egan (Altrincham)
L. Haslam (Rishton)

L. G. Leslie	Airdrieonians
D. MacKay	Celtic
E. Caldow (Captain)	Rangers
D. C. Mackay	Tottenham Hotspur
J. Plenderleith	Manchester City
J. Baxter	Rangers
G. Herd	Clyde
D. Law	Manchester City
A. Young	Heart of Midlothian
R. Brand	Rangers
D. Wilson	Rangers

Date. November 9, 1961
Venue. Hampden Park, Glasgow
Result. Scotland 5 Northern Ireland 2
Goalscorers. Scotland: Law, Caldow (pen.), Young, Brand (2)
N. Ireland: Blanchflower (pen.), McParland
Referee. K. Howley (Middlesbrough)
Linesmen. R. Egan (Altrincham)
L. Haslam (Rishton)

L. G. Leslie	Airdrieonians
D. MacKay	Celtic
E. Caldow (Captain)	Rangers
D. C. Mackay	Tottenham Hotspur
J. Plenderleith	Manchester City
J. Baxter	Rangers
G. Herd	Clyde
D. Law	Manchester City
A. Young	Heart of Midlothian
R. Brand	Rangers
D. Wilson	Rangers

Date. October 7, 1962
Venue. Windsor Park, Belfast
Result. Northern Ireland 1 Scotland 6
Goalscorers. N. Ireland: McLaughlin
Scotland: Scott (3), Wilson (2), Brand
Referee. J. Finney (Hereford)
Linesmen. W. G. Handley (Cannock)
L. D. D. Maddocks (Turnditch)

W. D. F. Brown	Tottenham Hotspur
D. MacKay	Celtic
E. Caldow (Captain)	Rangers
P. T. Crerand	Celtic
W. McNeill	Celtic
J. Baxter	Rangers
A. Scott	Rangers
J. A. White	Tottenham Hotspur
I. St John	Liverpool
R. Brand	Rangers
D. Wilson	Rangers

Date. November 7, 1963
Venue. Hampden Park, Glasgow
Result. Scotland 5 Northern Ireland 1
Goalscorers. Scotland: Law (4), Henderson
N. Ireland: Bingham
Referee. J. Finney (Hereford)
Linesmen. J. W. Hedley (Newcastle)
R. T. Clayton (Houghton-le-Spring)

W. D. F. Brown	Tottenham Hotspur
A. W. Hamilton	Dundee
E. Caldow (Captain)	Rangers
P. T. Crerand	Celtic
J. F. Ure	Dundee
J. Baxter	Rangers
W. Henderson	Rangers
J. A. White	Tottenham Hotspur
I. St John	Liverpool
D. Law	Manchester United
G. Mulhall	Sunderland

Date. October 12, 1964
Venue. Windsor Park, Belfast
Result. Northern Ireland 2 Scotland 1
Goalscorers. N. Ireland: Bingham, Wilson
Scotland: St John
Referee. J. K. Taylor (Wolverhampton)
Linesmen. G. W. Lee (Derby)
K. Cartwright (Nuneaton)

W. D. F. Brown	Tottenham Hotspur
A. W. Hamilton	Dundee
D. Provan	Rangers
P. T. Crerand	Manchester United
J. F. Ure	Arsenal
D. C. Mackay (Captain)	Tottenham Hotspur
W. Henderson	Rangers
J. A. White	Tottenham Hotspur
I. St John	Liverpool
D. Gibson	Leicester City
G. Mulhall	Sunderland

Date. November 25, 1965
Venue. Hampden Park, Glasgow
Result. Scotland 3 Northern Ireland 2
Goalscorers. Scotland: Wilson (2), Gilzean
N. Ireland: Irvine (2)
Referee. G. T. Powell (Newport)
Linesmen. L. A. Howells (Port Talbot)
R. Parker (Hope, nr. Wrexham)
Remarks. Match originally dated for November 18. Change made at request of the Irish F.A. to enable them to fix World Cup dates.

R. C. Forsyth	Kilmarnock
A. W. Hamilton	Dundee
J. Kennedy	Celtic
J. Greig	Rangers
J. McGrory	Kilmarnock
F. McLintock	Arsenal
W. Wallace	Heart of Midlothian
D. Law	Manchester United
A. J. Gilzean	Dundee
J. Baxter (Captain)	Rangers
D. Wilson	Rangers

Date. October 2, 1966
Venue. Windsor Park, Belfast
Result. Northern Ireland 3 Scotland 2
Goalscorers. N. Ireland: Dougan, Crossan, Irvine
Scotland: Gilzean (2)
Referee. J. K. Taylor (Wolverhampton)
Linesmen. W. J. Gow (Birmingham)
E. Garfield (Larkhill)

W. D. F. Brown	Tottenham Hotspur
A. W. Hamilton	Dundee
E. G. McCreadie	Chelsea
D. C. Mackay	Tottenham Hotspur
W. McNeill (Captain)	Celtic
J. Greig	Rangers
W. Henderson	Rangers
D. Law	Manchester United
A. J. Gilzean	Tottenham Hotspur
J. Baxter	Sunderland
J. Hughes	Celtic

Date. November 16, 1967
Venue. Hampden Park, Glasgow
Result. Scotland 2 Northern Ireland 1
Goalscorers. Scotland: Murdoch, Lennox
N. Ireland: Nicholson
Referee. J. K. Taylor (Wolverhampton)
Linesmen. M. J. Finney (Hereford)
J. Butler (Sunderland)

R. Ferguson	Kilmarnock
J. Greig (Captain)	Rangers
R. McKinnon	Rangers
J. Clark	Celtic
T. Gemmell	Celtic
R. Murdoch	Celtic
W. Bremner	Leeds United
W. Henderson	Rangers
S. Chalmers	Celtic
J. McBride	Celtic
R. Lennox	Celtic

Date. May 7, 1969 *Venue.* Hampden Park, Glasgow *Result.* Scotland 1 Northern Ireland 1 *Goalscorers.* Scotland: Stein N. Ireland: McMordie *Referee.* D. W. Smith (Stonehouse, Glos.) *Linesmen.* J. K. Taylor (Wolverhampton) J. K. Wright (Morecambe) *Remarks.* W. Johnston (Rangers) substituted for Cooke towards the end of the match	J. Herriot E. McCreadie T. Gemmell W. Bremner (Captain) J. Greig P. Stanton W. Henderson R. Murdoch C. Stein D. Law C. Cooke	Birmingham City Chelsea Celtic Leeds United Rangers Hibernian Rangers Celtic Rangers Manchester United Chelsea
Date. April 18, 1970 *Venue.* Windsor Park, Belfast *Result.* Northern Ireland 0 Scotland 1 *Goalscorer.* O'Hare *Referee.* E. T. Jennings (Stourbridge) *Linesmen.* N. C. H. Burtenshaw (Great Yarmouth) D. E. Bradbury (Runcorn) *Remarks.* C. Stein (Rangers) substituted for Gilzean late in the second half	R. Clark D. Hay W. Dickson F. McLintock (Captain) R. McKinnon R. Moncur T. McLean W. Carr J. O'Hare A. Gilzean W. Johnston	Aberdeen Celtic Kilmarnock Arsenal Rangers Newcastle United Kilmarnock Coventry City Derby County Tottenham Hotspur Rangers
Date. May 18, 1971 *Venue.* Hampden Park, Glasgow *Result.* Scotland 0 Northern Ireland 1 *Goalscorer.* Greig (o.g.) *Referee.* C. Thomas (Rhondda) *Linesmen.* J. G. D. Lewis (Port Talbot) W. D. Bond (Llangollen) *Remarks.* A. Jarvie and F. Munro were substituted for J. O'Hare and F. McLintock respectively, during the second half	R. Clark D. Hay J. Brogan J. Greig F. McLintock R. Moncur (Captain) P. Lorimer A. Green J. O'Hare H. Curran E. Gray	Aberdeen Celtic Celtic Rangers Arsenal Newcastle United Leeds United Blackpool Derby County Wolverhampton Wanderers Leeds United
Date. May 20, 1972 *Venue.* Hampden Park, Glasgow *Result.* Northern Ireland 0 Scotland 2 *Goalscorers.* Law, Lorimer *Referee.* C. Thomas (Treorchy) *Linesmen.* K. Sweet (Abercwmboi) G. D. Hellier (Cardiff) *Remarks.* J. Johnstone (Celtic) was substituted by P. Lorimer (Leeds United) during the second half	R. Clark J. Brownlie W. Donachie W. Bremner (Captain) W. McNeill R. Moncur J. Johnstone A. Gemmill J. O'Hare D. Law G. Graham	Aberdeen Hibernian Manchester City Leeds United Celtic Newcastle United Celtic Derby County Derby County Manchester United Arsenal

Date. March 25, 1876
Venue. Glasgow
Result. Scotland 4 Wales 0
Linesman. W. C. Mitchell

A. McGeoch	Dumbreck
J. Taylor	Queen's Park
R. Neil	Queen's Park
C. Campbell (Captain)	Queen's Park
A. Kennedy	Eastern
W. McKinnon	Queen's Park
T. Highet	Queen's Park
J. Ferguson	Vale of Leven
M. McNeil	Rangers
H. McNeil	Queen's Park
J. Lang	Clydesdale

Date. March 5, 1877
Venue. Wrexham
Result. Wales 0 Scotland 2
Linesmen. W. Dick (Hon. Sec. S.F.A.)
R. Mills (Wrexham)

A. McGeoch	Dumbreck
R. Neil	Queen's Park
T. Vallance	Rangers
C. Campbell (Captain)	Queen's Park
J. Phillips	Queen's Park
J. McDougall	Vale of Leven
J. McGregor	Vale of Leven
J. Smith	Mauchline
J. Hunter	Third Lanark
H. McNeil	Queen's Park
J. Ferguson	Vale of Leven

Date. March 23, 1878
Venue. Glasgow
Result. Scotland 9 Wales 0
Goalscorers. Campbell, Weir (2),
Ferguson (3), Baird, Watson
Referee. R. Gardner (Pres. S.F.A.)
Linesmen. J. J. Taylor (Queen's Park)
R. Mills (Wrexham)

R. Parlane	Vale of Leven
J. Duncan	A.A.C.
R. Neil (Captain)	Queen's Park
J. Phillips	Queen's Park
D. Davidson	Queen's Park
J. Ferguson	Vale of Leven
J. Baird	Vale of Leven
J. Lang	Third Lanark
J. Weir	Queen's Park
J. Watson	Rangers
P. Campbell	Rangers

Date. March 7, 1879
Venue. Wrexham
Result. Wales 0 Scotland 3
Linesman. W. C. Mitchell

R. Parlane	Vale of Leven
W. Somers	Third Lanark
T. Vallance	Rangers
D. Davidson	Queen's Park
J. McPherson	Vale of Leven
H. McNeil	Queen's Park
J. McDougal (Captain)	Vale of Leven
P. Campbell	Rangers
J. Smith	Mauchline
R. Paton	Vale of Leven
W. Beveridge	Ayr Academy

Date. April 3, 1880
Venue. Hampden Park, Glasgow
Result. Scotland 5 Wales 1
Goalscorers. Scotland: Davidson, Beveridge,
Lindsay, McAdam,
Campbell
Wales: Roberts
Referee. T. Lawrie (Queen's Park)
Linesmen. L. Kenrick (Druids)
Mr McQuarrie (3rd L.R.V.)

G. Gillespie	Rangers
W. Somers	Queen's Park
A. Lang	Dumbarton
D. Davidson (Captain)	Queen's Park
H. McIntyre	Rangers
J. Douglas	Renfrew
J. McAdam	3rd L.R.V.
E. Fraser	Queen's Park
J. Lindsay	Dumbarton
J. Campbell	South Western
W. Beveridge	Edinburgh University

Date. March 14, 1881
Venue. Wrexham
Result. Wales 1 Scotland 5
Goalscorers. Wales: Cross
Scotland: Ker (2), McNeil,
Bell (o.g.), Morgan (o.g.)

G. Gillespie	Rangers
A. Watson	Queen's Park
T. Vallance	Rangers
J. McPherson	Vale of Leven
D. Davidson (Captain)	Queen's Park
W. McGuire	Beith
D. Hill	Rangers
G. Ker	Queen's Park
J. Lindsay	Dumbarton
H. McNeil	Queen's Park
J. Smith	Queen's Park

Date. March 25, 1882
Venue. Hampden Park, Glasgow
Result. Scotland 5 Wales 0
Goalscorers. Kaye, Ker, Fraser (2), McAuley
Referee. D. Hamilton (Ayr)
Linesmen. J. Wallace (3rd L.R.V.)
F. H. Bancroft (Welsh Assoc.)

A. Rowan (Captain)	Queen's Park
A. Holm	Queen's Park
J. Duncan	Alexandra Athletic
C. Campbell	Queen's Park
A. Kennedy	Third Lanark
E. Fraser	Queen's Park
D. Hill	Rangers
G. Ker	Queen's Park
J. McAulay	Dumbarton
J. Kaye	Queen's Park
J. T. Richmond	Queen's Park

Date. March 12, 1883
Venue. Wrexham Racecourse
Result. Wales 1 Scotland 4
Referee. Mr Lithgoe

J. McAulay	Dumbarton
A. H. Holm	Queen's Park
W. Arnott	Queen's Park
P. Miller	Dumbarton
J. Smith	Edinburgh University
J. McPherson	Vale of Leven
E. Fraser	Queen's Park
W. Anderson	Queen's Park
J. Inglis	Rangers
J. Kaye	Queen's Park
W. McKinnon	Dumbarton

Date. March 29, 1884
Venue. Glasgow
Result. Scotland 4 Wales 1
Goalscorers. Scotland: Lindsay, Shaw, Kaye, ?
Wales: Shaw

T. Turner	Arthurlie
M. Paton	Dumbarton
J. Forbes	Vale of Leven
A. Kennedy	Third Lanark
J. McIntyre	Rangers
R. Brown	Dumbarton
F. Shaw	Pollockshields Athletic
S. Thomson	Lugar Boswell
J. Lindsay	Dumbarton
J. Kaye	Queen's Park
W. McKinnon	Dumbarton

Date. April 10, 1886
Venue. Hampden Park, Glasgow
Result. Scotland 4 Wales 1
Goalscorers. Scotland: McCormick, Allan,
McColl, ?
Wales: Lundie (o.g.)
Referee. J. Sinclair (Pres. Irish Assoc.)
Linesmen. A. Stuart (E.F.A.)
A. H. Hunter (Wrexham)

G. Gillespie	Queen's Park
J. Lundie	Hibernian
W. Semple (Captain)	Cambuslang
R. Kelso	Renton
W. Jackson	Cambuslang
J. Marshall	3rd L.R.V.
R. McCormick	Abercorn
J. McGhee	Hibernian
W. Harrower	Queen's Park
D. Allan	Queen's Park
J. McColl	Renton

Date. March 21, 1887
Venue. Wrexham
Result. Wales 0 Scotland 2
Goalscorers. Robertson, Allan
Referee. Mr Hull (England)
Linesmen. J. Roberts (Bangor)
R. Browne (Scotland)

J. McAulay (Captain)	Dumbarton
W. Arnott	Queen's Park
J. Forbes	Vale of Leven
J. Kelso	Renton
J. Auld	3rd L.R.V.
L. Keir	Dumbarton
J. Marshall	3rd L.R.V.
W. Robertson	Dumbarton
W. Sellar	Battlefield
J. McColl	Renton
J. Allan	Queen's Park

Date. March 10, 1888
Venue. Easter Road, Edinburgh
Result. Scotland 5 Wales 1
Goalscorers. Scotland: Latta (2), Groves, Paul, Monroe
Wales: Doughty

J. Wilson	Vale of Leven
A. Hannah	Renton
R. Smellie	Queen's Park
J. Johnston	Abercorn
J. Gourlay	Cambuslang
J. McLaren	Hibernian
A. Latta	Dumbarton
J. Groves	Hibernian
W. Paul	Partick Thistle
J. McPherson	Cowlairs
N. Monroe	Abercorn

Date. April 15, 1889
Venue. Wrexham Racecourse
Result. Wales 0 Scotland 0
Referee. Mr Walker

J. McLeod	Dumbarton
A. Thompson	Third Lanark
J. Rae	Third Lanark
A. Stewart	Queen's Park
A. Lochhead	Third Lanark
J. Auld	Third Lanark
F. Watt	Kilbirnie
J. Campbell	Rangers
W. Paul	Partick Thistle
W. Johnstone	Third Lanark
A. Hannah	Renton

Date. March 19, 1890
Venue. Underwood Park, Paisley
Result. Scotland 5 Wales 0
Goalscorers. Paul (3), Wilson
Referee. Mr Finlay (Belfast)
Linesmen. Mr Park (Scotland)
Mr Taylor (Wales)

G. Gillespie	Rangers
A. Whitelaw	Vale of Leven
J. Murray	Vale of Leven
M. McQueen	Leith Athletic
A. Brown	St Mirren
H. Wilson	Newmilns
J. Brown	Cambuslang
F. Watt	Kilbirnie
W. Paul	Partick Thistle
J. Dunlop	St Mirren
D. Bruce	Vale of Leven

Date. March 21, 1891
Venue. Wrexham
Result. Wales 3 Scotland 4
Referee. Mr Crump

J. McCorkindale	Partick Thistle
A. Ritchie	East Stirlingshire
J. Hepburn	Alloa Athletic
M. McQueen	Leith Athletic
R. Brown	Cambuslane
T. Robertson	Queen's Park
W. Gulliland	Queen's Park
R. Buchanan	Abercorn
J. Logan	Ayr United
R. Boyd	Mossend Swifts
A. Keillor	Montrose

Date. March 28, 1892
Venue. Tynecastle Park, Edinburgh
Result. Scotland 6 Wales 1
Referee. Mr Reid

R. Downie	Third Lanark
J. Adams	Heart of Midlothian
J. Orr	Kilmarnock
I. Begbie	Heart of Midlothian
J. Campbell	Kilmarnock
J. Hill	Heart of Midlothian
J. Taylor	Dumbarton
W. Thomson	Dumbarton
J. Hamilton	Queen's Park
J. McPherson	Rangers
D. Baird	Heart of Midlothian

Date. March 18, 1893
Venue. Wrexham
Result. Wales 0 Scotland 8
Referee. Mr Stacey

J. McLeod	Dumbarton
D. Doyle	Celtic
R. Foyers	St Bernard
D. Sillars	Queen's Park
A. McCreadie	Rangers
D. Stewart	Queen's Park
J. Taylor	Dumbarton
W. Thomson	Dumbarton
J. Madden	Celtic
J. Barker	Rangers
W. Lambie	Queen's Park

Date. March 24, 1894
Venue. Rugby Park, Kilmarnock
Result. Scotland 5 Wales 2
Referee. Mr McBride

A. Baird	Queen's Park
D. Crawford	St Mirren
R. Foyers	St Bernard
E. McBain	St Mirren
J. Kelly	Celtic
J. Johnstone	Kilmarnock
A. Stewart	Third Lanark
T. Chambers	Heart of Midlothian
D. Alexander	East Stirlingshire
D. Berry	Queen's Park
J. Barker	Rangers

Date. March 23, 1895
Venue. Wrexham
Result. Wales 2 Scotland 2
Referee. Mr Jope

F. Barret	Dundee
D. Sellars	Queen's Park
R. Glen	Renton
J. Simpson	Third Lanark
W. McColl	Renton
A. Keillor	Dundee
J. Fyfe	Third Lanark
J. Murray	Renton
J. Madden	Celtic
W. Sawers	Dundee
J. Divers	Celtic

Date. March 21, 1896
Venue. Carolina Port, Dundee
Result. Scotland 4 Wales 0
Goalscorers. Neil (2), Paton, Keillor
Referee. Mr McBride (Irish Assoc.)

R. McFarlane	Morton
D. McLean	St Bernards
R. Glen	Renton
J. Gillespie (Captain)	Queen's Park
R. Neil	Hibernian
W. Blair	Third Lanark
W. Thomson	Dundee
D. Paton	St Bernards
R. McColl	Queen's Park
A. King	Heart of Midlothian
A. Keillor	Dundee

Date. March 20, 1897
Venue. Wrexham
Result. Wales 2 Scotland 2
Goalscorers. Scotland: Ritchie (pen.), Jones (o.g.)

J. Patrick	St Mirren
J. Ritchie (Captain)	Queen's Park
D. Gardner	Third Lanark
B. Breslin	Hibernian
D. Russell	Celtic
A. Keillor	Dundee
J. Kennedy	Hibernian
P. Murray	Hibernian
J. Oswald	Rangers
J. McMillan	St Bernards
J. Walker	Heart ofMidlothian

Date. March 19, 1898
Venue. Motherwell
Result. Scotland 5 Wales 2
Goalscorers. Scotland: Gillespie (3), McKie (2)
Wales: Thomas, Morgan-Owen

W. Watson	Falkirk
N. Smith	Rangers
M. Scott	Airdrieonians
W. Thomson	Dumbarton
A. Christie	Queen's Park
P. Campbell	Morton
K. Gillespie	Third Lanark
J. Miller	Rangers
J. McKie	East Stirlingshire
H. Morgan	St Mirren
R. Findlay	Kilmarnock

Date. February 3, 1900
Venue. Aberdeen
Result. Scotland 5 Wales 2
Referee. Mr Sutcliffe

M. Dickie	Rangers
N. Smith	Rangers
D. Crawford	Rangers
J. Irons	Queen's Park
R. Neil	Rangers
J. Robertson	Rangers
J. Bell	Celtic
D. Wilson	Queen's Park
R. McColl	Queen's Park
R. Hamilton	Rangers
A. Smith	Rangers

Date. March 2, 1901
Venue. Wrexham
Result. Wales 1 Scotland 1

B. MacWattie	Queen's Park
N. Smith	Rangers
B. Battles	Celtic
N. Gibson	Rangers
D. Russell	Celtic
J. Robertson	Rangers
J. Bell	Celtic
R. Walker	Heart of Midlothian
R. McColl	Queen's Park
J. Campbell	Celtic
A. Smith	Rangers

Date. March 15, 1902
Venue. Cappielow Park, Greenock
Result. Scotland 5 Wales 1
Referee. J. McBride

H. Rennie	Hibernian
H. Allan	Heart of Midlothian
J. Drummond	Rangers
H. Wilson	Third Lanark
A. Buick	Heart of Midlothian
J. Robertson	Rangers
R. Walker	Heart of Midlothian
J. Campbell	Celtic
R. Hamilton	Rangers
A. McMahon	Celtic
A. Smith	Rangers

Date. March 9, 1903
Venue. Cardiff
Result. Wales 0 Scotland 1
Referee. F. Kirkham (Burslem)

H. Rennie	Hibernian
A. McCombie	Sunderland
J. Watson	Sunderland
A. Aitken	Newcastle United
A. Raisbeck	Liverpool
J. Robertson	Rangers
R. Templeton	Newcastle United
R. Walker	Heart of Midlothian
J. Campbell	Celtic
F. Speedie	Rangers
A. Smith	Rangers

Date. March 12, 1904
Venue. Dens Park, Dundee
Result. Scotland 1 Wales 1
Goalscorers. Scotland: Walker
Wales: Atherton
Referee. F. Kirkham (Burslem)

L. Skene	Queen's Park
T. Jackson	St Mirren
J. Sharp	Dundee
W. Orr	Celtic
T. Sloan	Third Lanark
J. Robertson	Rangers
J. Walker	Rangers
R. Walker	Heart of Midlothian
A. Bennett	Celtic
A. McFarlane	Dundee
G. Wilson	Heart of Midlothian

Date. March 6, 1905
Venue. Wrexham
Result. Wales 3 Scotland 1

H. Rennie	Hibernian
T. Jackson	St Mirren
A. McCombie	Newcastle United
A. Aitken	Newcastle United
C. Thomson	Heart of Midlothian
J. Robertson	Rangers
R. Templeton	Woolwich Arsenal
R. Walker	Heart of Midlothian
S. Kennedy	Partick Thistle
T. Fichie	Woolwich Arsenal
A. Smith	Rangers

Date. March 3, 1906
Venue. Tynecastle Park, Edinburgh
Result. Scotland 0 Wales 2

J. Raeside	Third Lanark
D. McLeod	Celtic
A. Richmond	Queen's Park
A. McNair	Celtic
C. Thomson	Heart of Midlothian
J. May	Rangers
G. Stewart	Hibernian
A. McFarlane	Dundee
J. Quinn	Celtic
T. Fichie	Woolwich Arsenal
G. Wilson	Heart of Midlothian

Date. March 4, 1907
Venue. Wrexham
Result. Wales 1 Scotland 0
Referee. Mr Mason

P. McBride	Preston North End
T. Jackson	St Mirren
J. Sharp	Arsenal
A. Aitken	Middlesbrough
C. Thomson	Heart of Midlothian
P. McWilliam	Newcastle United
G. Stewart	Manchester City
G. Livingstone	Manchester City
A. Young	Everton
T. Fichie	Queen's Park
A. Smith	Rangers

Date. March 7, 1908
Venue. Dundee
Result. Scotland 2 Wales 1
Goalscorers. Scotland: Bennett, Lennie
Wales: Jones

H. Rennie	Hibernian
W. Agnew	Kilmarnock
G. Chaplin	Dundee
A. McNair	Celtic
C. Thomson	Heart of Midlothian
J. Galt	Rangers
A. Bennett	Celtic
R. Walker	Heart of Midlothian
J. Speirs	Rangers
A. McFarlane	Dundee
W. Lennie	Aberdeen

Date. March 1, 1909
Venue. Wrexham
Result. Wales 3 Scotland 2
Goalscorers. Wales: Davies (2), Jones
Scotland: Walker, Somers

P. McBride	Preston North End
T. Collins	Heart of Midlothian
J. Sharp	Fulham
J. May	Rangers
C. Thomson	Sunderland
P. McWilliam	Newcastle United
A. Bennett	Rangers
R. Walker	Heart of Midlothian
J. Hunter	Dundee
P. Somers	Celtic
H. Paul	Queen's Park

Date. March 5, 1910
Venue. Kilmarnock
Result. Scotland 1 Wales 0
Goalscorer. Devine

J. Brownlie	Third Lanark
G. Law	Rangers
J. Mitchell	Kilmarnock
A. McNair	Celtic
W. Loney	Celtic
J. Hay (Captain)	Celtic
A. Bennett	Rangers
J. McMenemy	Celtic
J. Quinn	Celtic
A. Devine	Falkirk
G. Robertson	Motherwell

Date. March 7, 1911
Venue. Ninian Park, Cardiff
Result. Wales 2 Scotland 2
Goalscorers. Wales: A. Morris (2)
Scotland: Hamilton (2)

J. Brownlie	Third Lanark
D. Colman	Aberdeen
J. Walker	Swindon Town
T. Tait	Sunderland
W. Low	Newcastle United
P. McWilliam	Newcastle United
A. Bennett	Rangers
J. McMenemy	Celtic
W. Reid	Rangers
A. McFarlane	Dundee
R. Hamilton	Dundee

Date. March 2, 1912
Venue. Tynecastle Park, Edinburgh
Result. Scotland 1 Wales 0
Goalscorer. Quinn

J. Brownlie	Third Lanark
A. McNair	Celtic
J. Walker	Swindon Town
R. Mercer	Heart of Midlothian
C. Thomson	Sunderland
J. Hay	Newcastle United
G. Sinclair	Heart of Midlothian
J. McMenemy	Celtic
J. Quinn	Celtic
R. Walker	Heart of Midlothian
G. Robertson	Sheffield Wednesday

Date. March 3, 1913
Venue. Wrexham
Result. Wales 0   Scotland 0

J. Brownlie	Third Lanark
R. Orrock	Falkirk
J. Walker	Swindon Town
J. Gordon	Rangers
C. Thomson	Sunderland
J. Campbell	Sheffield Wednesday
A. McAtee	Celtic
R. Walker	Heart of Midlothian
W. Reid	Rangers
A. Wilson	Sheffield Wednesday
R. Templeton	Kilmarnock

Date. February 28, 1914
Venue. Celtic Park, Glasgow
Result. Scotland 0   Wales 0

J. Brownlie	Third Lanark
T. Kelso	Dundee
J. Dodds	Celtic
P. Nellies	Heart of Midlothian
P. Pursell	Queen's Park
H. Anderson	Raith Rovers
A. Donaldson	Bolton Wanderers
J. McMenemy	Celtic
J. Reid	Airdrieonians
J. Croal	Falkirk
J. Browning	Celtic

Date. February 26, 1920
Venue. Cardiff
Result. Wales 1   Scotland 1
Goalscorers. Wales: Evans
Scotland: Cairns
Referee. J. Mason

K. Campbell	Liverpool
A. McNair	Celtic
D. Thomson	Dundee
J. Gordon	Rangers
W. Cringan	Celtic
J. McMullan	Partick Thistle
J. Reid	Airdrieonians
J. Crosbie	Ayr United
A. Wilson	Dunfermline Athletic
T. Cairns	Rangers
A. Morton	Queen's Park

Date. February 12, 1921
Venue. Aberdeen
Result. Scotland 2   Wales 1
Goalscorers. Scotland: Wilson (2)
Wales: Collier
Referee. J. Mason

K. Campbell	Partick Thistle
J. Marshall	Middlesbrough
W. McStay	Celtic
J. Harris	Partick Thistle
C. Pringle	St Mirren
J. McMullan	Partick Thistle
A. Archibald	Rangers
A. Cunningham	Rangers
A. Wilson	Dunfermline Athletic
J. Cassidy	Celtic
A. Troup	Dundee

Date. February 4, 1922
Venue. Wrexham
Result. Wales 2   Scotland 1
Goalscorers. Wales: L. Davies, S. Davies
Scotland: Archibald
Referee. A. Ward (Kirkham)

K. Campbell	Partick Thistle
J. Marshall	Middlesbrough
D. McKinlay	Liverpool
D. Meiklejohn	Rangers
M. Gilhooley	Hull City
W. Collier	Raith Rovers
A. Archibald	Rangers
J. White	Albion Rovers
A. Wilson	Middlesbrough
F. Walker	Third Lanark
A. Morton	Rangers

Date. March 17, 1923
Venue. Paisley
Result. Scotland 2 Wales 0
Goalscorer. Wilson (2)
Referee. I. Baker (England)
Remarks. Match postponed from February 3

W. Harper	Hibernian
J. Hutton	Aberdeen
J. Blair	Cardiff City
J. McNab	Liverpool
W. Cringan	Celtic
D. Steele	Huddersfield Town
H. Ritchie	Hibernian
A. Cunningham	Rangers
A. Wilson	Middlesbrough
T. Cairns	Rangers
A. Morton	Rangers

Date. February 16, 1924
Venue. Ninian Park, Cardiff
Result. Wales 2 Scotland 0
Goalscorers. W. Davies, L. Davies
Referee. H. W. Andrews (Prestwich)

W. Harper	Hibernian
J. Marshall	Llanelly
J. Blair	Cardiff City
D. Meiklejohn	Rangers
N. McBain	Everton
T. Muirhead	Rangers
A. Archibald	Rangers
W. Russell	Airdrieonians
J. Cassidy	Celtic
J. McKay	Blackburn Rovers
A. Morton	Rangers

Date. February 14, 1925
Venue. Tynecastle Park, Edinburgh
Result. Scotland 3 Wales 1
Goalscorers. Scotland: Meiklejohn, Gallacher (2)
Wales: Williams
Referee. A. Ward (Kirkham)

W. Harper	Hibernian
J. Nelson	Cardiff City
W. McStay	Celtic
D. Meiklejohn	Rangers
D. Morris	Raith Rovers
R. Bennie	Airdrieonians
A. Jackson	Aberdeen
J. Dunn	Hibernian
H. Gallacher	Airdrieonians
T. Cairns	Rangers
A. Morton	Rangers

Date. October 31, 1926
Venue. Ninian Park, Cardiff
Result. Wales 0 Scotland 3
Goalscorers. Duncan, McLean, Clunas
Referee. E. Pinckston (Birmingham)

W. Robb	Rangers
J. Hutton	Aberdeen
W. McStay	Celtic
W. Clunas	Sunderland
T. Townsley (Captain)	Falkirk
J. McMullan	Partick Thistle
A. Jackson	Huddersfield Town
J. Duncan	Leicester City
H. Gallacher	Airdrieonians
A. James	Preston North End
A. McLean	Celtic

Date. October 25, 1927
Venue. Ibrox Park
Result. Scotland 3 Ireland 0
Goalscorers. Jackson (2), Gallacher

A. McClory	Motherwell
W. McStay	Celtic
W. Wiseman	Queen's Park
J. Gibson	Partick Thistle
R. Gillespie	Queen's Park
J. McMullan (Captain)	Manchester City
A. Jackson	Huddersfield Town
A. Cunningham	Rangers
H. Gallacher	Newcastle United
T. MacInally	Celtic
A. McLean	Ccltic

Date. October 29, 1928
Venue. Wrexham
Result. Wales 2 Scotland 2
Goalscorers. Wales: Curtiss, Gibson (o.g.)
Scotland: Gallacher, Hutton
Referee. A. H. Kingscott (Long Eaton)

W. Robb	Hibernian
J. Hutton	Blackburn Rovers
W. McStay	Celtic
D. Meiklejohn	Rangers
J. Gibson	Aston Villa
J. McMullan (Captain)	Manchester City
A. Jackson	Huddersfield Town
R. McKay	Newcastle United
H. Gallacher	Newcastle United
G. Stevenson	Motherwell
A. Morton	Rangers

Date. October 27, 1929
Venue. Ibrox Park, Glasgow
Result. Scotland 4 Wales 2
Goalscorers. Scotland: Gallacher (3), Dunn
Wales: W. Davies (2)
Referee. A. H. Kingscott (Long Eaton)

J. Harkness	Heart of Midlothian
D. Gray	Rangers
D. Blair	Clyde
T. Muirhead	Rangers
W. King	Queen's Park
J. McMullan	Manchester City
A. Jackson	Huddersfield Town
J. Dunn	Everton
H. Gallacher	Newcastle United
R. McPhail	Rangers
A. Morton	Rangers

Date. October 26, 1930
Venue. Ninian Park, Cardiff
Result. Wales 2 Scotland 4
Goalscorers. Wales: O'Callaghan, L. Davies
Scotland: Gallacher (2), James, Gibson
Referee. W. McLean (Ireland)

J. Harkness	Heart of Midlothian
D. Gray	Rangers
J. Nibloe	Kilmarnock
J. Gibson	Aston Villa
J. Johnstone	Heart of Midlothian
T. Craig	Rangers
A. Jackson	Huddersfield Town
T. Muirhead	Rangers
H. Gallacher	Newcastle United
A. James	Arsenal
A. Morton	Rangers

Date. October 25, 1931
Venue. Ibrox Park, Glasgow
Result. Scotland 1 Wales 1
Goalscorers. Scotland: Battles
Wales: Bamford
Referee. C. E. Lines (Birmingham)

J. Thomson	Celtic
D. Gray	Rangers
J. Gilmour	Dundee
C. McNab	Dundee
R. Gillespie (Captain)	Queen's Park
F. Hill	Aberdeen
D. McRorie	Morton
G. Brown	Rangers
B. Battles	Heart of Midlothian
G. Stevenson	Motherwell
A. Morton	Rangers

Date. October 31, 1932
Venue. Wrexham
Result. Wales 2 Scotland 3
Goalscorers. Wales: Curtis (2)
Scotland: Stevenson, Thomson, McGrory
Referee. I. Caswell (Blackburn)

J. Harkness	Heart of Midlothian
D. Blair	Clyde
R. McAulay	Rangers
A. Massie	Heart of Midlothian
D. Meiklejohn	Rangers
G. Brown	Rangers
R. Thomson	Celtic
G. Stevenson	Motherwell
J. McGrory	Celtic
R. McPhail	Rangers
A. Morton	Rangers

Date. October 26, 1933
Venue. Tynecastle Park, Edinburgh
Result. Scotland 2 Wales 5
Goalscorers. Scotland: Dewar, Duncan
Wales: O'Callaghan (2), Astley, Griffiths, J. Thomson (o.g.)
Referee. W. P. Harper (Stourbridge)

A. McLaren	St Johnstone
D. Gray	Rangers
D. Blair	Aston Villa
H. Wales	Motherwell
J. Johnstone	Heart of Midlothian
J. Thomson	Everton
J. Crawford	Queen's Park
A. Thomson	Celtic
N. Dewar	Third Lanark
A. James	Arsenal
D. Duncan	Derby County

Date. October 4, 1934
Venue. Cardiff
Result. Wales 3 Scotland 2
Goalscorers. Wales: Evans, Robbins, Astley
Scotland: McFadyen, Duncan

J. Harkness	Heart of Midlothian
A. Anderson	Heart of Midlothian
D. Urquhart	Hibernian
M. Busby	Manchester City
J. Blair	Motherwell
J. McLuckie	Manchester City
F. McGurk	Birmingham City
J. McMenemy	Motherwell
W. McFadyen	Motherwell
J. Easson	Portsmouth
D. Duncan	Derby County

Date. November 21, 1935
Venue. Pittodrie Park, Aberdeen
Result. Scotland 3 Wales 2
Goalscorers. Scotland: Duncan, Napier (2)
Wales: Phillips, Astley

A. McClory	Motherwell
A. Anderson	Heart of Midlothian
W. McGonagle	Celtic
A. Massie	Heart of Midlothian
J. Simpson	Rangers
G. Brown	Rangers
W. Cook	Bolton Wanderers
T. Walker	Heart of Midlothian
D. McCulloch	Heart of Midlothian
C. Napier	Celtic
D. Duncan	Derby County

Date. October 5, 1936
Venue. Ninian Park, Cardiff
Result. Wales 1 Scotland 1
Goalscorers. Wales: Phillips
Scotland: Duncan

J. Jackson	Chelsea
A. Anderson	Heart of Midlothian
G. Cummings	Partick Thistle
A. Massie	Heart of Midlothian
J. Simpson	Rangers
G. Brown	Rangers
J. Delaney	Celtic
T. Walker	Heart of Midlothian
M. Armstrong	Aberdeen
W. Mills	Aberdeen
D. Duncan	Derby County

Date. December 2, 1937
Venue. Dens Park, Dundee
Result. Scotland 1 Wales 2
Goalscorers. Scotland: Walker
Wales: Glover (2)
Referee. Dr A. W. Barton (England)

J. Dawson	Rangers
A. Anderson	Heart of Midlothian
R. Ancell	Newcastle United
A. Massie	Aston Villa
J. Simpson	Rangers
G. Brown	Rangers
A. Munro	Heart of Midlothian
T. Walker	Heart of Midlothian
D. McCulloch	Brentford
W. Mills	Aberdeen
D. Duncan	Derby County

Date. October 30, 1938
Venue. Ninian Park, Cardiff
Result. Wales 2 Scotland 1
Goalscorers. Wales: B. Jones, Morris
Scotland: Massie
Referee. C. E. Argent (St Albans)

J. Dawson	Rangers
A. Anderson	Heart of Midlothian
G. Cummings	Aston Villa
A. Massie	Aston Villa
J. Simpson	Rangers
G. Brown	Rangers
R. Main	Rangers
T. Walker	Heart of Midlothian
F. O'Donnell	Preston North End
R. McPhail	Rangers
D. Duncan	Derby County

Date. November 9, 1939
Venue. Tynecastle Park, Edinburgh
Result. Scotland 3 Wales 2
Goalscorers. Scotland: Walker (2), Gillick
Wales: Astley, L. Jones

J. Brown	Clyde
A. Anderson	Heart of Midlothian
A. Beattie	Preston North End
W. Shankly	Preston North End
R. Baxter	Middlesbrough
A. Miller	Heart of Midlothian
J. Delaney	Celtic
T. Walker	Heart of Midlothian
D. McCulloch	Derby County
R. Beattie	Preston North End
T. Gillick	Everton

Date. November 10, 1946
Venue. Hampden Park, Glasgow
Result. Scotland 2 Wales 0
Goalscorers. Dodds, Waddell
Referee. M. C. Dale (Glasgow)
Linesmen. W. Adam (Glasgow)
W. Brown (Bellshill)

R. Brown	Queen's Park
J. McPhee	Falkirk
J. Shaw	Rangers
W. Campbell	Greenock Morton
A. Paton	Motherwell
G. Paterson	Celtic
W. Waddell	Rangers
G. Smith	Hibernian
E. Dodds	Blackpool
J. Deakin	St Mirren
W. Liddell	Liverpool

Date. October 19, 1947
Venue. Wrexham
Result. Wales 3 Scotland 1
Goalscorer. Scotland: Waddell
Referee. W. H. Evans (Liverpool)
Linesman. A. Young (Dumfries)

W. Miller	Celtic
J. F. Stephen	Bradford
D. Shaw	Hibernian
H. Brown	Partick Thistle
F. Brennan	Newcastle United
J. Husband	Partick Thistle
W. Waddell	Rangers
N. Dougal	Birmingham City
W. Thornton	Rangers
J. Blair	Blackpool
W. Liddell	Liverpool

Date. November 12, 1948
Venue. Hampden Park, Glasgow
Result. Scotland 1 Wales 2
Goalscorer. Scotland: McLaren
Referee. A. E. Ellis (Halifax)
Linesman. L. G. McDonald (Stirling)

W. Miller	Celtic
J. Govan	Hibernian
J. F. Stephen	Bradford
A. Macaulay	West Ham United
W. Woodburn	Rangers
A. Forbes	Sheffield United
G. Smith	Hibernian
A. McLaren	Preston North End
J. Delaney	Manchester United
W. Steel	Derby County
W. Liddell	Liverpool

Date. October 23, 1949
Venue. Cardiff
Result. Wales 1 Scotland 3
Goalscorers. Scotland: Waddell (2), Howie
Referee. D. Maxwell (Belfast)
Linesman. W. Morrison (Clydebank)

J. Cowan	Greenock Morton
H. Howie	Hibernian
D. Shaw	Hibernian
R. Evans	Celtic
G. Young	Rangers
W. Redpath	Motherwell
W. Waddell	Rangers
J. Mason	Third Lanark
L. Reilly	Hibernian
W. Steel	Derby County
J. Kelly	Barnsley

Date. November 9, 1950
Venue. Hampden Park, Glasgow
Result. Scotland 2 Wales 0
Goalscorers. McPhail, Linwood
Referee. S. E. Law (West Bromwich)
Linesmen. P. F. Power (York)
J. W. Bowes (Huddersfield)

J. Cowan	Greenock Morton
G. Young	Rangers
S. Cox	Rangers
R. Evans	Celtic
W. Woodburn	Rangers
G. Aitken	East Fife
W. Liddell	Liverpool
J. McPhail	Celtic
A. Linwood	Clyde
W. Steel	Derby County
L. Reilly	Hibernian

Date. October 21, 1951
Venue. Cardiff
Result. Wales 1 Scotland 3
Goalscorers. Scotland: Reilly (2), Liddell
Referee. A. E. Ellis (Halifax)
Linesmen. W. T. Marsh (Devon)
W. R. Rodgers (Birmingham)

J. Cowan	Greenock Morton
G. Young	Rangers
W. McNaught	Raith Rovers
I. McColl	Rangers
W. Woodburn	Rangers
A. Forbes	Arsenal
R. Collins	Celtic
J. McPhail	Celtic
L. Reilly	Hibernian
W. Steel	Dundee
W. Liddell	Liverpool

Date. November 14, 1952
Venue. Hampden Park, Glasgow
Result. Scotland 0 Wales 1
Referee. P. Morris (Belfast)
Linesmen. J. Davidson (Newtonards)
T. J. Mitchell (Lurgan)

J. Cowan	Greenock Morton
G. Young	Rangers
S. Cox	Rangers
T. H. Docherty	Preston North End
W. Woodburn	Rangers
A. Forbes	Arsenal
W. Waddell	Rangers
T. Orr	Greenock Morton
L. Reilly	Hibernian
W. Steel	Dundee
W. Liddell	Liverpool

Date. October 18, 1953
Venue. Cardiff
Result. Wales 1 Scotland 2
Goalscorers. Scotland: Brown, Liddell
Referee. A. Bond (London)
Linesmen. G. W. Pullin (Bristol)
W. H. Davey (Torquay)

G. Farm	Blackpool
G. Young	Rangers
S. Cox	Rangers
J. Scoular	Portsmouth
F. Brennan	Newcastle United
G. Aitken	Sunderland
T. Wright	Sunderland
A. Brown	Blackpool
L. Reilly	Hibernian
W. Steel	Dundee
W. Liddell	Liverpool

Date. November 4, 1954
Venue. Hampden Park, Glasgow
Result. Scotland 3 Wales 3
Goalscorers. Scotland: Brown, Johnstone, Reilly
Referee. T. J. Mitchell
Linesmen. J. Davidson
R. J. Quail

G. Farm	Blackpool
G. Young	Rangers
S. Cox	Rangers
R. Evans	Celtic
W. Telfer	St Mirren
D. Cowie	Dundee
J. McKenzie	Partick Thistle
R. Johnstone	Hibernian
L. Reilly	Hibernian
A. Brown	Blackpool
W. Liddell	Liverpool

Date. October 16, 1955
Venue. Cardiff
Result. Wales 0 Scotland 1
Goalscorer. Buckley
Referee. W. Ling (Stapleford)
Linesmen. G. Pankhurst (Warwick)
T. Jepson (Mansfield)

W. Fraser	Sunderland
G. Young	Rangers
W. Cunningham	Preston North End
T. Docherty	Preston North End
J. Davidson	Partick Thistle
D. Cowie	Dundee
W. Waddell	Rangers
H. Yorston	Aberdeen
P. Buckley	Aberdeen
W. Fernie	Celtic
T. Ring	Clyde

Date. November 9, 1956
Venue. Hampden Park, Glasgow
Result. Scotland 2 Wales 0
Goalscorer. Johnstone (2)
Referee. R. J. Leafe (Nottingham)
Linesmen. J. Mitchell (Whitson)
W. W. Sutcliffe (Halifax)

T. Younger	Hibernian
A. H. Parker	Falkirk
J. McDonald	Sunderland
R. Evans	Celtic
G. Young	Rangers
D. Cowie	Dundee
G. Smith	Hibernian
R. Johnstone	Manchester City
L. Reilly	Hibernian
R. Collins	Celtic
J. Henderson	Portsmouth

Date. October 20, 1957
Venue. Cardiff
Result. Wales 2 Scotland 2
Goalscorers. Scotland: Fernie, Reilly
Referee. R. H. Mann (Worcester)
Linesmen. E. Jennings (Stourbridge)
E. G. Dodge (Bath)

T. Younger	Liverpool
A. H. Parker	Falkirk
J. Hewie	Charlton Athletic
I. McColl	Rangers
G. Young	Rangers
D. Cowie	Dundee
G. Leggat	Aberdeen
J. Mudie	Blackpool
L. Reilly	Hibernian
R. Collins	Celtic
W. Fernie	Celtic

Date. November 13, 1958
Venue. Hampden Park, Glasgow
Result. Scotland 1 Wales 1
Goalscorers. Scotland: Collins
Wales: Medwin
Referee. J. H. Clough (Bolton)
Linesmen. H. Hawthorne (Crook)
J. Bruce (Newcastle)

T. Younger	Liverpool
A. H. Parker	Falkirk
E. Caldow	Rangers
T. Docherty (Captain)	Preston North End
R. Evans	Celtic
W. Fernie	Celtic
A. Scott	Rangers
R. Collins	Celtic
J. I. Gardiner	Motherwell
J. K. Mudie	Blackpool
T. Ewing	Partick Thistle

Date. October 18, 1959
Venue. Ninian Park, Cardiff
Result. Wales 0 Scotland 3
Goalscorers. Leggat, Law, Collins
Referee. R. J. Leafe (Nottingham)
Linesmen. W. J. Paradise (Frome)
J. Hemming (Chesterfield)

W. D. F. Brown	Dundee
J. Grant	Hibernian
E. Caldow	Rangers
D. C. Mackay (Captain)	Heart of Midlothian
W. Toner	Kilmarnock
T. Docherty	Arsenal
G. Leggat	Fulham
R. Collins	Everton
D. Herd	Arsenal
D. Law	Huddersfield Town
J. Henderson	Arsenal

Date. October 22, 1960
Venue. Hampden Park, Glasgow
Result. Scotland 1 Wales 1
Goalscorer. Leggat

W. D. F. Brown	Dundee
E. Caldow	Rangers
D. C. Mackay	Heart of Midlothian
J. Hewie	Charlton
A. Evans	Celtic
R. MacCann	Motherwell
G. Leggat	Aberdeen
J. A. White	Tottenham Hotspur
I. St. John	Motherwell
D. Law	Huddersfield
R. Auld	Rangers

Date. October 22, 1961
Venue. Ninian Park, Cardiff
Result. Wales 2 Scotland 0
Goalscorers. Jones, Vernon
Referee. A. Holland (Barnsley)
Linesmen. F. Alford (Tiverton)
R. Stevens (Midsomer Norton)

L. G. Leslie	Airdrieonians
D. MacKay	Celtic
E. Caldow (Captain)	Rangers
J. Gabriel	Everton
J. Martis	Motherwell
D. C. Mackay	Tottenham Hotspur
G. Herd	Clyde
J. A. White	Tottenham Hotspur
A. Young	Heart of Midlothian
W. Hunter	Motherwell
D. Wilson	Rangers

Date. November 8, 1962
Venue. Hampden Park, Glasgow
Result. Scotland 2 Wales 0
Goalscorer. St John (2)
Referee. A. Holland (Barnsley)
Linesmen. A. Gorton (Macclesfield)
J. A. Russell (Leeds)
Remarks. First match in British International Championship to be played fully by floodlight

W. D. F. Brown	Tottenham Hotspur
A. W. Hamilton	Dundee
E. Caldow (Captain)	Rangers
P. T. Crerand	Celtic
J. F. Ure	Dundee
J. Baxter	Rangers
A. Scott	Rangers
J. A. White	Tottenham Hotspur
I. St John	Liverpool
R. Brand	Rangers
D. Wilson	Rangers

Date. October 20, 1963
Venue. Ninian Park, Cardiff
Result. Wales 2 Scotland 3
Goalscorers. Wales: Allchurch, J. Charles
Scotland: Caldow (pen.), Law, Henderson
Referee. K. Dagnall (Bolton)
Linesmen. K. R. B. Hall (Bristol)
L. E. Hewlett (Solihull)

W. D. F. Brown	Tottenham Hotspur
A. W. Hamilton	Dundee
E. Caldow (Captain)	Rangers
P. T. Crerand	Celtic
J. F. Ure	Dundee
J. Baxter	Rangers
W. Henderson	Rangers
J. A. White	Tottenham Hotspur
I. St John	Liverpool
D. Law	Manchester United
D. Wilson	Rangers

Date. November 20, 1964
Venue. Hampden Park, Glasgow
Result. Scotland 2 Wales 1
Goalscorers. Scotland: White, Law
Wales: B. Jones
Referee. W. Clements (West Bromwich)
Linesmen. J. Butler (Sunderland)
H. Ashton (St Helens)

W. D. F. Brown	Tottenham Hotspur
A. W. Hamilton	Dundee
J. Kennedy	Celtic
D. C. Mackay (Captain)	Tottenham Hotspur
W. McNeill	Celtic
J. Baxter	Rangers
W. Henderson	Rangers
J. A. White	Tottenham Hotspur
A. J. Gilzean	Dundee
D. Law	Manchester United
A. Scott	Everton

Date. November 24, 1965
Venue. Hampden Park, Glasgow
Result. Scotland 4 Wales 1
Goalscorers. Scotland: Murdoch (2), Henderson, Greig
Wales: Allchurch
Referee. J. Finney (Hereford)
Linesmen. H. G. Wilson (Stockton-on-Tees)
A. Hetherington (Blyth)

R. Ferguson	Kilmarnock
J. Greig	Rangers
E. G. McCreadie	Chelsea
R. Murdoch	Celtic
R. McKinnon	Rangers
J. Baxter (Captain)	Sunderland
W. Henderson	Rangers
C. Cooke	Dundee
J. Forrest	Rangers
A. J. Gilzean	Tottenham Hotspur
W. Johnston	Rangers

Date. November 24, 1966
Venue. Hampden Park, Glasgow
Result. Scotland 4 Wales 1
Goalscorers. Scotland: Murdoch (2), Henderson, Greig
Wales: Allchurch
Referee. J. Finney (Hereford)
Linesmen. H. G. Wilson (Stockton-on-Tees)
A. Hetherington (Blyth)

R. Ferguson	Kilmarnock
J. Greig	Rangers
E. G. McCreadie	Chelsea
R. Murdoch	Celtic
R. McKinnon	Rangers
J. Baxter (Captain)	Sunderland
W. Henderson	Rangers
C. Cooke	Dundee
J. Forrest	Rangers
A. J. Gilzean	Tottenham Hotspur
W. Johnston	Rangers

Date. October 22, 1967
Venue. Ninian Park, Cardiff
Result. Wales 1 Scotland 1
Goalscorers. Wales: R. Davies
Scotland: Law
Referee. K. Dagnall (Bolton)
Linesmen. N. C. H. Burtenshaw (Great Yarmouth)
L. Newsome (London)

R. Ferguson	Kilmarnock
J. Greig (Captain)	Rangers
T. Gemmell	Celtic
W. Bremner	Leeds United
R. McKinnon	Rangers
J. Clark	Celtic
J. Johnstone	Celtic
D. Law	Manchester United
J. McBride	Celtic
J. Baxter	Sunderland
W. Henderson	Rangers

Date. November 22, 1968
Venue. Hampden Park, Glasgow
Result. Scotland 3 Wales 2
Goalscorers. Scotland: Gilzean (2), McKinnon
Wales: Durban 2
Referee. J. Finney (Hereford)
Linesmen. G. McCabe (Sheffield)
W. B. Johnson (Westmorland)

R. Clark	Aberdeen
J. Craig	Celtic
E. McCreadie	Chelsea
J. Greig (Captain)	Rangers
R. McKinnon	Rangers
J. Baxter	Sunderland
J. Johnstone	Celtic
W. Bremner	Leeds United
A. Gilzean	Tottenham Hotspur
W. Johnston	Rangers
R. Lennox	Celtic

Date. May 3, 1969 *Venue*. Wrexham *Result*. Wales 3 Scotland 5 *Goalscorers*. Wales: Davies (2), Toshack Scotland: McNeil, Stein, Gilzean, Bremner, McLean *Referee*. J. Finney (Hereford) *Linesmen*. E. T. Jennings (Stourbridge) E. Loukes (Sheffield) *Remarks*. J. Herriot (Birmingham City) substituted for Lawrence who was injured during the second half	T. Lawrence T. Gemmell E. McCreadie W. Bremner (Captain) W. McNeil J. Greig T. McLean R. Murdoch C. Stein A. Gilzean C. Cooke	Liverpool Celtic Chelsea Leeds United Celtic Rangers Kilmarnock Celtic Rangers Tottenham Hotspur Chelsea
Date. April 22, 1970 *Venue*. Hampden Park, Glasgow *Result*. Scotland 0 Wales 0 *Referee*. D. W. Smith (Stonehouse) *Linesmen*. K. H. Burns (Wordsley) J. Bell (Newcastle) *Remarks*. R. Lennox (Celtic) substituted for McLean during the second half	J. Cruickshank W. Callaghan W. Dickson J. Greig (Captain) R. McKinnon R. Moncur T. McLean D. Hay C. Stein J. O'Hare W. Carr	Heart of Midlothian Dunfermline Athletic Kilmarnock Rangers Rangers Newcastle United Kilmarnock Celtic Rangers Derby County Coventry City
Date. May 15, 1971 *Venue*. Ninian Park, Cardiff *Result*. Wales 0 Scotland 0 *Referee*. J. K. Taylor (England) *Linesmen*. K. E. Walker (England) J. E. Griffiths (England) *Remarks*. J. Greig (Rangers) was substituted for W. Bremner during the second half	R. Clark D. Hay J. Brogan W. Bremner F. McLintock R. Moncur (Captain) P. Lorimer P. Cormack D. Robb J. O'Hare E. Gray	Aberdeen Celtic Celtic Leeds United Arsenal Newcastle United Leeds United Nottingham Forest Aberdeen Derby County Leeds United
Date. May 24, 1972 *Venue*. Hampden Park, Glasgow *Result*. Scotland 1 Wales 0 *Goalscorer*. Lorimer *Referee*. J. Lawther (Bangor) *Linesmen*. H. Wright (Portadown) H. Wilson (Belfast) *Remarks*. R. Hartford (West Bromwich Albion) was substituted for A. Gemmill in the first half, and L. Macari (Celtic) was substituted for J. O'Hare in the second half	R. Clark P. Stanton M. Buchan W. Bremner (Captain) W. McNeill R. Moncur P. Lorimer A. Gemmill J. O'Hare D. Law A. Green	Aberdeen Hibernian Manchester United Leeds United Celtic Newcastle United Leeds United Derby County Derby County Manchester United Newcastle United

Date. May 16, 1931
Venue. Vienna
Result. Austria 5 Scotland 0
Goalscorers. Schall, Gischek (2), Vogel, Simdelwar
Referee. P. Ruoff (Switzerland)

J. Jackson	Partick Thistle
D. Blair (Captain)	Clyde
J. Nibloe	Kilmarnock
C. McNab	Dundee
G. Walker	St Mirren
J. McDougall	Liverpool
A. Love	Aberdeen
J. Robertson	Dundee
J. Paterson	Cowdenbeath
J. Easson	Portsmouth
D. Liddle	East Fife

Date. November 29, 1933
Venue. Hampden Park, Glasgow
Result. Scotland 2 Austria 2
Goalscorers. Scotland: Seszta (o.g.), McFadyen
Austria: Zischek, Schall
Referee. J. Langenus (Belgium)

J. Kennaway	Celtic
A. Anderson	Heart of Midlothian
W. McGonagle	Celtic
D. Meiklejohn	Rangers
P. Watson	Blackpool
G. Brown	Rangers
D. Ogilvie	Motherwell
R. Bruce	Middlesbrough
W. McFadyen	Motherwell
R. McPhail	Rangers
D. Duncan	Derby County

Date. May 9, 1937
Venue. Vienna
Result. Austria 1 Scotland 1
Goalscorers. Austria: Sindelar
Scotland: O'Donnell

J. Dawson	Rangers
A. Anderson	Heart of Midlothian
A. Beattie	Preston North End
A. Massie	Aston Villa
J. Simpson	Rangers
A. McNab	Sunderland
J. Delaney	Celtic
T. Walker	Heart of Midlothian
F. O'Donnell	Preston North End
C. Napier	Derby County
T. Gillick	Everton

Date. December 13, 1950
Venue. Hampden Park, Glasgow
Result. Scotland 0 Austria 1
Goalscorer. Mechior
Referee. W. Ling (Stapleford)
Linesmen. R. Meikle (Hamilton)
J. C. Dyer (Greenock)
Remarks. This was the first occasion on which one of the four British Associations lost at home to a foreign country

J. Cowan	Morton
G. Young (Captain)	Rangers
W. McNaught	Raith Rovers
R. Evans	Celtic
W. A. Woodburn	Rangers
A. Forbes	Arsenal
R. Collins	Celtic
E. Turnbull	Hibernian
J. McPhail	Celtic
W. Steel	Dundee
W. B. Liddell	Liverpool

Date. May 27, 1951
Venue. Vienna
Result. Austria 4 Scotland 0

J. Cowan	Greenock Morton
G. Young	Rangers
S. Cox	Rangers
J. Scoular	Portsmouth
W. Woodburn	Rangers
W. Redpath	Motherwell
W. Waddell	Rangers
J. Mason	Third Lanark
G. Hamilton	Aberdeen
W. Steel	Dundee
L. Reilly	Hibernian

Date. May 19, 1955
Venue. Vienna
Result. Austria 1 Scotland 4
Goalscorers. Scotland: Smith, Robertson, Reilly, Liddell

T. Younger	Hibernian
A. H. Parker	Falkirk
A. Kerr	Partick Thistle
T. H. Docherty	Preston North End
R. Evans	Celtic
D. Cowie	Dundee
G. Smith	Hibernian
R. Collins	Celtic
L. Reilly	Hibernian
A. Robertson	Clyde
W. Liddell	Liverpool

Date. May 2, 1956
Venue. Hampden Park, Glasgow
Result. Scotland 1 Austria 1
Goalscorers. Scotland: Conn
Austria: Wagner
Referee. J. Bronkhurst (Holland)
Linesmen. C. G. Van Doorn (Holland)
G. G. Florin (Holland)

T. Younger	Hibernian
A. H. Parker	Falkirk
J. Hewie	Charlton Athletic
R. Evans	Celtic
G. Young (Captain)	Rangers
D. Cowie	Dundee
J. McKenzie	Partick Thistle
A. Conn	Heart of Midlothian
L. Reilly	Hibernian
H. Baird	Airdrieonians
M. Cullen	Luton Town

Date. May 29, 1960
Venue. Vienna
Result. Austria 4 Scotland 1
Goalscorers. Austria: Hanappi (2), Hof (2)
Scotland: D. C. Mackay
Referee. A. Dusch (Germany)
Linesmen. L. Fischer (Germany)
R. Kreitlen (Germany)
Remarks. Law was injured after 11 minutes and was replaced by A. Young (Heart of Midlothian)

W. D. F. Brown	Tottenham Hotspur
D. MacKay	Celtic
E. Caldow	Rangers
D. C. Mackay	Tottenham Hotspur
R. Evans (Captain)	Celtic
J. Cumming	Heart of Midlothian
G. Leggat	Fulham
J. A. White	Tottenham Hotspur
I. St John	Motherwell
D. Law	Manchester City
A. Weir	Motherwell

Date. May 8, 1963
Venue. Hampden Park, Glasgow
Result. Scotland 4 Austria 1
Goalscorers. Scotland: Wilson (2), Law (2)
Austria: Linhart
Referee. J. Finney (Hereford)
Linesmen. A. E. Ellis (Halifax)
E. Henderson (Consett)
Remarks. The referee abandoned the game in the seventy-ninth minute because, in terms of his report, 'The Austrian players and officials were bringing the game into disrepute'.

W. D. F. Brown	Tottenham Hotspur
A. W. Hamilton	Dundee
D. D. Holt	Heart of Midlothian
D. C. Mackay (Captain)	Tottenham Hotspur
J. F. Ure	Dundee
J. Baxter	Rangers
W. Henderson	Rangers
D. Gibson	Leicester City
J. Millar	Rangers
D. Law	Manchester United
D. Wilson	Rangers

Versus Belgium 1946–1951

Date. January 23, 1946
Venue. Hampden Park, Glasgow
Result. Scotland 2 Belgium 2
Goalscorers. Scotland: Delaney (2)
Referee. J. Jackson (Glasgow)
Linesman. W. G. Livingstone (Glasgow)

R. Brown	Queen's Park
J. McGowan	Partick Thistle
J. Shaw	Rangers
W. Campbell	Greenock Morton
A. Paton	Motherwell
G. Paterson	Celtic
G. Smith	Hibernian
A. Baird	Aberdeen
J. Delaney	Celtic
J. Deakin	St Mirren
J. Walker	Heart of Midlothian

Date. May 18, 1947
Venue. Brussels
Result. Belgium 2 Scotland 1
Goalscorer. Scotland: Steel

W. Miller	Celtic
G. Young	Rangers
J. Shaw	Rangers
H. Brown	Partick Thistle
W. Woodburn	Rangers
A. Forbes	Sheffield United
R. Campbell	Falkirk
A. McLaren	Preston North End
R. Flavell	Airdrieonians
W. Steel	Greenock Morton
T. Pearson	Newcastle United

Date. April 28, 1948
Venue. Hampden Park, Glasgow
Result. Scotland 2 Belgium 0
Goalscorers. Combe, Duncan
Referee. W. Ling (Stapleford)
Linesmen. R. M. Main (Glasgow)
J. de Rees (Belgium)

J. Cowan	Morton
J. Govan	Hibernian
D. Shaw	Hibernian
W. Campbell	Morton
G. Young (Captain)	Rangers
A. R. Macaulay	Arsenal
G. Smith	Hibernian
R. Combe	Hibernian
L. Johnstone	Clyde
E. Turnbull	Hibernian
D. Duncan	East Fife

Date. May 21, 1951
Venue. Brussels
Result. Belgium 0 Scotland 5
Goalscorers. Hamilton (3), Mason, Waddell

J. Cowan	Greenock Morton
G. Young	Rangers
S. Cox	Rangers
I. McColl	Rangers
W. Woodburn	Rangers
W. Redpath	Motherwell
W. Waddell	Rangers
J. Mason	Third Lanark
G. Hamilton	Aberdeen
W. Steel	Dundee
L. Reilly	Hibernian

Versus Brazil 1966

Date. May 25, 1966
Venue. Hampden Park, Glasgow
Result. Scotland 1 Brazil 1
Goalscorers. Scotland: Chalmers
Brazil: Servilio
Referee. J. Finney (Hereford)
Linesmen. E. Crawford (Doncaster)
D. F. Morgan (Rotherham)

R. Ferguson	Kilmarnock
J. Greig (Captain)	Rangers
W. Bell	Leeds United
W. Bremner	Leeds United
R. McKinnon	Rangers
J. Clark	Celtic
A. Scott	Everton
C. Cooke	Chelsea
S. Chalmers	Celtic
J. Baxter	Sunderland
P. Cormack	Hibernian

Versus Czechoslovakia 1937

Date. May 22, 1937
Venue. Prague
Result. Czechoslovakia 1 Scotland 3
Goalscorers. Czechoslovakia: Puc
Scotland: Simpson, McPhail, Gillick
Referee. Dr P. J. Bauwens (Germany)

J. Dawson	Rangers
Hogg	Celtic
A. Beattie	Preston North End
Thomson	Sunderland
J. Simpson	Rangers
G. Brown	Rangers
J. Delaney	Celtic
T. Walker	Heart of Midlothian
F. O'Donnell	Preston North End
R. McPhail	Rangers
T. Gillick	Everton

Date. August 8, 1937
Venue. Ibrox Park, Glasgow
Result. Scotland 5 Czechoslovakia 0
Goalscorers.. McCulloch (2), Buchanan, Black, Kinnear
Referee. T. Thompson (Northumberland)
Linesmen. H. Watson (Glasgow)
M. C. Hutton (Glasgow)

W. Waugh	Heart of Midlothian
A. Anderson	Heart of Midlothian
G. Cummings	Aston Villa
G. Robertson	Kilmarnock
R. Johnstone	Sunderland
G. C. P. Brown	Rangers
P. Buchanan	Chelsea
T. Walker	Heart of Midlothian
D. McCulloch	Brentford
A. Black	Heart of Midlothian
D. Kinnear	Rangers

Versus Denmark 1951–1968

Date. May 12, 1951
Venue. Hampden Park, Glasgow
Result. Scotland 3 Denmark 1
Goalscorers. Scotland: Steel, Reilly Mitchell
Denmark: W. Hansen
Referee. W. E. Evans (Lancashire)
Linesmen. A. B. Henry (Peebles)
J. McTaggart (Glasgow)

J. Cowan	Morton
G. Young (Captain)	Rangers
S. R. Cox	Rangers
J. Scoular	Portsmouth
W. A. Woodburn	Rangers
W. Redpath	Motherwell
W. Waddell	Rangers
R. Johnstone	Hibernian
L. Reilly	Hibernian
W. Steel	Dundee
R. Mitchell	Newcastle United

Date. May 25, 1952
Venue. Copenhagen
Result. Denmark 1 Scotland 2
Goalscorers. Scotland: Reilly, Thornton

J. Cowan	Greenock Morton
G. Young	Rangers
S. Cox	Rangers
J. Scoular	Portsmouth
A. Paton	Motherwell
A. Forbes	Arsenal
L. Reilly	Hibernian
I. McMillan	Airdrieonians
W. Thornton	Rangers
A. Brown	Blackpool
W. Liddell	Liverpool

Date. October 16, 1968
Venue. Idraetspark, Copenhagen
Result. Denmark 0 Scotland 1
Goalscorer. Lennox
Referee. H. Carlsson (Sweden)
Linesmen. L. Ekfeldt (Sweden)
S. Lindquist (Sweden)
Remarks. P. Cormack (Hibernian) substituted for J. McCalliog shortly before the end of the game

J. Herriot	Birmingham City
T. Gemmell	Celtic
E. McCreadie	Chelsea
W. Bremner (Captain)	Leeds United
R. MacKinnon	Rangers
J. Greig	Rangers
T. McLean	Kilmarnock
J. McCalliog	Sheffield Wednesday
C. Stein	Hibernian
R. Hope	West Bromwich Albion
R. Lennox	Celtic

Versus Finland 1954

Date. May 25, 1954
Venue. Helsinki
Result. Finland 1 Scotland 2
Goalscorers. Scotland: Ormond, Johnstone

J. Anderson	Leicester City
A. Wilson	Portsmouth
W. Cunningham	Preston North End
R. Evans	Celtic
D. Cowie	Dundee
D. Mathers	Partick Thistle
J. McKenzie	Partick Thistle
R. Johnstone	Hibernian
A. Brown	Blackpool
W. Fernie	Celtic
W. Ormond	Hibernian

Versus France 1930–1951

Date. May 18, 1930
Venue. Paris
Result. France 0 Scotland 2
Goalscorer. Gallacher (2)

J. Thomson	Celtic
J. Nelson	Cardiff City
J. Crapnell	Airdrieonians
P. Wilson	Celtic
G. Walker	St Mirren
F. Hill	Aberdeen
A. Jackson	Huddersfield Town
A. Cheyne	Aberdeen
H. Gallacher	Newcastle United
G. Stevenson	Motherwell
J. Connor	Sunderland

Date. May 8, 1932
Venue. Paris
Result. France 1 Scotland 3
Goalscorers. France: Langiller (pen.)
Scotland: Dewar (3)
Referee. A. Carraro (Italy)

J. D. Harkness	Queen's Park
J. Crapnell	Airdrieonians
J. Nibloc	Kilmarnock
A. Massie	Heart of Midlothian
R. Gillespie (Captain)	Queen's Park
J. Miller	St Mirren
J. Crawford	Queen's Park
A. Thomson	Celtic
N. Dewar	Third Lanark
R. McPhail	Rangers
A. Morton	Rangers

Date. May 23, 1948
Venue. Paris
Result. France 3 Scotland 0

J. Cowan	Greenock Morton
J. Govan	Hibernian
D. Shaw	Hibernian
W. Campbell	Greenock Morton
G. Young	Rangers
A. Macaulay	Arsenal
E. Rutherford	Rangers
W. Steel	Derby County
G. Smith	Hibernian
J. Cox	Heart of Midlothian
D. Duncan	East Fife

Date. April 27, 1949
Venue. Hampden Park, Glasgow
Result. Scotland 2 France 0
Goalscorer. Steel (2)
Referee. W. Ling (Stapleford)
Linesmen. F. Thurman (Preston)
F. H. Gerrard (Preston)

J. Cowan	Morton
G. Young (Captain)	Rangers
S. R. Cox	Rangers
R. Evans	Celtic
W. A. Woodburn	Rangers
G. Aitken	East Fife
W. Waddell	Rangers
W. Thornton	Rangers
W. Houliston	Queen of the South
W. Steel	Derby County
L. Reilly	Hibernian

Date. May 27, 1950
Venue. Paris
Result. France 0 Scotland 1
Goalscorer. Brown

J. Cowan	Morton
G. Young (Captain)	Rangers
S. R. Cox	Rangers
J. McColl	Rangers
W. Woodburn	Rangers
A. Forbes	Arsenal
R. Campbell	Chelsea
A. Brown	East Fife
L. Reilly	Hibernian
W. Steel	Derby County
W. Liddell	Liverpool

Date. May 16, 1951
Venue. Hampden Park, Glasgow
Result. Scotland 1 France 0
Goalscorer. Reilly
Referee. R. A. Mortimer (Huddersfield)
Linesmen. R. Wood (Sunderland)
H. Trenholme (Stockton)

J. Cowan	Morton
G. Young (Captain)	Rangers
S. R. Cox	Rangers
J. Scoular	Portsmouth
W. A. Woodburn	Rangers
W. Redpath	Motherwell
W. Waddell	Rangers
R. Johnstone	Hibernian
L. Reilly	Hibernian
W. Steel	Dundee
R. Mitchell	Newcastle United

Versus Germany 1936–1964

Date. October 14, 1936
Venue. Ibrox Park, Glasgow
Result. Scotland 2 Germany 0
Goalscorer. Delaney (2)
Referee. H. Nattrass (New Seaham)
Linesmen. Dr A. W. Barton (Repton)
J. M. Wiltshire (Dorset)

J. Dawson	Rangers
A. Anderson	Heart of Midlothian
G. Cummings	Aston Villa
A. Massie	Aston Villa
J. Simpson (Captain)	Rangers
G. C. P. Brown	Rangers
J. Delaney	Celtic
T. Walker	Heart of Midlothian
M. Armstrong	Aberdeen
R. McPhail	Rangers
D. Duncan	Derby County

Date. May 22, 1957
Venue. Stuttgart
Result. Germany 1 Scotland 3
Goalscorers. Germany: Siedl
Scotland: Collins (2), Mudie
Referee. H. Dienst (Switzerland)
Linesmen. A. Andres (Switzerland)
A. Renschler (Switzerland)

T. Younger	Liverpool
E. Caldow	Rangers
J. Hewie	Charlton Athletic
I. McColl	Rangers
R. Evans	Celtic
T. Docherty (Captain)	Preston North End
A. Scott	Rangers
R. Collins	Celtic
J. K. Mudie	Blackpool
S. Baird	Rangers
T. Ring	Clyde

Date. May 6, 1959
Venue. Hampden Park, Glasgow
Result. Scotland 3 Germany 2
Goalscorers. Scotland: White, Weir, Leggat
Germany: Juskowiak (pen.), Seeler
Referee. A. E. Ellis (Halifax)
Linesmen. K. R. Tuck (Clusterfield)
J. W. Hedley (Newcastle)

G. Farm	Blackpool
D. MacKay	Celtic
E. Caldow	Rangers
D. C. Mackay	Tottenham Hotspur
R. Evans (Captain)	Celtic
R. J. McCann	Motherwell
G. Leggat	Fulham
J. A. White	Falkirk
I. St John	Motherwell
R. Collins	Everton
A. Weir	Motherwell

Date. May 12, 1964
Venue. Hanover
Result. Germany 2 Scotland 2
Goalscorers. Germany: Seeler (2)
Scotland: Gilzean (2)
Referee. E. Poulsen (Denmark)
Linesmen. H. Asmussen (Denmark)
G. Hansen (Denmark)
Remarks. Hamilton was injured during the first half and was replaced by D. D. Holt (Heart of Midlothian)

J. F. Cruickshank	Heart of Midlothian
A. W. Hamilton	Dundee
J. Kennedy	Celtic
J. Greig	Rangers
W. McNeill (Captain)	Celtic
J. Baxter	Rangers
W. Henderson	Rangers
J. A. White	Tottenham Hotspur
A. J. Gilzean	Dundee
D. Law	Manchester United
D. Wilson	Rangers

Versus Hungary 1938–1960

Date. December 7, 1938
Venue. Ibrox Stadium, Glasgow
Result. Scotland 3 Hungary 1
Goalscorers. Scotland: Black, Walker, Gillick
Hungary: Sarosi

J. Dawson	Rangers
A. Anderson	Heart of Midlothian
A. Beattie	Preston North End
W. Shankly	Preston North End
R. Baxter	Middlesbrough
J. Symon	Rangers
A. McSpadyen	Partick Thistle
T. Walker	Heart of Midlothian
D. McCulloch	Derby County
A. Black	Heart of Midlothian
T. Gillick	Everton

Date. December 8, 1954
Venue. Hampden Park, Glasgow
Result. Scotland 2 Hungary 4
Goalscorers. Scotland: Ring, Johnstone
Hungary: Hedegkuti, Haddock (o.g.), Sandor, Kocsis
Referee. L. Horn (Holland)
Linesmen. A. P. Formanoy (Holland)
J. C. Van Gelder (Holland)

F. Martin	Aberdeen
W. Cunningham (Captain)	Preston North End
H. Haddock	Clyde
T. Docherty	Preston North End
J. Davidson	Partick Thistle
J. Cumming	Heart of Midlothian
J. McKenzie	Partick Thistle
R. Johnstone	Hibernian
L. Reilly	Hibernian
J. Wardhaugh	Heart of Midlothian
T. Ring	Clyde

Date. May 29, 1955
Venue. Budapest
Result. Hungary 3 Scotland 1
Goalscorer. Scotland: Smith

T. Younger	Hibernian
A. Kerr	Partick Thistle
H. Haddock	Clyde
T. H. Docherty	Preston North End
R. Evans	Celtic
D. Cowie	Dundee
G. Smith	Hibernian
R. Collins	Celtic
L. Reilly	Hibernian
A. Robertson	Clyde
W. Liddell	Liverpool

Date. May 7, 1958
Venue. Hampden Park, Glasgow
Result. Scotland 1 Hungary 1
Goalscorers. Scotland: Mudie
Hungary: Fenyvesi
Referee. J. H. Clough (Bolton)
Linesmen. T. S. Blenkinsop (South Shields)
W. Crossley (Lancaster)

T. Younger (Captain)	Liverpool
E. Caldow	Rangers
J. Hewie	Charlton Athletic
E. Turnbull	Hibernian
R. Evans	Celtic
D. Cowie	Dundee
G. Leggat	Aberdeen
J. Murray	Heart of Midlothian
J. K. Mudie	Blackpool
R. Collins	Celtic
S. Imlach	Nottingham Forest

Date. June 5, 1960
Venue. Nepstadion, Budapest
Result. Hungary 3 Scotland 3
Goalscorers. Hungary: Sandor, Gorocs, Tichy
Scotland: Hunter, Herd, Young
Referee. A. E. Ellis (Halifax)
Linesmen. J. Powell (Rotherham)
B. T. Wickham (Trowbridge)

W. D. F. Brown	Tottenham Hotspur
D. MacKay	Celtic
E. Caldow	Rangers
J. Cumming	Heart of Midlothian
R. Evans (Captain)	Celtic
D. C. Mackay	Tottenham Hotspur
G. Leggat	Fulham
G. Herd	Clyde
A. Young	Heart of Midlothian
W. Hunter	Motherwell
A. Weir	Motherwell

Versus Italy 1931

Date. May 20, 1931
Venue. Rome
Result. Italy 3 Scotland 0
Goalscorers. Constantino, Meazza, Orsi
Referee. P. J. Bauwens (Germany)

J. Jackson	Partick Thistle
D. Blair	Clyde
J.Nibloe	Kilmarnock
C. McNab	Dundee
J. McDougall (Captain)	Liverpool
J. Miller	St Mirren
A. Love	Aberdeen
J. Paterson	Cowdenbeath
W. Boyd	Clyde
J. Robertson	Dundee
D. Liddle	East Fife

Versus Luxembourg 1947

Date. May 24, 1947
Venue. Luxembourg
Result. Luxembourg 0 Scotland 6
Goalscorers. Scotland: McLaren (2), Steel (2), Flavell (2)

W. Miller	Celtic
G. Young	Rangers
J. Shaw	Rangers
H. Brown	Partick Thistle
W. Woodburn	Rangers
A. Forbes	Sheffield United
J. McFarlane	Heart of Midlothian
A. McLaren	Preston North End
R. Flavell	Airdrieonians
W. Steel	Greenock Morton
R. Campbell	Falkirk

Versus Netherlands 1938–1971

Date. May 21, 1938
Venue. Amsterdam
Result. Netherlands 1 Scotland 3
Goalscorers. Netherlands: Van Spaandouck
Scotland: Black, Murphy, Walker
Referee. C. E. Argent (England)

J. Dawson	Rangers
A. Anderson	Heart of Midlothian
J. Carabine	Third Lanark
T. McKillop	Rangers
J. Dykes	Heart of Midlothian
G. Brown	Rangers
A. Munro	Blackpool
T. Walker	Heart of Midlothian
F. O'Donnell	Blackpool
A. Black	Heart of Midlothian
Murphy	Celtic

Date. May 27, 1959
Venue. Olympic Stadium, Amsterdam
Result. Netherlands 1 Scotland 2
Goalscorers. Netherlands: van der Gyp
Scotland: Collins, Leggat
Referee. S. Campos (Portugal)
Linesmen. H. Soaves (Portugal)
E. Gouveia (Portugal)
Remarks. Auld was ordered off by the referee in the closing minutes of the match

G. Farm	Blackpool
D. MacKay	Celtic
E. Caldow	Rangers
J. E. Smith	Celtic
R. Evans (Captain)	Celtic
J. Hewie	Charlton Athletic
G. Leggat	Fulham
R. Collins	Everton
J. A. White	Falkirk
D. Law	Huddersfield Town
R. Auld	Celtic

Date. May 11, 1966
Venue. Hampden Park, Glasgow
Result. Scotland 0 Netherlands 3
Goalscorers. Nuninga, Kuijlen (2)
Referee. K. Dagnall (Bolton)
Linesmen. J. K. Taylor (Wolverhampton)
F. M. Barr (Hull)
Remarks. Proceeds of match devoted to Winston Churchill Memorial Appeal

R. Ferguson	Kilmarnock
J. Greig (Captain)	Rangers
D. Provan	Rangers
P. G. Stanton	Hibernian
R. McKinnon	Rangers
D. B. Smith	Aberdeen
W. Henderson	Rangers
A. Penman	Dundee
J. Scott	Hibernian
W. S. B. Wallace	Heart of Midlothian
W. Johnston	Rangers

Date. May 30, 1968
Venue. Olympic Stadium, Amsterdam
Result. Netherlands 0 Scotland 0
Referee. K. Riegg (West Germany)
Linesmen. F. Wengenmayer (West Germany)
H. Guller (West Germany)
Remarks. R. Hope was injured in the first half and was replaced by J. Smith (Aberdeen)

R. Clark	Aberdeen
D. Fraser	West Bromwich Albion
E. McCreadie	Chelsea
R. Moncur	Newcastle United
R. McKinnon	Rangers
D. Smith	Rangers
W. Henderson	Rangers
R. Hope	West Bromwich Albion
G. McLean	Dundee
J. Greig (Captain)	Rangers
C. Cooke	Chelsea

Date. December 1, 1971
Venue. Olympic Stadium, Amsterdam
Result. Netherlands 2 Scotland 1
Goalscorers. Netherlands: Cruyff, Hulshoff
Scotland: Graham
Referee. F. Biwerst (West Germany)
Linesmen. W. Engel (West Germany)
G. Linn (West Germany)
Remarks. J. O'Hare (Derby County) and P. Cormack (Nottingham Forest) were substituted for J. Johnstone and E. Gray respectively during the second half

R. Wilson	Arsenal
W. Jardine	Rangers
E. Colquhoun	Sheffield United
P. Stanton	Hibernian
D. Hay	Celtic
W. Bremner (Captain)	Leeds United
G. Graham	Arsenal
A. Gemmill	Derby County
J. Johnstone	Celtic
K. Dalgleish	Celtic
E. Gray	Leeds United

Versus Norway 1954–1963

Date. May 5, 1954
Venue. Hampden Park, Glasgow
Result. Scotland 1 Norway 0
Goalscorer. Hamilton

F. Martin	Aberdeen
W. Cunningham	Preston North End
J. Aird	Burnley
T. H. Docherty	Preston North End
J. Davidson	Partick Thistle
R. Evans	Celtic
R. Johnstone	Hibernian
G. Hamilton	Aberdeen
P. Buckley	Aberdeen
A. Brown	Blackpool
W. Ormond	Hibernian

Date. May 19, 1954
Venue. Oslo
Result. Norway 1 Scotland 1
Goalscorer. Scotland: McKenzie

F. Martin	Aberdeen
W. Cunningham	Preston North End
J. Aird	Burnley
T. H. Docherty	Preston North End
J. Davidson	Partick Thistle
D. Cowie	Dundee
J. McKenzie	Partick Thistle
G. Hamilton	Aberdeen
J. Henderson	Portsmouth
A. Brown	Blackpool
N. Mochan	Celtic

Date. June 4, 1963
Venue. Bergen
Result. Norway 4 Scotland 3
Goalscorers. Norway: Nilsen, Johansen,
Pederson, Krogh
Scotland: Law (3)
Referee. H. Oskarsson (Iceland)
Linesmen. H. Granlund (Norway)
S. E. Olsen (Norway)
Remarks. Mackay retired injured, towards the end of the first half, and was replaced by F. McLintock (Leicester City)

A. Blacklaw	Burnley
A. W. Hamilton	Dundee
D. D. Holt	Heart of Midlothian
D. C. Mackay (Captain)	Tottenham Hotspur
J. F. Ure	Dundee
J. Baxter	Rangers
W. Henderson	Rangers
D. Gibson	Leicester City
I. St John	Liverpool
D. Law	Manchester United
D. Wilson	Rangers

Date. November 7, 1963	W. D. F. Brown	Tottenham Hotspur
Venue. Hampden Park, Glasgow	A. W. Hamilton	Dundee
Result. Scotland 6 Norway 1	D. Provan	Rangers
Goalscorers. Scotland: Law (4), Mackay (2)	D. C. Mackay (Captain)	Tottenham Hotspur
Norway: Kristoffersen	J. F. Ure	Arsenal
Referee. K. Howley (Billingham)	J. Baxter	Rangers
Linesmen. D. Wilkie (Dundee)	A. Scott	Everton
R. H. Young (Aberdeen)	J. A. White	Tottenham Hotspur
Remarks. The match was arranged for November 6	A. J. Gilzean	Dundee
1963 but, because of fog, was postponed.	D. Law	Manchester United
Baxter was injured and retired at the interval.	W. Henderson	Rangers
Mackay was moved to left-half in place of Baxter.		
J. Gabriel (Everton) replaced Mackay		

Versus Peru 1972

Date. April 26, 1972	A. Hunter	Kilmarnock
Venue. Hampden Park, Glasgow	J. Brownlie	Hibernian
Result. Scotland 2 Peru 0	W. Donachie	Manchester City
Goalscorers. O'Hare, Law	W. Carr	Coventry City
Referee. P. Partridge (Middlesbrough)	E. Colquhoun	Sheffield United
Linesmen. T. Farley (Newton Aycliffe)	R. Moncur	Newcastle United
R. Chadwick (Darwen)	W. Morgan	Manchester United
	D. Law (Captain)	Manchester United
	J. O'Hare	Derby County
	A. Gemmill	Derby County
	R. Hartford	West Bromwich Albion

Versus Poland 1958–1960

Date. June 1, 1958	T. Younger (Captain)	Liverpool
Venue. Warsaw	E. Caldow	Rangers
Result. Poland 1 Scotland 2	J. Hewie	Charlton Athletic
Goalscorers. Poland: Cieslik	E. Turnbull	Hibernian
Scotland: Collins (2)	R. Evans	Celtic
Referee. E. Sramko (Hungary)	D. Cowie	Dundee
Linesmen. F. Holyst (Hungary)	G. Leggat	Aberdeen
G. Aleksandrowicz (Hungary)	J. Murray	Heart of Midlothian
	J. K. Mudie	Blackpool
	R. Collins	Celtic
	S. Imlach	Nottingham Forest

Date. May 4, 1960	W. D. F. Brown	Tottenham Hotspur
Venue. Hampden Park, Glasgow	D. MacKay	Celtic
Result. Scotland 2 Poland 3	J. Hewie	Charlton Athletic
Goalscorers. Scotland: Law, St John	J. Cumming	Heart of Midlothian
Poland: Baskiewicz (2), Brychczy	R. Evans (Captain)	Celtic
Referee. A. Holland (Barnsley)	D. C. Mackay	Tottenham Hotspur
Linesmen. H. Hawksworth (Bolton)	G. Leggat	Fulham
C. S. Wilkinson (Rotherham)	J. A. White	Tottenham Hotspur
	I. St John	Motherwell
	D. Law	Manchester City
	A. Weir	Motherwell

Versus Portugal 1950–1966

Date. May 21, 1950	J. Cowan	Morton
Venue. Lisbon	G. Young (Captain)	Rangers
Result. Portugal 2 Scotland 2	S. Cox	Rangers
Goalscorers. Scotland: Bauld, Brown	R. Evans	Celtic
	W. Woodburn	Rangers
	A. Forbes	Arsenal
	R. Campbell	Chelsea
	A. Brown	East Fife
	W. Bauld	Heart of Midlothian
	W. Steel	Derby County
	W. Liddell	Liverpool

Date. May 4, 1955
Venue. Hampden Park, Glasgow
Result. Scotland 3 Portugal 0
Goalscorers. Gemmell, Liddell, Reilly
Referee. D. J. Gardeazabal (Spain)
Linesmen. R. Azow (Spain)
M. Asensi (Spain)

T. Younger	Hibernian
A. H. Parker	Falkirk
H. Haddock	Clyde
R. Evans	Celtic
G. Young (Captain)	Rangers
J. Cumming	Heart of Midlothian
G. Smith	Hibernian
A. Robertson	Clyde
L. Reilly	Hibernian
T. Gemmell	St Mirren
W. B. Liddell	Liverpool

Date. June 3, 1959
Venue. Lisbon
Result. Portugal 1 Scotland 0
Goalscorer. Matateu
Referee. D. Zariquiegui (Spain)
Linesmen. Mosquera (Spain)
F. Birigay (Spain)

G. Farm	Blackpool
D. MacKay	Celtic
E. Caldow	Rangers
J. E. Smith	Celtic
R. Evans (Captain)	Celtic
J. Hewie	Charlton Athletic
A. Scott	Rangers
R. Collins	Everton
J. A. White	Falkirk
D. Law	Huddersfield Town
R. Auld	Celtic

Date. June 18, 1966
Venue. Hampden Park, Glasgow
Result. Scotland 0 Portugal 1
Goalscorer. Torres
Referee. G. McCabe (Sheffield)
Linesmen. W. Clements (West Bromwich)
D. J. Farrow (Bury St Edmunds)
Remarks. A. Young was injured during the match and replaced by S. Chalmers (Celtic)

R. Ferguson	Kilmarnock
W. Bell	Leeds United
E. McCreadie	Chelsea
J. Greig (Captain)	Rangers
F. McGrory	Kilmarnock
W. Bremner	Leeds United
A. Scott	Everton
C. Cooke	Chelsea
A. Young	Everton
J. Baxter	Sunderland
J. Sinclair	Leicester City

Versus Republic of Ireland 1963–1969

Date. June 9, 1963
Venue. Dalymount Park, Dublin
Result. Republic of Ireland 1 Scotland 0
Goalscorer. Cantwell
Referee. K. Howley (Middlesbrough)
Linesmen. P. J. Woodland (Weymouth)
M. Matthews (Sheffield)
Remarks. Millar retired injured shortly before the end of the first half and was replaced by I. St John (Liverpool)

T. Lawrence	Liverpool
A. W. Hamilton	Dundee
D. D. Holt	Heart of Midlothian
F. McLintock	Leicester City
W. McNeill	Celtic
J. Baxter	Rangers
W. Henderson	Rangers
D. Gibson	Leicester City
J. Millar	Rangers
D. Law (Captain)	Manchester United
D. Wilson	Rangers

Date. September 21, 1969
Venue. Dalymount Park, Dublin
Result. Republic of Ireland 1 Scotland 1
Goalscorers. Republic of Ireland: Givens
Scotland: Stein
Referee. N. C. H. Burtenshaw (England)
Linesmen. M. Quinn (Republic of Ireland)
T. Barry (Republic of Ireland)
Remarks. E. McGarr was injured in the first half and was replaced by J. Herriot (Birmingham City). W. Callaghan (Dunfermline Athletic) substituted for T. Gemmell, injured, in the second half

E. McGarr	Aberdeen
J. Greig	Rangers
T. Gemmell	Celtic
P. Stanton	Hibernian
R. McKinnon	Rangers
R. Moncur	Newcastle United
W. Henderson	Rangers
W. Bremner (Captain)	Leeds United
C. Stein	Rangers
P. Cormack	Hibernian
J. Hughes	Celtic

Versus Spain 1963–1965

Date. June 13, 1963
Venue. Madrid
Result. Spain 2 Scotland 6
Goalscorers. Spain: Adalardo, Veloso
Scotland: Henderson, Gibson, St John, Law, Wilson, McLintock
Referee. G. Campanati (Italy)
Linesmen. E. Carminati (Italy)
G. Roversi (Italy)

A. Blacklaw	Burnley
W. McNeill	Celtic
D. D. Holt	Heart of Midlothian
F. McLintock	Leicester City
J. F. Ure	Dundee
J. Baxter	Rangers
W. Henderson	Rangers
D. Gibson	Leicester City
I. St John	Liverpool
D. Law (Captain)	Manchester United
D. Wilson	Rangers

Date. May 8, 1965
Venue. Hampden Park, Glasgow
Result. Scotland 0 Spain 0
Referee. K. Howley (Billingham)
Linesmen. J. K. Taylor (Wolverhampton)
J. W. D. Wilkes (Solihull)

W. D. F. Brown	Tottenham Hotspur
A. W. Hamilton	Dundee
E. G. McCreadie	Chelsea
W. J. Bremner	Leeds United
W. McNeill (Captain)	Celtic
J. Greig	Rangers
W. Henderson	Rangers
R. Collins	Leeds United
D. Law	Manchester United
A. J. Gilzean	Tottenham Hotspur
J. Hughes	Celtic

Versus Sweden 1952–1953

Date. May 30, 1952
Venue. Stockholm
Result. Sweden 3 Scotland 1
Goalscorer. Scotland: Liddell

J. Cowan	Greenock Morton
G. Young	Rangers
S. Cox	Rangers
J. Scoular	Portsmouth
A. Paton	Motherwell
A. Forbes	Arsenal
L. Reilly	Hibernian
W. Humphries	Motherwell
W. Thornton	Rangers
A. Brown	Blackpool
W. Liddell	Liverpool

Date. May 6, 1953
Venue. Hampden Park, Glasgow
Result. Scotland 1 Sweden 2
Goalscorers. Scotland: Johnstone
Sweden: Lofgren, Eriksson
Referee. W. Ling (Cambridge)
Linesmen. D. R. Minto (Hurlford)
J. W. Paton (Bellshill)

G. Farm	Blackpool
G. Young (Captain)	Rangers
J. Little	Rangers
R. Evans	Celtic
D. Cowie	Dundee
T. Docherty	Preston North End
J. Henderson	Portsmouth
R. Johnstone	Hibernian
L. Reilly	Hibernian
W. Steel	Dundee
T. Ring	Clyde

Versus Switzerland 1931–1950

Date. May 24, 1931
Venue. Geneva
Result. Switzerland 2 Scotland 3
Goalscorers. Switzerland: Buche, Fauguel
Scotland: Easson, Boyd, Love
Referee. A. Carraro (Italy)

J. Jackson	Partick Thistle
J. Crapnell (Captain)	Airdrieonians
J. Nibloe	Kilmarnock
C. McNab	Dundee
G. Walker	St Mirren
J. Miller	St Mirren
A. Love	Aberdeen
J. Paterson	Cowdenbeath
W. Boyd	Clyde
J. Easson	Portsmouth
D. Liddle	East Fife

Date. May 15, 1946
Venue. Hampden Park, Glasgow
Result. Scotland 3 Switzerland 1
Goalscorers. Scotland: Liddell (2), Delaney

R. Brown	Rangers
D. Shaw	Hibernian
J. Shaw	Rangers
W. Campbell	Greenock Morton
F. Brennan	Airdrieonians
J. Husband	Partick Thistle
W. Waddell	Rangers
W. Thornton	Rangers
J. Delaney	Manchester United
T. Walker	Heart of Midlothian
W. Liddell	Liverpool

Date. May 17, 1948
Venue. Berne
Result. Switzerland 2 Scotland 1
Goalscorer. Scotland: Johnstone

J. Cowan	Greenock Morton
J. Govan	Hibernian
D. Shaw	Hibernian
W. Campbell	Greenock Morton
G. Young	Rangers
A. Macaulay	Arsenal
G. Smith	Hibernian
R. Combe	Hibernian
L. Johnstone	Clyde
E. Turnbull	Hibernian
D. Duncan	East Fife

Date. April 26, 1950
Venue. Hampden Park, Glasgow
Result. Scotland 3 Switzerland 1
Goalscorers. Scotland: Bauld, Campbell, Brown
Referee. G. Reader (Southampton)
Linesmen. G. Bowman (Clydebank)
J. McMillan (Glasgow)

J. Cowan	Greenock Morton
G. Young	Rangers
S. Cox	Rangers
R. Evans	Celtic
R. Dougan	Heart of Midlothian
G. Aitken	East Fife
R. Campbell	Chelsea
A. Brown	East Fife
W. Bauld	Heart of Midlothian
W. Steel	Derby County
L. Reilly	Hibernian

Versus Turkey 1960

Date. June 8, 1960
Venue. Ankara
Result. Turkey 4 Scotland 2
Goalscorers. Turkey: Lefter (2), Matin, Senol
Scotland: Caldow (pen.), Young
Referee. E. Steiner (Austria)
Linesmen. H. Guruz (Turkey)
C. Basar (Turkey)

W. D. F. Brown	Tottenham Hotspur
D. MacKay	Celtic
E. Caldow	Rangers
J. Cumming	Heart of Midlothian
R. Evans (Captain)	Celtic
D. C. Mackay	Tottenham Hotspur
J. A. White	Tottenham Hotspur
G. Herd	Clyde
A. Young	Heart of Midlothian
W. Hunter	Motherwell
A. Weir	Motherwell

Versus Uruguay 1962

Date. May 2, 1962
Venue. Hampden Park, Glasgow
Result. Scotland 2 Uruguay 3
Goalscorers. Scotland: Baxter, Brand
Uruguay: Sasia, Luis Cubillas (2)
Referee. A. Holland (Barnsley)
Linesmen. G. E. Readle (Manchester)
H. Hawksworth (Bolton)

E. Connachan	Dunfermline Athletic
A. W. Hamilton	Dundee
E. Caldow (Captain)	Rangers
P. T. Crerand	Celtic
W. McNeill	Celtic
J. Baxter	Rangers
A. Scott	Rangers
P. Quinn	Motherwell
I. St John	Liverpool
R. Brand	Rangers
D. Wilson	Rangers

Versus U.S.A. 1952

Date. April 30, 1952
Venue. Hampden Park, Glasgow
Result. Scotland 6 U.S.A. 0
Goalscorers. Reilly (3), McMillan (2), O'Connell (o.g.)
Referee. D. Gerrard (Aberdeen)
Linesmen. A. P. Gow (Edinburgh)
J. Lackie (Perth)

J. Cowan	Morton
G. Young (Captain)	Rangers
S. R. Cox	Rangers
J. Scoular	Portsmouth
W. A. Woodburn	Rangers
H. T. Kelly	Blackpool
G. Smith	Hibernian
J. L. McMillan	Airdrieonians
L. Reilly	Hibernian
A. Brown	Blackpool
W. B. Liddell	Liverpool

Versus U.S.S.R. 1967–1971

Date. May 10, 1967
Venue. Hampden Park, Glasgow
Result. Scotland 0 U.S.S.R. 2
Goalscorers. Gemmell (o.g.), Medvid
Referee. L. van Ravens (Holland)
Linesmen. T. Boosten (Holland)
A. Vangemert (Holland)
Remarks. Law retired injured at the interval and was replaced by W. Wallace (Celtic)

R. Simpson	Celtic
T. Gemmell	Celtic
E. McCreadie	Chelsea
J. Clark	Celtic
W. McNeil	Celtic
J. Baxter (Captain)	Sunderland
J. Johnstone	Celtic
F. McLintock	Arsenal
J. McCalliog	Sheffield Wednesday
D. Law	Manchester United
R. Lennox	Celtic

Date. June 14, 1971
Venue. Lenin Stadium, Moscow
Result. U.S.S.R. 1 Scotland 0
Goalscorer. Yevruzhikhin
Referee. F. Marschall (Austria)
Linesmen. A. Kessler (Austria)
Dr F. Bauer (Austria)
Remarks. H. Curran (Wolverhampton Wanderers) substituted for C. Stein during the second half

R. Clark	Aberdeen
J. Brownlie	Hibernian
W. Dickson	Kilmarnock
F. Munro	Wolverhampton Wanderers
R. McKinnon	Rangers
P. Stanton (Captain)	Hibernian
J. Forrest	Aberdeen
R. Watson	Motherwell
C. Stein	Rangers
D. Robb	Aberdeen
J. Scott	Dundee

Versus Yugoslavia 1955–1956

Date. May 15, 1955
Venue. Belgrade
Result. Yugoslavia 2 Scotland 2
Goalscorers. Scotland: Reilly, Smith

T. Younger	Hibernian
A. H. Parker	Falkirk
H. Haddock	Clyde
R. Evans	Celtic
G. Young	Rangers
J. Cumming	Heart of Midlothian
G. Smith	Hibernian
R. Collins	Celtic
L. Reilly	Hibernian
T. Gemmell	St Mirren
W. Liddell	Liverpool

Date. November 21, 1956
Venue. Hampden Park, Glasgow
Result. Scotland 2 Yugoslavia 0
Goalscorers. Mudie, Baird
Referee. P. P. Roomer (Holland)
Linesmen. K. Schipper (Holland)
W. Beltman (Holland)

T. Younger	Liverpool
A. H. Parker	Falkirk
J. Hewie	Charlton Athletic
I. McColl	Rangers
G. Young (Captain)	Rangers
T. Docherty	Preston North End
A. Scott	Rangers
J. K. Mudie	Blackpool
L. Reilly	Hibernian
S. Baird	Rangers
W. Fernie	Celtic

Scotland World Cup Teams

Versus Austria 1954

Date. June 16, 1954
Venue. Zurich
Result. Scotland 0 Austria 1

F. Martin	Aberdeen
W. Cunningham	Preston North End
J. Aird	Burnley
T. H. Docherty	Preston North End
J. Davidson	Partick Thistle
D. Cowie	Dundee
J. McKenzie	Partick Thistle
W. Fernie	Celtic
N. Mochan	Celtic
A. Brown	Blackpool
W. Ormond	Hibernian

Versus Uruguay 1954

Date. June 19, 1954
Venue. Basle
Result. Scotland 0 Uruguay 7

F. Martin	Aberdeen
W. Cunningham	Preston North End
J. Aird	Burnley
T. H. Docherty	Preston North End
J. Davidson	Partick Thistle
D. Cowie	Dundee
J. McKenzie	Partick Thistle
W. Fernie	Celtic
N. Mochan	Celtic
A. Brown	Blackpool
W. Ormond	Hibernian

Versus Spain 1957

Date. May 8, 1957
Venue. Hampden Park, Glasgow
Result. Scotland 4 Spain 2
Goalscorers. Scotland: Mudie (3), Hewie (pen.)
Spain: Kubala, Suarez
Referee. A. Dusch (Germany)
Linesmen. G. Baumgartel (Germany)
W. Zimmerman (Germany)

T. Younger	Liverpool
E. Caldow	Rangers
J. Hewie	Charlton Athletic
I. McColl	Rangers
G. Young (Captain)	Rangers
T. Docherty	Preston North End
G. Smith	Hibernian
R. Collins	Celtic
J. K. Mudie	Blackpool
S. Baird	Rangers
T. Ring	Clyde

Date. May 26, 1957
Venue. Madrid
Result. Spain 4 Scotland 1
Goalscorers. Spain: Mateos, Kubala, Basora (2)
Scotland: Smith
Referee. R. J. Leafe (Nottingham)
Linesmen. F. Cowen (Manchester)
N. E. Fox (Bristol)

T. Younger	Liverpool
E. Caldow	Rangers
J. Hewie	Charlton Athletic
D. C. Mackay	Heart of Midlothian
R. Evans	Celtic
T. Docherty (Captain)	Preston North End
G. Smith	Hibernian
R. Collins	Celtic
J. K. Mudie	Blackpool
S. Baird	Rangers
T. Ring	Clyde

Versus Switzerland 1957

Date. May 19, 1957
Venue. Basle
Result. Switzerland 1 Scotland 2
Goalscorers. Switzerland: Vonlanden
Scotland: Mudie, Collins
Referee. F. Seipelt (Austria)
Linesmen. R. Roman (Austria)
D. Landa (Austria)

T. Younger	Liverpool
E. Caldow	Rangers
J. Hewie	Charlton Athletic
I. McColl	Rangers
G. Young (Captain)	Rangers
T. Docherty	Preston North End
G. Smith	Hibernian
R. Collins	Celtic
J. K. Mudie	Blackpool
S. Baird	Rangers
T. Ring	Clyde

Date. November 6, 1957
Venue. Hampden Park, Glasgow
Result. Scotland 3 Switzerland 2
Goalscorers. Scotland: Robertson, Mudie, Scott
Switzerland: Riva, Vonlanden
Referee. R. J. Leafe (Nottingham)
Linesmen. G. M. Harley (Bradford)
K. Howley (Middlesbrough)

T. Younger	Liverpool
A. H. Parker	Falkirk
E. Caldow	Rangers
W. Fernie	Celtic
R. Evans	Celtic
T. Docherty (Captain)	Preston North End
A. Scott	Rangers
R. Collins	Celtic
J. K. Mudie	Blackpool
A. Robertson	Clyde
T. Ring	Clyde

Versus Yugoslavia 1958

Date. June 8, 1958
Venue. Vasteras
Result. Scotland 1 Yugoslavia 1
Goalscorers. Scotland: Murray
Yugoslavia: Petakovi
Referee. P. Wysaling (Switzerland)
Linesmen. W. Macko (Czechoslovakia)
V. Orlandini (Italy)

T. Younger (Captain)	Liverpool
E. Caldow	Rangers
J. Hewie	Charlton Athletic
E. Turnbull	Hibernian
R. Evans	Celtic
D. Cowie	Dundee
G. Leggat	Aberdeen
J. Murray	Heart of Midlothian
J. K. Mudie	Blackpool
R. Collins	Celtic
S. Imlach	Nottingham Forest

Versus Paraguay 1958

Date. June 11, 1958
Venue. Norrkoping
Result. Scotland 2 Paraguay 3
Goalscorers. Scotland: Mudie, Collins
Paraguay: Aguero, Re, Parodi
Referee. V. Orlandini (Italy)
Linesmen. J. Gardeazabal (Spain)
B. Andren (Sweden)

T. Younger (Captain)	Liverpool
A. H. Parker	Falkirk
E. Caldow	Rangers
E. Turnbull	Hibernian
R. Evans	Celtic
D. Cowie	Dundee
G. Leggat	Aberdeen
R. Collins	Celtic
J. K. Mudie	Blackpool
A. Robertson	Clyde
W. Fernie	Celtic

Versus France 1958

Date. June 15, 1958
Venue. Orebro
Result. Scotland 1 France 2
Goalscorers. Scotland: Baird
France: Kopa, Fontaine
Referee. J. Brozzi (Argentine)
Linesmen. V. Orlandini (Italy)
P. Wyssling (Switzerland)

W. D. F. Brown	Dundee
E. Caldow	Rangers
J. Hewie	Charlton Athletic
E. Turnbull	Hibernian
R. Evans (Captain)	Celtic
D. C. Mackay	Heart of Midlothian
R. Collins	Celtic
J. Murray	Heart of Midlothian
J. K. Mudie	Blackpool
S. Baird	Rangers
S. Imlach	Nottingham Forest

Versus Republic of Ireland 1961

Date. May 3, 1961
Venue. Hampden Park, Glasgow
Result. Scotland 4 Republic of Ireland 1
Goalscorers. Scotland: Brand (2), Herd (2)
Republic of Ireland: Haverty
Referee. M. Guigue (France)
Linesmen. R. Deban (France)
P. Mourat (France)

L. G. Leslie	Airdrieonians
R. Shearer	Rangers
E. Caldow (Captain)	Rangers
P. T. Crerand	Celtic
W. McNeill	Celtic
J. Baxter	Rangers
J. M. Macleod	Hibernian
P. Quinn	Motherwell
D. Herd	Arsenal
R. Brand	Rangers
D. Wilson	Rangers

Date. May 7, 1961
Venue. Dalymount Park, Dublin
Result. Republic of Ireland 0 Scotland 3
Goalscorers. Young (2), Brand
Referee. G. Grandain (Belgium)
Linesmen. E. Calonne (Belgium)
J. Dupont (Belgium)

L. G. Leslie	Airdrieonians
R. Shearer	Rangers
E. Caldow (Captain)	Rangers
P. T. Crerand	Celtic
W. McNeill	Celtic
J. Baxter	Rangers
J. M. Macleod	Hibernian
P. Quinn	Motherwell
A. Young	Everton
R. Brand	Rangers
D. Wilson	Rangers

Versus Czechoslovakia 1961

Date. May 14, 1961
Venue. Bratislava
Result. Czechoslovakia 4 Scotland 0
Goalscorers. Pospichal (2), Kvasnak, Kadraba
Referee. E. Steiner (Austria)
Linesmen. A. Haberfellner (Austria)
J. Stoll (Austria)

L. G. Leslie	Airdrieonians
R. Shearer	Rangers
E. Caldow (Captain)	Rangers
P. T. Crerand	Celtic
W. McNeill	Celtic
J. Baxter	Rangers
J. M. Macleod	Hibernian
J. L. McMillan	Rangers
D. Herd	Arsenal
R. Brand	Rangers
D. Wilson	Rangers

Date. September 26, 1961
Venue. Hampden Park, Glasgow
Result. Scotland 3 Czechoslovakia 2
Goalscorers. Scotland: St John, Law (2)
Czechoslovakia: Kvasnak, Scherer
Referee. L. Gulliksen (Norway)
Linesmen. A. Nilsen (Norway)
T. Dahlgren (Norway)

W. D. F. Brown	Tottenham Hotspur
D. MacKay	Celtic
E. Caldow (Captain)	Rangers
P. T. Crerand	Celtic
W. McNeill	Celtic
J. Baxter	Rangers
A. Scott	Rangers
J. A. White	Tottenham Hotspur
I. St John	Liverpool
D. Law	Turin
D. Wilson	Rangers

Date. November 29, 1961
Venue. Heysel Stadium, Brussels
Result. Czechoslovakia 4 Scotland 2
Goalscorers. Czechoslovakia: Hledik, Scherer, Pospichal, Kvasnak
Scotland: St John (2)
Referee. G. Versyp (Belgium)
Linesmen. J. Hannet (Belgium)
M. Raeymaekers (Belgium)
Remarks. Extra-time required. Score after ninety minutes was 2–2. This was the third match to decide which country would qualify to play in the Final series in Chile

E. D. Connachan	Dunfermline Athletic
A. W. Hamilton	Dundee
E. Caldow (Captain)	Rangers
P. T. Crerand	Celtic
J. F. Ure	Dundee
J. Baxter	Rangers
R. Brand	Rangers
J. A. White	Tottenham Hotspur
I. St John	Liverpool
D. Law	Turin
H. Robertson	Dundee

Versus Finland 1964

Date. October 21, 1964
Venue. Hampden Park, Glasgow
Result. Scotland 3 Finland 1
Goalscorers. Scotland: Law, Chalmers, Gibson
Finland: Peltonen
Referee. J. Hannet (Belgium)
Linesmen. J. Casteleyn (Belgium)
M. Bertrand (Belgium)

R. C. Forsyth	Kilmarnock
A. W. Hamilton	Dundee
J. Kennedy	Celtic
J. Greig	Rangers
J. McGrory	Kilmarnock
J. Baxter	Rangers
J. Johnstone	Celtic
D. Gibson	Leicester City
S. Chalmers	Celtic
D. Law (Captain)	Manchester United
A. Scott	Everton

Versus Poland 1965

Date. May 23, 1965
Venue. Slaski Stadium, Chorzow
Result. Poland 1 Scotland 1
Goalscorers. Poland: Liberda
Scotland: Law
Referee. S. Alimov (Russia)
Linesmen. S. Arhipov (Russia)
K. Andzulis (Russia)

W. D. F. Brown	Tottenham Hotspur
A. W. Hamilton	Dundee
E. G. McCreadie	Chelsea
J. Greig	Rangers
W. McNeill (Captain)	Celtic
P. T. Crerand	Manchester United
W. Henderson	Rangers
R. Y. Collins	Leeds United
N. Martin	Hibernian
D. Law	Manchester United
J. Hughes	Celtic

Versus Finland 1965

Date. May 27, 1965
Venue. Olympic Stadium, Helsinki
Result. Finland 1 Scotland 2
Goalscorers. Finland: Hyvarinan
Scotland: Wilson, Greig
Referee. E. Vetter (East Germany)
Linesmen. W. Riedel (East Germany)
G. Mannig (East Germany)

W. D. F. Brown	Tottenham Hotspur
A. W. Hamilton	Dundee
E. G. McCreadie	Chelsea
P. T. Crerand	Manchester United
W. McNeill (Captain)	Celtic
J. Greig	Rangers
W. Henderson	Rangers
D. Law	Manchester United
N. Martin	Hibernian
W. M. Hamilton	Hibernian
D. Wilson	Rangers

Versus Poland 1965

Date. October 13, 1965
Venue. Hampden Park, Glasgow
Result. Scotland 1 Poland 2
Goalscorers. Scotland: McNeill
Poland: Liberda, Sadek
Referee. H. Carlsson (Sweden)
Linesmen. C. Liedberg (Sweden)
E. Johansson (Sweden)

W. D. F. Brown	Tottenham Hotspur
A. W. Hamilton	Dundee
E. G. McCreadie	Chelsea
P. T. Crerand	Manchester United
W. McNeill (Captain)	Celtic
J. Greig	Rangers
W. Henderson	Rangers
W. J. Bremner	Leeds United
A. J. Gilzean	Tottenham Hotspur
D. Law	Manchester United
W. Johnston	Rangers

Versus Italy 1965

Date. November 9, 1965
Venue. Hampden Park, Glasgow
Result. Scotland 1 Italy 0
Goalscorer. Greig
Referee. R. Kreitlein (West Germany)
Linesmen. R. Jakobi (West Germany)
F. Seiler (West Germany)

W. D. F. Brown	Tottenham Hotspur
J. Greig	Rangers
D. Provan	Rangers
R. Murdoch	Celtic
R. McKinnon	Rangers
J. Baxter (Captain)	Sunderland
W. Henderson	Rangers
W. J. Bremner	Leeds United
A. J. Gilzean	Tottenham Hotspur
N. Martin	Sunderland
J. Hughes	Celtic

Date. December 7, 1965
Venue. San Paolo Stadium, Naples
Result. Italy 3 Scotland 0
Goalscorers. Pascutti, Faschetti, Mora
Referee. I. Zsolt (Hungary)
Linesmen. G. Emsberger (Hungary)
G. Vadas (Hungary)

A. Blacklaw	Burnley
D. Provan	Rangers
E. G. McCreadie	Chelsea
R. Murdoch	Celtic
R. McKinnon	Rangers
J. Greig (Captain)	Rangers
J. Forrest	Rangers
W. J. Bremner	Leeds United
R. Yeats	Liverpool
C. Cooke	Dundee
J. Hughes	Celtic

Versus Austria 1968

Date. November 6, 1968
Venue. Hampden Park, Glasgow
Result. Scotland 2 Austria 1
Goalscorers. Scotland: Law, Bremner
Austria: Starek
Referee. B. Lööw (Sweden)
Linesmen. E. Bostroem (Sweden)
G. Karlstrand (Sweden)
Remarks. In the last twenty minutes of the match, A. Gilzean (Tottenham Hotspur) substituted for D. Law who was injured

R. Simpson	Celtic
T. Gemmell	Celtic
E. McCreadie	Chelsea
W. Bremner (Captain)	Leeds United
R. McKinnon	Rangers
J. Greig	Rangers
J. Johnstone	Celtic
C. Cooke	Chelsea
D. Law	Manchester United
R. Lennox	Celtic
J. Hughes	Celtic

Versus Cyprus 1968

Date. December 11, 1968
Venue. Nicosia
Result. Cyprus 0 Scotland 5
Goalscorers. Gilzean (2), Murdoch,
Koreas (o.g.), Theodorou (o.g.)
Referee. P. Bonnet (Malta)
Linesmen. A. Lentini (Malta)
E. Borg (Malta)
Remarks. W. McNeill (Celtic) replaced R. McKinnon at the interval, and R. Lennox (Celtic) replaced C. Cooke 10 minutes from the end of the match

J. Herriot	Birmingham City
D. Fraser	West Bromwich Albion
E. McCreadie	Chelsea
W. Bremner (Captain)	Leeds United
R. McKinnon	Rangers
J. Greig	Rangers
T. McLean	Kilmarnock
R. Murdoch	Celtic
C. Stein	Rangers
A. Gilzean	Tottenham Hotspur
C. Cooke	Chelsea

Versus West Germany 1969

Date. April 16, 1969
Venue. Hampden Park, Glasgow
Result. Scotland 1 West Germany 1
Goalscorers. Scotland: Murdoch
West Germany: Muller
Referee. J. Gardeazabal (Spain)
Linesmen. A. Rigo (Spain)
A. Herrero (Spain
Remarks. C. Cooke (Chelsea) replaced R. Lennox early in the second half

T. Lawrence	Liverpool
T. Gemmell	Celtic
E. McCreadie	Chelsea
R. Murdoch	Celtic
R. McKinnon	Rangers
J. Greig	Rangers
J. Johnstone	Celtic
W. Bremner (Captain)	Leeds United
D. Law	Manchester United
A. Gilzean	Tottenham Hotspur
R. Lennox	Celtic

Versus Cyprus 1969

Date. May 17, 1969
Venue. Hampden Park, Glasgow
Result. Scotland 8 Cyprus 0
Goalscorers. Gray, McNeill, Stein (4),
Henderson, Gemmell
Referee. P. P. Coates (Dublin)
Linesmen. O. McCarthy (Cork)
D. Barrett (Cork)

J. Herriot	Birmingham City
E. McCreadie	Chelsea
T. Gemmell	Celtic
W. Bremner (Captain)	Leeds United
W. McNeill	Celtic
J. Greig	Rangers
W. Henderson	Rangers
C. Cooke	Chelsea
C. Stein	Rangers
A. Gilzean	Tottenham Hotspur
E. Gray	Leeds United

Versus Austria 1969

Date. November 5, 1969
Venue. Prater Stadium, Vienna
Result. Austria 2 Scotland 0
Goalscorer. Redl (2)
Referee. K. Karlo (U.S.S.R.)
Linesmen. B. Tofik (U.S.S.R.)
A. Sergey (U.S.S.R.)
Remarks. P. Lorimer (Leeds United) and C. Stein (Rangers) replaced C. Cooke and H. Curran respectively, late in the second half

E. McGarr	Aberdeen
J. Greig	Rangers
F. Burns	Manchester United
P. Stanton	Hibernian
R. McKinnon	Rangers
R. Murdoch	Celtic
C. Cooke	Chelsea
W. Bremner (Captain)	Leeds United
H. Curran	Wolverhampton Wan.
A. Gilzean	Tottenham Hotspur
E. Gray	Leeds United

Versus West Germany 1969

Date. October 22, 1969
Venue. Hamburg
Result. West Germany 3 Scotland 2
Goalscorers. West Germany: Fitchel, Muller, Libuda
Scotland: Johnstone, Gilzean
Referee. G. Droz (Switzerland)
Linesmen. M. Despland (Switzerland)
G. Racine (Switzerland)

J. Herriot	Birmingham City
J. Greig	Rangers
T. Gemmell	Celtic
W. Bremner (Captain)	Leeds United
R. McKinnon	Rangers
W. McNeill	Celtic
J. Johnstone	Celtic
P. Cormack	Hibernian
C. Stein	Rangers
A. Gilzean	Tottenham Hotspur
E. Gray	Leeds United

Scottish F.A. Cup Winners

Year	*Winners*	*Runners-up*	*Score*
1874	Queen's Park	Clydesdale	2–0
1875	Queen's Park	Renton	3–0
1876	Queen's Park	Third Lanark	2–0 after 1–1 draw
1877	Vale of Leven	Rangers	3–2 after 0–0 and 1–1 draws
1878	Vale of Leven	Third Lanark	1–0
1879	*Vale of Leven	Rangers	
1880	Queen's Park	Thornlibank	3–0
1881	†Queen's Park	Dumbarton	3–1
1882	Queen's Park	Dumbarton	4–1 after 2–2 draw
1883	Dumbarton	Vale of Leven	2–1 after 2–2 draw
1884	‡Queen's Park	Vale of Leven	
1885	Renton	Vale of Leven	3–1 after 0–0 draw
1886	Queen's Park	Renton	3–1
1887	Hibernian	Dumbarton	2–1
1888	Renton	Cambuslang	6–1
1889	§Third Lanark	Celtic	2–1
1890	Queen's Park	Vale of Leven	2–1 after 1–1 draw
1891	Hearts	Dumbarton	1–0
1892	§Celtic	Queen's Park	5–1
1893	Queen's Park	Celtic	2–1
1894	Rangers	Celtic	3–1
1895	St Bernard's	Renton	2–1
1896	Hearts	Hibernian	3–1
1897	Rangers	Dumbarton	5–1
1898	Rangers	Kilmarnock	2–0
1899	Celtic	Rangers	2–0
1900	Celtic	Queen's Park	4–3
1901	Hearts	Celtic	4–3
1902	Hibernian	Celtic	1–0
1903	Rangers	Hearts	2–0 after 1–1 and 0–0 draws
1904	Celtic	Rangers	3–2
1905	Third Lanark	Rangers	3–1 after 0–0 draw
1906	Hearts	Third Lanark	1–0
1907	Celtic	Hearts	3–0
1908	Celtic	St Mirren	5–1
1909 ¶			
1910	Dundee	Clyde	2–1 after 2–2 and 0–0 draws
1911	Celtic	Hamilton Academicals	2–0 after 0–0 draw
1912	Celtic	Clyde	2–0
1913	Falkirk	Raith Rovers	2–0
1914	Celtic	Hibernian	4–1 after 0–0 draw
1920	Kilmarnock	Albion Rovers	3–2
1921	Partick Thistle	Rangers	1–0
1922	Morton	Rangers	1–0
1923	Celtic	Hibernian	1–0
1924	Airdrieonians	Hibernian	2–0
1925	Celtic	Dundee	2–1
1926	St Mirren	Celtic	2–0
1927	Celtic	East Fife	3–1
1928	Rangers	Celtic	4–0
1929	Kilmarnock	Rangers	2–0
1930	Rangers	Partick Thistle	2–1 after 0–0 draw
1931	Celtic	Motherwell	4–2 after 2–2 draw
1932	Rangers	Kilmarnock	3–0 after 1–1 draw
1933	Celtic	Motherwell	1–0
1934	Rangers	St Mirren	5–0
1935	Rangers	Hamilton Academicals	2–1
1936	Rangers	Third Lanark	1–0
1937	Celtic	Aberdeen	2–1
1938	East Fife	Kilmarnock	4–2 after 1–1 draw
1939	Clyde	Motherwell	4–0

1947	Aberdeen	Hibernian	2–1	1961	Dunfermline Athletic	Celtic	2–0 after 0–0 draw
1948	Rangers	Morton	1–0 after 1–1 draw	1962	Rangers	St Mirren	2–0
1949	Rangers	Clyde	4–1	1963	Rangers	Celtic	3–0 after 1–1 draw
1950	Rangers	East Fife	3–0				
1951	Celtic	Motherwell	1–0	1964	Rangers	Dundee	3–1
1952	Motherwell	Dundee	4–0	1965	Celtic	Dunfermline Athletic	3–2
1953	Rangers	Aberdeen	1–0 after 1–1 draw	1966	Rangers	Celtic	1–0 after 0–0 draw
1954	Celtic	Aberdeen	2–1				
1955	Clyde	Celtic	1–0 after 1–1 draw	1967	Celtic	Aberdeen	2–0
				1968	Dunfermline Athletic	Hearts	3–1
1956	Hearts	Celtic	3–1				
1957	Falkirk	Kilmarnock	2–1 after 1–1 draw	1969	Celtic	Rangers	4–0
				1970	Aberdeen	Celtic	3–1
1958	Clyde	Hibernian	1–0	1971	Celtic	Rangers	2–1 after 1–1 draw
1959	St Mirren	Aberdeen	3–1				
1960	Rangers	Kilmarnock	2–0	1972	Celtic	Hibernian	6–1

* Vale of Leven awarded cup, Rangers failed to appear for replay after 1–1 draw.
† After Protest game, Queen's Park 2 Dumbarton 1.
‡ Queen's Park awarded cup, Vale of Leven failing to appear.
§ After replay ordered by Scottish F.A.
§ After Protested Game.
¶ Owing to riot, the cup was withheld after two drawn games – Celtic 2,1 Rangers 2,1

Scotland Teams in the European Football Championship Henri Delaunay Cup

Versus Denmark 1970

Date. November 11, 1970
Venue. Hampden Park, Glasgow
Result. Scotland 1 Denmark 0
Goalscorer. O'Hare
Referee. E. Linemayr (Austria)
Linesmen. A. Kessler (Austria)
H. Schram (Austria)
Remarks. J. O'Hare and D. Hay were replaced by P. Cormack (Nottingham Forest) and W. Jardine (Rangers), respectively, towards the end of the match

J. Cruickshank	Heart of Midlothian
D. Hay	Celtic
J. Greig	Rangers
P. Stanton	Hibernian
R. McKinnon	Rangers
R. Moncur (Captain)	Newcastle United
J. Johnstone	Celtic
W. Carr	Coventry City
C. Stein	Rangers
J. O'Hare	Derby County
W. Johnston	Rangers

Versus Belgium 1971

Date. February 3, 1971
Venue. Liege
Result. Belgium 3 Scotland 0
Goalscorers. McKinnon (o.g.), van Himst (2)
Referee. A. Sbardella (Italy)
Linesmen. C. Gussoni (Italy)
A. Picasso (Italy)
Remarks. J. Forrest (Aberdeen) and A. Green (Blackpool) were substituted for C. Stein and P. Stanton respectively during the second half

J. Cruickshank	Heart of Midlothian
D. Hay	Celtic
T. Gemmell	Celtic
P. Stanton	Hibernian
R. McKinnon	Rangers
R. Moncur (Captain)	Newcastle United
C. Cooke	Chelsea
J. Greig	Rangers
C. Stein	Rangers
J. O'Hare	Derby County
A. Gemmill	Derby County

Versus Portugal 1971

Date. April 21, 1971
Venue. Estadia da Luz, Lisbon
Result. Portugal 2 Scotland 0
Goalscorers. Stanton (o.g.), Eusebio
Referee. M. Kitabdjian (France)
Linesmen. M. Frauciel (France)
R. Lefebvre (France)
Remarks. A. Jarvie (Airdrieonians) was substituted for J. McCalliog and A. Green (Blackpool) was substituted for P. Stanton during the second half

R. Clark	Aberdeen
D. Hay	Celtic
J. Brogan	Celtic
P. Stanton	Hibernian
R. McKinnon	Rangers
R. Moncur (Captain)	Newcastle United
W. Henderson	Rangers
J. McCalliog	Wolverhampton Wanderers
D. Robb	Aberdeen
P. Cormack	Nottingham Forest
A. Gilzean	Tottenham Hotspur

Versus Denmark 1971

Date. June 9, 1971
Venue. Copenhagen
Result. Denmark 1 Scotland 0
Goalscorer. Laudrup
Referee. W. Riedel (East Germany)
Linesmen. H. Einbeck (East Germany)
H. Schulz (East Germany)
Remarks. T. Forsyth and J. Forrest were replaced by D. Robb (Aberdeen) and J. Scott Dundee) respectively in the second half

R. Clark	Aberdeen
F. Munro	Wolverhampton Wanderers
W. Dickson	Kilmarnock
P. Stanton	Hibernian
R. McKinnon	Rangers
R. Moncur (Captain)	Newcastle United
T. McLean	Rangers
T. Forsyth	Motherwell
C. Stein	Rangers
H. Curran	Wolverhampton Wanderers
J. Forrest	Aberdeen

Versus Portugal 1971

Date. October 13, 1971
Venue. Hampden Park, Glasgow
Result. Scotland 2 Portugal 1
Goalscorers. Scotland: O'Hare, Gemmill
Portugal: Rodrigues
Referee. B. Piotrowicz (Poland)
Linesmen. J. Lazowski (Poland)
W. Karolak (Poland)
Remarks. M. Buchan (Aberdeen) was substituted for E. Colquhoun, who was injured, in the second half

R. Wilson	Arsenal
W. Jardine	Rangers
D. Hay	Celtic
W. Bremner (Captain)	Leeds United
E. Colquhoun	Sheffield United
P. Stanton	Hibernian
J. Johnstone	Celtic
A. Cropley	Hibernian
J. O'Hare	Derby County
G. Graham	Arsenal
A. Gemmill	Der by County

Versus Belgium 1971

Date. November 10, 1971
Venue. Pittodrie Park, Aberdeen
Result. Scotland 1 Belgium 0
Goalscorer. O'Hare
Referee. E. Bostrom (Sweden)
Linesmen. O. Dahlberg (Sweden)
M. Forsman (Sweden)
Remarks. Cropley and Johnstone were substituted by K. Dalgleish (Celtic) and J. Hansen (Partick Thistle), respectively during the second half. Belgium were eventual winners of this section

R. Clark	Aberdeen
W. Jardine	Rangers
D. Hay	Celtic
W. Bremner (Captain)	Leeds United
M. Buchan	Aberdeen
P. Stanton	Hibernian
J. Johnstone	Celtic
S. Murray	Aberdeen
J. O'Hare	Derby County
E. Gray	Leeds United
A. Cropley	Hibernian